"The power to live with joy and victory,"
says Norman Vincent Peale, "is available to
you and me. This power can lead you to a
solution to your problems, help you to meet
your difficulties successfully and fill your
heart with peace and contentment."

The
Amazing Results
of
Positive Thinking

by Norman Vincent Peale

FAWCETT CREST • NEW YORK

THE AMAZING RESULTS OF POSITIVE THINKING

THIS BOOK CONTAINS THE COMPLETE TEXT OF
THE ORIGINAL HARDCOVER EDITION.

Published by Fawcett Crest Books, CBS Educational and
Professional Publishing, a division of CBS Inc., by arrangement with Prentice-Hall, Inc.

ISBN: 0-449-23773-7

Printed in the United States of America

36   35   34   33   32   31   30   29   28   27

TO CHERISHED ASSOCIATES
   Smiley Blanton
   Daniel A. Poling
   Herman L. Barbery
   Eugene McKinley Pierce
   Donald Wayne Hoffman
   Mary F. Brinig

A Word to the Reader

HUNDREDS OF PEOPLE wrote this book. I have simply put together the combined experiences of many men and women.

This is a result book. It is the story of thrilling things which took place in the lives of thousands of people when they applied the principles of dynamic change.

Since publication of *The Power of Positive Thinking*, a book which teaches effective living through right thinking and practical religious faith, thousands of readers have communicated with me. They told how, by the application of positive thinking principles to their own life situations, they have mastered fear, healed personal relationships, found better health, overcome inner conflicts and gained strong new confidence.

Writers of these letters invariably expressed themselves in terms of joy and faith in God. Readers repeatedly said that they started reading the Bible, and they told how it took on new meaning. Indeed, they declared that they drew from it faith and happiness they had not previously known. They discovered new values in the church, and the use of practical spiritual techniques became an exciting adventure. These letters came from Catholics, Protestants and Jews alike, and told how God had become a living reality. Many referred to experiencing Jesus Christ in their lives, and this spiritual phenomenon is described with deep feeling as being very warm, rich and personal. New potentials were found in spiritual living, especially in the power of prayer. Some who had gone regularly to church for years, but with no joy or sense of lift, spoke wonderingly of fresh discoveries in faith.

What excitement, what sense of wonder, what new life, what love of their fellow men, and of life itself, these people told about.

While readers have graciously expressed appreciation of the teachings outlined in *The Power of Positive Thinking*, many have found either new uses for the suggested methods or, in some cases, exciting new formulas for effective living, which in their enthusiasm they sent to me. These discoveries of fresh techniques should, I felt, be passed on to others for the helpfulness they are certain to bring.

So wonderful were the letters and word-of-mouth statements concerning the workability of the positive way of life that, when I gathered many of them together in book form, a natural title was *The Amazing Results of Positive Thinking*. This book is a laboratory demonstration of the real experiences of many people with formulas that actually changed lives.

Through these formulas thousands of people have discovered a way of thinking and living that changed sorrow to joy, weakness to strength, failure to success, despair to hope, and defeat to victory. This new book explains how the same principles can help you. And, after reading these results, perhaps you will want to put these powerful techniques to work in your life. Then won't you write me about your own results, that I may pass them on to encourage and help others.

To you, my reader and friend, God bless and guide you always. And He will, too.

Norman Vincent Peale

Contents

The
Amazing Results
of
Positive Thinking

Chapter I

Does Positive Thinking Always Work?

DOES POSITIVE THINKING ALWAYS WORK?

Yes.

Now, I realize this is a rather bold statement. And someone may object: "Is that so. I had lots of problems. I read positive thinking and I still have problems." Someone else may say, "Well, I had a business that was in the doldrums, and I tried positive thinking, and my business is still in the doldrums. Positive thinking didn't change the facts. Failure exists. If you deny that, you're just being an ostrich, burying your head in the sand."

So often, people don't really understand the nature of positive thinking. A positive thinker does not refuse to *recognize* the negative, he refuses to *dwell* on it. Positive thinking is a form of thought which habitually looks for the best results from the worse conditions. It is possible to look for something to build on; it is possible to expect the best for yourself even though things look bad. And the remarkable fact is that when you seek good, you are very likely to find it.

This seeking-the-positive is a deliberate process, and a matter of choice. Not long ago I received word that a friend of mine had been fired. In talking with Bill, I learned the circumstances. He had been summarily dismissed. No explanation was given except there had been a policy change, and he was no longer needed. To make matters worse, nine months earlier Bill had received a handsome offer from a competing firm, he had talked the matter over with his boss, and his boss had persuaded him to stay on, saying: "We need you here, Bill. And frankly, things look pretty good for you."

Well, of course, Bill reacted rather bitterly to all of this. He went around feeling unwanted, insecure, rejected. His ego had been hurt. He became morose and resentful, and in a state of mind like that, he wasn't in a very good condition to look for another job.

This is exactly the kind of situation where positive thinking can do its best. One day, Bill dug out an old copy of *The Power of Positive Thinking,* and read it through. What possible good was there in his condition, he wondered? He didn't know. But he could see plenty of negative factors, and he clearly realized that these negative emotions were dragging him down. If he was going to put positive thinking to work, the first thing he had to do was get rid of the negative feelings.

Here, at least, was a place he could begin. So he practiced the principle of thought replacement. That is, he deliberately filled his mind with positive affirmations and crowded out the negative thoughts. He began a systematic program of prayer and told the Lord: "I believe You have a plan for my life, so there must be some purpose in my getting fired. Instead of railing against my fate, I humbly ask You to show me the purpose in what has happened." Once he began to believe there had been a reason and some meaning behind what had happened to him, it was easier to rid himself of resentment against his former employers. And once that happened he was "employable" again.

One day, shortly after he had reached this point in his thinking, Bill met an old friend. They got to talking, and the friend asked how things were.

"Oh, I've just been fired," Bill said, casually.

The friend was surprised. "Well you're certainly honest enough about it," he said. "What happened?"

Bill told him, and he finished by saying: ". . . and I know the Lord has a job for me somewhere else."

"The *Lord!* Aren't you worried?"

"Not at all. Something better will turn up. In my philosophy, when one door shuts another will open if you just have faith and put it in God's hands."

A few days later Bill received a telephone call from his friend, saying that there was a long-unfilled opening in his company, and asking him if he wanted the job—salarywise it wasn't as good as his last position, but it had potential. Bill took it. There was no doubt about the fact that in his new job he was in a better position to be of service to people. He realized this very shortly and soon discovered that his new activity was one he had always wanted. He became stimulated and excited about his work in a way that he had almost forgotten at his previous place of employment. He would grow. This, he felt sure, was part of the plan that God had in mind.

Now the important thing to analyze here is *why* positive thinking worked. It's not that some magic entered the picture and created a job out of the ether. There was a definite scientific principle at work. When Bill had his mind filled with resentments and angers and hatreds, he was destroying his own value as an employee. He was making it impossible for himself to do this best at the business of job-seeking. On the day Bill met his friend, if he had been bitter and full of sly defenses, do you think his friend would have considered him a good person to recommend for the new job? There is no mysticism at work here. This way of thinking and of acting is, above all, down-to-earth common sense.

Positive thinking is looking at events with the knowledge that there will be both good and bad in life, but that it is better to emphasize the good. And as you do that, good seems to increase.

The other day I went out the door of my office and hailed a cab. As soon as I got in the taxi, I could tell that my driver was a happy man. He was whistling. First he whistled a tune from, "My Fair Lady," and then he launched himself into a version of "Stars and Stripes Forever." After a while I said to him, "You seem to be in a happy mood."

"Why shouldn't I be?" he said. "I've just learned something. I've learned that there's no percentage in getting excited, or in the dumps, because things average out."

And he went on to explain what he meant. Early that morning he had taken his cab out, hoping to take advantage of the morning rush hour. It was a bitterly cold day. The driver said it was ". . . the kind of temperature where, if you touch metal, your hand will stick to it." And as luck would have it, no sooner had he started his day than he had a flat tire. He was angry. Muttering, he got out his jack and lug wrench and tried to take off the tire. It was so cold he could only work for a few minutes at a time. And while he was struggling, a truck stopped. The driver jumped out and, much to the taxi-driver's surprise, began to help him. When the tire was back in place, the trucker gruffly waved off the cabby's thanks, got in his truck and drove off.

"Well, this put me in a high mood," the cabby said to me. "Already things were averaging out. First, I was angry with the flat, then I felt good because of that trucker's help and right away things started going good. Even the money had averaged out. I've never had a busier morning, one fare after another in and out of the cab. Things average out, Mister. Don't get excited when a situation gets rocky; things average out."

Here was a positive thinker, all right. He said he was never again going to let life's mishaps annoy him. He was just going to live by the theory that things average out OK. That is real positive thinking, and it will work, too, because things always come around to a brighter view when you wait them out and work them out optimistically. The law of averages is always on the positive thinker's side. A positive thinker chooses to keep his mind fixed on the bright future that is always just around the corner, and in this way he helps make the dark moments more cheerful, productive and creative. That attitude gets you around the "corner" quicker, too.

It is a fact of life that all of us will come face to face with plenty of frustration, difficulty and trouble. But there isn't one of us who needs to be defeated by these obstacles. If you face life with the sincere faith that through the aid of the Almighty you can overcome your troubles, then you will keep defeat at arm's length. And this applies in all the circumstances life can bring.

One evening in San Francisco, I had the pleasure of dining in the home of a charming lady named Elena Zelayeta. I have never attended a dinner party presided over by an individual of happier personality or more irresistible gaiety. Elena is Mexican, and the dinner she served that evening was a 17-course Mexican dinner (small courses)—the most delicious repast I could hope to experience. She cooked it herself—and she is totally blind.

Elena Zelayeta once ran a restaurant in San Francisco. It was a beautiful place, full of color and life. Then her eyesight began to fail. Soon she was blind, living in darkness. One day the telephone rang and she groped her way to answer it and received the shocking news that her husband had just been killed in an accident.

Blindness—and now her husband suddenly dead. She sat by the telephone, utterly crushed, wondering what she was going to do. She was dejected for weeks, living in helplessness. But in this most complete darkness, emotionally and physically, she perceived finally, by the help of her strong faith, that there was something positive to which she could attach herself. She did not choose to dwell on the negative, she sought the positive, and she found it in a most remarkable way. As she struggled in shock and sorrow, suddenly she felt "as if a great, strong hand gripped her and lifted her up."

Putting sincere faith and strong positive thinking against her sad conditions, she determined that she would conquer her grief, loneliness and handicap. So complete was her ultimate victory that presently she picked up her life again as a career woman. How well Elena Zelayeta succeeded is shown by the fact that in recent years she has lectured on cooking up and down the West Coast, sometimes to as many as a thousand women at a time. She has written three successful cook books and a book of inspiration. She operates a frozen food business with her two sons and goes to the office every day.

She had to cook by sense of feel and taste and smell. But these, she says with a smile, are what cooking is all about anyway. This inspiring woman is one of the most marvelous examples of positive thinking I have ever ran across. Naturally I sought for her secret of conquering adversity. While we were having dinner at her home, Mrs. Zelayeta made this powerful statement which is the guiding principle of her life. It is the formula through which she found victory. "Always act," she said, "as if it were impossible to fail and God will see you through."

Always act as if it were *impossible* to fail!

Elena Zelayeta is the type of person William James the philosopher-psychologist would call "tough minded." The world, according to this great thinker, is made up of two kinds of people—the "tough-minded" and "tender-minded." The tender-minded are the ones who wilt under obstacles and difficulties. They are cut to the quick by criticism and lose heart. They are the ones who whine and fail. But the tough-minded individuals are not like that. They are people from all walks of life, the manual workers and the merchants, the mothers and the fathers, the teachers, the old people, and the young people too, who have a strong element of toughness built into them by Almighty God. By toughness is meant the inner power to stand up to a difficulty; to have what it takes to take it.

Up in the little town of Carmel, New York, where we publish *Guideposts* magazine, lived a boy named Jim Mackey. Jim was fourteen years old; a lovable boy and real man, one of the truly tough-minded people of this world. He was a natural born athlete, one of the very best. But early in his high school career, be began to limp. It soon developed that he had a cancer. An operation was required, and Jim's leg was amputated. As soon as he was out of the hospital, he went around to the high school on his crutches, talking cheerfully about how he was going to have a wooden leg soon. "Then I'll be able to hold up my socks with a thumb tack," he said. "None of you guys can do that!"

As soon as the football season started, Jim went to the coach and asked if he could be one of the team managers. For weeks he appeared regularly for practice, carrying the coach's set of plays and infusing the team with his contagious, fiery courage. Then one afternoon he missed a practice. The coach was worried. He checked, and learned that Jim was in the hospital having another examination. Later, he learned that the examination had revealed lung cancer. "Jim will be dead," said the doctor, "within six weeks."

Jim's parents decided not to tell the boy about his death sentence; they wanted him to live as normal a life as he could for the last few weeks. So, Jim was soon back at practice again with his big smile and his offering of enthusiasm and courage. With his inspiration the team raced through the season undefeated, and to celebrate they decided to throw a banquet. Jim was to receive a victory football autographed by each member of the team. The banquet, however, was not the success it should have been. Jim was not there. He was too weak to attend.

A few weeks later, however, Jim was back again, this time at a basketball game. He was pale, very pale, but aside from that he was the same old Jim, smiling, laughing, making jokes. When, after the game, he went to the coach's office the entire football team was there. The coach scolded him gently for missing the banquet. "I'm on a diet, Coach," said Jim with a grin that covered his pain. Then one of the team members presented him with the victor's football. "We won it because of you, Jim," he said. Jim said a quiet thanks with tears in his eyes. The coach and Jim and the other boys talked about plans for the next season, and then it was time to go. Jim turned, and at the door he said, looking at the coach with a steady, level gaze:

"Good-bye, Coach."

"Don't you mean, 'so long,' Jim?" the coach asked.

Jim's eyes lighted up and his steady gaze turned into a smile. "Don't worry, Coach," he said. "I'm all set." And with that he was gone.

Two days later, he was dead.

Jim had known all along about his death sentence. But he could take it, for you see he was a tough-minded positive thinker. He made of this sad and tragic fact a creative experience. But, someone might say, he died; his positive thinking didn't get him very much. This is not true. Jim knew how to reach out for faith and how to create something warm and uplifting from the worse possible situation. He wasn't burying his head in the sand; he knew full well what was in store for him, and yet he chose not to be defeated! Jim was never defeated. He took his life, short as it was, and used it to instill courage, faith and laughter, permanently, into the lives and minds of the people who knew him. Could you, in any possible way, say that a person who succeeded in doing that with his life had been a failure?

That's what positive thinking is; it is tough-mindedness. It is refusing to be defeated. It is making the most of what you have to deal with in life. I have always been a reader of the works of the apostle of tough-mindedness: Thomas Carlyle. Recently I went up to Ecclefechan, the little Scotch village where he was born, to see if I might find there something of the strength of mind and character he possessed. Carlyle was the son of a stone mason. He started off to Edinburgh for his education with a shilling in his pocket and he walked into immortality.

Carlyle grew up in the little town of Ecclefechan, halfway between the Scottish border and the town of Dumfries. He loved Ecclefechan and Dumfrieshire. He might have been buried in Westminster Abbey but he preferred Ecclefechan. Queen Victoria once asked Carlyle what he considered the most beautiful road in Britain, and he answered, "The road from Ecclefechan to Dumfries." And then she asked him what he considered the second most beautiful road, and he answered, "Why, it's the road back to Ecclefechan."

I visited Carlyle's grave in the cemetery of his beloved Ecclefechan and sat at his graveside reading some of his words. Carlyle's message came to me anew—the essence of which is never give up; never give in; stand up to it—fight it through. God will aid you. According to Carlyle's understanding, life asks of each of us, "Will you be a hero, or will you be a coward?" It is just that direct and forthright. Where did Carlyle get such ideas? Of course, from the most rugged Book ever put together. "Be strong and of good courage; be not afraid, neither be thou dismayed; for the Lord thy God is with thee whithersoever thou goest." (Joshua 1:9)

Will you be a hero, or will you be a coward? Will you be tough-minded or tender-minded. The positive thinker will not be a coward. He believes in himself, in life, in humanity and in God. He knows his own capacity and his own ability. He is undaunted and invincible. He will draw the best from whatever comes.

The formula he uses is one by which he is changed from weakness to strength. Some time ago the Chase Manhattan Bank started excavation for a new skyscraper. Most of Manhattan Island is composed of solid bed-rock. This is the reason we can have structures that pierce the sky. But early excavations revealed that this site was not solid rock, as had been supposed, but contained a large pocket of quicksand! And of course it would be very difficult indeed to build a skyscraper on such a base.

So the bank people called in experts to suggest ways for meeting this situation constructively. One expert suggested pilings; another said to seal it off with caissons; but the cost would be prohibitive. Geologists were consulted: How long would it take to turn quicksand into sandstone? About a million years, the geologists answered. Well, the bank didn't feel they could wait that long. They then called in some soil solidification people, and this is where their search ended. These experts knew how to handle the quicksand problem. They sank pipes down into the quicksand and pumped into it a solution of sodium silicate and calcium chloride. In a few days the quicksand solidified into sandstone hard enough to permit the erection of a sixty-floor skyscraper building.

Does this seem miraculous? No, because it was done according to a sound, scientific principle; a proven, scientific formula. But I have seen "miracles" that make this achievement fade into insignificance. I have seen weak, defeated personalities who have had infused into them a special mental-spiritual formula called positive thinking, and I have seen them become as solid as rock. They have become strong people, well able to bear the weight of life most successfully.

This kind of transformation is available to all of us. It is in this sense that positive thinking always works. Positive thinking is able to transform us from cowards to heroes, from tender-minded to tough-minded individuals, from weak, negative, vacillating people to men of positive strength.

Although the life-changing power of positive thinking is available to all, some people experience difficulty in making it work. This is because of some strange psychological barrier that stands between them and the full use of positive thinking. One that keeps cropping up, is simply that they do not *want* it to work. They do not want to succeed. Actually, they are afraid to succeed. It's easier to wallow in self-pity. So, we create our own failure, and when a suggestion (such as positive thinking) comes along that will help overcome that failure, we subconsciously see to it that the suggestion doesn't work, and so we believe the principle, rather than ourselves is at fault. But when we understand such unhealthy mental reactions, then positive thinking begins to work. Recently I received this letter from a reader who lives in Petaluna, California:

> For the first time in my life I can see where I have created my own bad luck by my thought pattern. Since reading your book about positive thinking and trying to clear my mind, I find little resentments cropping up I thought I'd forgotten years ago. Such silly little things to carry along with me all these years.
> Certainly if you have helped me rub out these little termites, I owe you a great deal for showing me the way. I, too, have a pattern of failure and defeat. I never expected the best and I never got it, either. From here on out I'm going to go after the things I want, with confidence.
> I feel God gave me a good chance and I just didn't have sense enough to use it. My faith will certainly deepen as I remove these mental blocks that I have so industriously set up. Believe me I built them strong!

This woman states that, for the first time, she sees that she has been creating her own bad luck by her thoughts. We have to stop creating our own failure. We have to stop being afraid that success will come our way.

I have a very good friend who is outstanding in the field of industrial medicine. He is the medical director of one of the nation's giant companies. He has come up from the worst kind of failure to the finest kind of success. Like the quicksand, he was made into rock, but by a spiritual formula of great strength. The other day I received a letter from him which had this paragraph in it:

> I struggle constantly with success. For me, it has an insidious sweetness far more difficult to handle than the bitterness of failure, and much more uncertain as a stepping stone to spiritual progress.

I will call this man simply Dr. Tom, because he has such a spectacular story hidden in his past that I cannot name him fully. His was a dramatic struggle with success. He did not want it. It frightened him so thoroughly that he came close to killing himself rather than face it. In 1938 Dr. Tom was on the staff of a state mental hospital. Exactly ten years later he was paroled from this same hospital *as a patient!*

Dr. Tom started out in life with all the advantages. In fact, he had so many advantages that they got him in trouble. He had social position, a fine education, wealth, health and good looks. A nurse sat beside him in private school until he was nine years old; his father gave him an open checkbook when he was in high school. If Tom wanted anything, he just wrote a check; it was as simple as that. But along with this ease went trouble. People were always watching him, expecting great things from him because he came of such an outstanding family and "wonderful" environment. Nothing that Tom did seemed to live up to people's expectations. He never got any satisfaction out of success; in fact; success always seemed to get people annoyed with him: "Of course he's successful," they'd snap. "He ought to be!"

So Tom's subconscious mind did the thing that so many of our minds do. It said, "All right. If I can't get satisfaction from success, I'll get it from failure." And he proceeded to fail magnificently. When he was in college he started drinking. At medical school, his drinking became excessive. Drug addiction compounded his troubles. He married, set up a practice and had a child; the degeneration continued. In about ten years he reached the place where "just one" drink would start him off on a wild, blind drinking orgy that would last for days, even weeks. After one of his long disappearances, Dr. Tom came home to find that commitment papers had been made out against him. He was put in the violent ward of the state hospital, the same hospital where he had served as a doctor only a few years earlier.

"For forty-five days," Tom says, "I was out of my mind with D.T.'s. I was in solitary confinement, eating out of a tin plate like an animal. Then I began to come out of it and for another eighty-six days I lay in a comatose state, halfway between life and death. Surely this was as low as a man could sink. And then, suddenly—my heart still pounds when I think of it—I heard words spoken very slowly, and very distinctly. 'As far as the east is from the west, so far have I removed your transgressions from you.' (Psalm 103:12) Nothing has been the same for me since."

What had happened? Tom didn't know. He only knew that he had changed. He became calm. He was released from solitary confinement and allowed the comparative freedom of the ward. There he met two men who befriended him, and introduced him to Alcoholics Anonymous. In time, under the sponsorship of his AA friends, he was paroled from the hospital.

It was at this point that I met Tom at a religious conference where I was speaking. Scarcely have I ever known a man so thirsty for the water of life, so hungry for the bread of life. He wanted God, and God wanted him, and they found each other.

Dr. Tom did not go back to his practice right away. He felt he wasn't ready for that. He wanted to get a job on his own, one that had no relation to his childhood education. The only work he could find was a manual laboring job in the city dump. Think of that! A highly skilled, wealthy young man working as a laborer on the city dump and in the very southern community of his birth. But it was what Tom wanted. He wanted to see if he could be accepted for himself, and not for his family or his money.

One day while he was working, several of the "city fathers" came down to the dump for an inspection. Dr. Tom recognized some of his former schoolmates. He was suddenly filled with shame that they might recognize him, and he turned his back, bent down, and pretended to be working with something on the ground. A Negro fellow-worker saw him do this, and at the same time saw the neatly dressed city fathers. He must have sized up the situation quickly because, without saying a word, he turned and did Dr. Tom's work for him until the visitors left. To my mind that is one of the greatest, kindliest acts of understanding and brotherhood that I have ever heard about. Dr. Tom and his Negro friend never spoke about it, but it created a bond between them that was to have a wonderful effect on the young doctor. He took from it the strength that he needed.

"That man's name was Frank," Dr. Tom told me. "Frank will never know what he did for me. He accepted me. He taught me that I could be accepted for myself. First I had the acceptance of God, there in the hospital's solitary ward. Then I had the acceptance of man. It was what I needed in order to start again."

Today, Dr. Tom is again practicing medicine very successfully. He has a kind of enthusiasm about him, and a basic solidarity that comes from the new tough-mindedness that he has found. He was transformed from a "coward" to a "hero," to use Carlyle's terms. Of course, not many of us have such dramatic experiences with our fear of success, but it is nonetheless true that we often *don't want* positive thinking to work. We subconsciously see to it that our failure patterns remain intact.

But this is not the only block that can keep positive thinking from being effective. Sometimes there are strong negative elements in our lives that we refuse to clean out. We make feeble efforts to put positive forces to work, but they get stymied behind negative forces.

One night after I finished speaking at a dinner meeting in a hotel ballroom a man came up to me with the challenge: "I've been reading your stuff," he said, "I've tried it and it won't work."

"Why won't it work?" I asked him.

"That's what I'd like to know," he blustered.

Having a little time before taking a late plane I invited him to my hotel room for a talk. "I didn't mean to be impolite," he said as we sat down to chat. "But I'm trying to find out what's wrong. I seem to have lost my grip. I'm nervous and tense. I have a wonderful wife and family, a good business, a nice home, and I go to church. You'd think I'd be happy. But . . ." The recital went on and on. One trouble after another. And positive thinking, he said, did him no good at all.

After some discussion it occurred to me to throw out this question: "Are you doing anything wrong?"

"Nothing much," he muttered.

"What?" I asked.

"There's no point in going into that. I'm not doing anything that is in any way connected with my troubles. I'm only doing what everybody does."

"What does everybody else do?" I asked.

"Well," he said, "there is a little affair with a woman in Milwaukee."

"How little?" I asked.

He hesitated, "Well, maybe not so little."

"Maybe we had better face it. The plain truth is that you know you are doing something wrong, something you are ashamed of, something that could very well be the reason positive thinking isn't working for you."

"But how?" he demanded, on the defensive.

"Because guilt has a way of closing off your personality," I continued. "It sprouts fear and self-doubt; it restricts the power that gives vitality to the thought-flow. Constructive thinking becomes more difficult. Also, there is the self-punishment mechanism to deal with. When you are doing something wrong, you want to punish yourself to get relief from conscience distress. So actually, you try to make yourself fail, strange as it may sound. Of course all this blocks the positive feelings and thoughts that you do have. It's possible that all your misery and conflict stems from this sour area in your life."

"Well, what do I do about it?" he asked. Then he continued, "I guess I know the answer—stop doing it, get forgiveness—is that it?"

"That's it," I agreed. "And then you must forgive yourself. Do you want to start now?" He nodded. I could see that he was in earnest so I prayed, and he prayed. I made him pray out loud because he really had a lot to unload. And because he was sincere in his desire for change, God came into the picture and poured spiritual strength into him. Then his positive thinking really started working. Gone now is the woman in Milwaukee. Gone are the guilt and conflict feelings. As he became spiritually organized he found that it was quite possible for him to apply the principles of positive thinking with effective results. Naturally, this change did not happen all at once, but it *did* happen, and of course that's the important thing. One of the greatest facts in this world is that when a man changes, really changes in the God-centered way, everything changes.

Again, there is nothing mysterious about this. It is just common sense. We do something wrong, we feel guilty about it, and we expect punishment. If this remains uncorrected, the tendency is to punish ourselves, often through failures. That is the way the human mind is made. To correct the situation we must first clean out the wrong-doings; then the guilt feelings disappear and the need to punish ourselves with failures is thus eliminated. When this process has been completed, the principles of positive thinking can be tremendously effective.

One of the most important reasons why positive thinking seems not to work sometimes is that it has not really been put to a test. Positive thinking requires training and study and long perseverance. You have to be willing to work at it, sometimes for a long while, as was the case of a woman who spent four months of good solid, even painful effort before she got the results she sought. She wrote the following:

Dear Dr. Peale:

On the morning of January 21, 1956, I awoke with a headache. I am a registered nurse and I didn't think much of it at the time. A headache for a mother of three children is not an unheard of thing. Little did I know, as I downed a couple of aspirins, that this one was to be my constant companion for the next eight months.

Why should I have a headache? Seven doctors later, a badly depleted bank account, and a skin full of the newest drugs found me fifteen pounds lighter, an almost raving maniac, the sight badly impaired in one eye, blood pressure sky high and the headache.

My husband and I are devout Catholics. I was beyond the ability to pray so my husband prayed for both of us. He prayed God would direct him to help for me. It was in a chiropractor's office that I learned the power of positive thinking. I did not believe all this doctor told me, but when your book, *The Power of Positive Thinking*, fell into my hands I began to believe it might be so. Fortified with the spoken word of this sage doctor, plus the written material in your book, I began to apply to myself the principles.

To the degree I was able to understand and change my concepts from negative to positive—my headaches lessened. It took four months. I took no medication during this time and by September of that same year I had the last of the headaches.

I must add, our medical expenses have dropped about 80 per cent since I've changed my pattern of thinking. Do you know how a nurse thinks? Well, I'll tell you. One of the children has a running nose. Now, to the average person it is a running nose, but not to a nurse. It's pneumonia! She shoots that concept out into the air, and into the child's head. The child accepts it and puts the picture into reality.

How do I know this—because I did it. Hospital insurance records will bear me out. I was so good at it I was able to put not one of our children in the hospital, but all three of them at once, plus myself.

Now when they get a cold I look at it for what it is, a cold. And you know something—that's just as far as it goes. They throw it off in a couple of days.

Notice that it took four months of hard work to get results. This registered nurse understood the principle of positive thinking all right, but it wasn't until she was willing to put it to a test, go all out with it, make an effort really to change herself that she got rid of her headaches and experienced radical change within herself.

Ben Hogan, one of the greatest golfers of all time, practices what he calls muscle memory. He gets out on the links and swings the very same golf shot over, and over, and yet over again until his muscles "memorize" the exact pattern they have to follow. It is the same with our thinking habits. They have to be trained by a deliberate learning process to react the way we want them to react when we are faced with life's problems. Our mind has to be *trained* to think positively.

A final thing that I would like to mention has to do with belief. Positive thinking will not work unless you believe it will work. You have to bring your faith to bear on your thinking processes. The reason a lot of people do not get anywhere with positive thinking is that their faith is diluted. They water it down with timid little doubts. They do not dare to believe! But when you *do* believe, what amazing results you have.

There is D. H. Metzger, for example. But first let me refer to one of the most effective positive thinkers I have ever been privileged to know, my friend, Roger Burman, New York Sales Manager for the National Cash Register Company. Roger has a passion for helping others. He is always bringing out latent possibilities and guiding men in overcoming difficulties.

Roger Burman's teaching of positive thinking was a godsend to one of his top salesmen, D. H. Metzger, who suddenly was afflicted with a growth in the throat. During the days of crisis Dave Metzger was able to say, "My mind was alerted to think right and have faith. I knew my life was at stake, but the feeling of doing right at the right time added confidence as to my future."

Then Dave Metzger encountered an even greater crisis, learning to speak again. How could he ever sell unless he could speak? Roger Burman told him that, with God's help, he could and would; and he did, too. In fact he became a top salesman, one of the most successful in his line. In his desire to help others Dave said:

In order that I may be helpful to others who may find themselves in a similar predicament, more or less, I would like to emphasize that I put into practice Dr. Norman Vincent Peale's philosophy as outlined in his *Power of Positive Thinking,* of getting to the point of emptying one's mind of all negative thoughts, all unhappy thoughts and all pessimistic thinking and filling that vacuum with happy thoughts, filling the mind with a determination to get well at all costs. I pictured in my mind a return of my former faculties and good health. By following the specialist's prescribed exercises, I visualized my return as a leading salesman for my company once again.

"Faith power works wonders" and I quote it from Dr. Peale's book. I cannot stress the value of this philosophy, the magic power of positive thinking for anyone who has any kind of a problem.

This whole new experience has renewed the statement: "Salesmen talk too much." Finding it necessary to say the "mostest" in the "leastest" number of words I have framed my word story in such a manner and in such a tone that the results have been most gratifying. I speak slower and lower, and find the customer leaning forward if he misses a word. I am not dominating the situation and giving the customer a chance to say "yes" much sooner than before. In this way I do not tax my strength. I "word plan" my sentence and now give the buyer a chance to be part of the sales. I confess I used to be part of that Etc., Etc., and Etc.

Conrad Hilton, an inspiring friend of mine for many years, magnificently demonstrated positive thinking in his victory over adversity in the building of his vast hotel empire. In his dynamic book, *Be My Guest,* he tells us that his parents gave him a two-part formula to which he owes much of his success. His mother said "pray" and his father said "work." Pray and work; how wise!

My own parents helped me similarly. My father said "think" and my mother said "believe." What power is in those four words when taken together; pray, work, think, believe!

Belief that is bold and daring—there is the formula. It carries all before it. Nothing can permanently stand against it. It magnificently focuses power. "If ye have faith . . . nothing shall be impossible unto you." (Matthew 17:20) Faith in God, faith in God's power in you, faith in life itself—that is the essence of positive thinking; not timid doubt, not weak speculation, but big, bold, daring faith—this is the victory.

Does positive thinking always work?

Of course it does; positive thinking will work if you are willing to work at it. It is not an easy discipline. It takes hard work and hard belief. It takes honest living, and a strong desire to succeed. And you will need to keep working at it constantly to achieve success in applying positive thinking. Just when you believe you have mastered it, you will have to develop it again.

My friend Justin Dart, head of Rexall Drugs, one of our greatest salesmen and business leaders said, "Positive thinking is just like golf. You get a good stroke or two, and you think you've mastered the game. But the next thing you know, you flub your shots again. So, with positive thinking you have to work at it again and then again, ever relearning it."

How right Mr. Dart is. You must do a day-to-day job on yourself, conditioning and reconditioning your thinking. But the results are really amazing. They are worth all the effort and change-in-habit that is required, as I will demonstrate in the chapters that follow.

Chapter II

PRECONDITION YOUR MIND TO SUCCESS

YOU CAN precondition your mind to success. This is a basic principle of positive thinking. You can actually forecast what your future failure or success will be by your present type of thinking.

And right here I think it is important to define what we mean by success. Naturally we do not mean mere achievement, but rather the more difficult feat of handling your life efficiently. It means to be a success as a person; controlled, organized, not part of the world's problem but part of its cure. This is the goal we should have for ourselves: the goal of successful living, of being a creative individual.

I learned a valuable lesson in successful living from a Pullman porter. I had a speaking date in Olean, New York, and my travel schedule called for an overnight trip on the Erie Railroad. My journey got off to a wonderful start the moment I stepped into the sleeping car. I was greeted by the porter, a big, genial, friendly man.

"Good evening, sir," he said. "Are you ready for a good night's sleep?"

"I sure am," I replied. "I can't wait to get into bed."

As he showed me into my compartment I saw that the bed was already made up. It was really an inviting sight. The sheets and covers were tight and neatly turned back, the bedroom was immaculate with a generous supply of towels, the temperature was exactly right. "You certainly know how to prepare an attractive room," I commented. I got into bed, read a few verses from my Bible, and then fell into a deep sleep. The next thing I knew it was nine o'clock and I usually wake up automatically at seven.

"Good morning, sir," said the porter as I was going in to breakfast. "How did you sleep?"

"Fine," I said, "just fine."

"Well, I'm not surprised; I knew you would. But you should have seen the man who got on just after you. First thing he said was, 'I know I'm not going to sleep, porter.' And then nothing was right. He wanted to be moved to the center of the car. He didn't like the way his bed was facing. The room was too cold and then it was too hot. Do you know the difference between you two gentlemen and why you slept well and he didn't?"

"No. I'm interested."

"You slept well because you had made up your mind to it. That other man had made up his mind not to sleep. A long time ago I discovered that those who ride with me sleep if they think they are going to sleep. They precondition their minds to sleep."

It was worth making the trip just to get that remark which contained such amazing insight. You can precondition your mind. You can precondition it to sleep, or to insomnia. You can precondition it to success, or to failure. In other words, that which you constantly think is going to happen, tends to happen. At this very minute, as you are reading this book, you are what your thoughts have made you over a long period of time. And it is possible to figure out, almost scientifically, what kind of person you will be ten years from now by analyzing the kind of thoughts you are now holding in your mind. Are they negative, destructive thoughts? Are you preconditioning yourself to failure? Or are they positive, healthy thoughts, so that you are forecasting your own success?

Let me tell you about a friend of mine, Norman A. McGee. Better still, here's a story from the *Savannah Morning News* about him:

Ten years ago, the Southland Oil Corporation was just an idea in the fertile brain of Norman A. McGee. Today it is a flourishing Savannah corporation occupying 24 acres at the Georgia State Port with fixed assets topping the $2,000,000 mark.

"I've been lucky many times," the 43-year-old McGee says. "On the other hand, I've resorted to prayer often, too. I believe anybody could have done it with persistence and faith —and a wife like mine."

McGee had this idea about forming a corporation for the distribution of oil products and he had worked hard to interest others in it. The prospects looked good, but McGee had no income and he was down to his last $1,000 in the bank.

"I asked my wife," McGee recalls, "what should I do? Keep on trying, or give up and take a job?"

Her answer made Southland Oil possible. "Keep on trying," she said. "Don't ever give up!"

What is McGee's secret? He thinks, he prays, he believes, he works and he has a wife who would never let him quit. What marvelous assets! He preconditioned himself to success. And he isn't working only for himself either. He is active in the Presbyterian Church and was elected to the legislature.

Now listen, my friend. You can also gain success. Stop thinking failure. Start thinking success. Think and pray and work. Get a goal, clearly define it, and never give up. But first start working on your thoughts. Precondition them with sound positive thinking. When you precondition your mind, you are in the process of transforming your life. We transform our lives by how we think. The Bible says ". . . be ye transformed by the renewing of your mind." (Romans 12:2) Thoughts are things. Thoughts are dynamic, thoughts are vital and creative, thoughts actually change conditions. If you hold defeatist thoughts, hate thoughts, dishonest thoughts, failure thoughts—these are destructive. If you have honest thoughts, love thoughts, if you have service thoughts, success thoughts—these are creative. By the renewing of your mind you can be transformed as a person. Your condition may be transformed by the substitution of positive thinking for negative thinking. This is being done every day as my contacts reveal. The following letter is an example:

Five years ago, right after my husband returned from the service, I had a complete physical and nervous breakdown. I was not able to face life. I became weak and nauseated after having given a simple devotional for our Sunday school class.

I became panicky and made excuses when asked to do things socially. When more than one or two unusual things faced me at a time, I would go to bed with nervous chills and a real and intense sickness. Then depression would set in, and I would feel so guilty and bad about leaving my family in the lurch and at upsetting them, that I would have a long hard battle before I could again face a full day's routine. I was miserable.

All this time my husband was taking his place in the community. Civic clubs, church and business were demanding more and more of his time and talent. I knew that as far as our marriage was concerned, I was being outgrown and the years would see us with nothing in common . . . he an active and happy person away from home and I more of a recluse each day.

Then came help! I found out about positive thinking. My husband ordered some literature about positive thinking, and here it was! I started reading with the feeling of, "I might as well try this, too." But this was new. Real. Something definite to work with.

Now time has passed. Six months ago when they asked me to be president of our Sunday school class I said no. I had no more than hung up the phone than I realized that this was God giving me a chance to overcome my sense of defeat. After a prayer, I phoned the committee and accepted the nomination. Then, until I took office, I prayed daily that God would let it be His work.

I have never faced that class with anything except a perfect calm and peace of heart. I am now secretary of our School Parents; work two days a week for my husband; bowl every week and do all my own housework. I seldom have even an hour of depression. My husband loves his home and we do civic work together. Thank you, Dr. Peale, and God bless you.

Here is a woman whose life was completely changed by a change in her thought pattern. She changed the conditions of her life by changing the conditions of her mental life. Disraeli, the great English statesman, made this wise remark: "Nurture your mind with great thoughts for you will never go any higher than you think." Therefore, think big. I believe the trouble with all of us is that we have a tendency to think only little thoughts about everything: about ourselves, our family, our children, our business. So we get little results.

I really believe it is a law—you will get no bigger results than your thoughts are big. Big thoughts get big results; little thoughts get little results. One of the most successful men I have ever known was William Danforth, who headed the Purrina Company. When Mr. Danforth was a boy he was puny. He would have qualified well for one of the "before" pictures in a body building advertisement. He has told me that he was small in thought, too. He did not think well of himself, and this insecurity was compounded by the slenderness of his physique.

But all this changed. William had a teacher in school who must have been one of the world's great builders of men. Privately, one day his teacher took him aside and said, "William, your thinking is all wrong. You think of yourself as a weakling and you are becoming one. But this need not be. I *dare* you to be a strong boy."

"What do you mean?" the boy asked. "You can't just dare yourself strong."

"Oh, yes, you can. Stand up here in front of me." Young Danforth stood up before the teacher. "Now take your posture, for instance. It shows that you are thinking weakness. What I want you to do is to think strength. Pull in your stomach, draw it up under your rib cage. Now. Do this. Think tall. Believe tall. Act tall. Dare tall. Stand on your own two feet and live tall like a man."

And that is what William Danforth did. The last time I saw him he was eighty-five years old. He was vigorous, healthy, active. And the last thing he said to me as we were parting was: "Remember, stand tall."

Justin Dart, head of the Rexall Drug Company, once played guard for Northwestern University. Before an important game the coach called him aside and said, "Go out there today and play as a great guard should. You can do it!"

Justin told me, "I know the coach overestimated me, but he gave me a new mental concept of myself. I shall never forget how I ran out on the field, running tall."

Big thinking, tall thinking. It is this that makes men big and conditions them to success.

One of my readers describes himself as a business doctor. John, as I shall designate him, takes ailing businesses and makes them well again. And he tells me that in nine out of ten cases there is nothing much wrong with the business except the personnel. "A sick business is usually run by sick men," he says. "The trick is to get the men to thinking of themselves as successful; and then the business will be successful."

John told me about a boy he met at one of the companies he was doctoring. This boy was about as low on the totem pole of that business as he could possibly be. He was the fifth assistant to the shipping clerk; he spent his days sticking on labels. But there was something appealing about him, and one day my friend said to the boy, "I see no reason why you couldn't be a great success if you *thought* you could be. You are a bright boy. You have the brains and the personality. I hope you're not content with sticking on labels. Have you ever thought of becoming a salesman?"

"Oh no, no. I couldn't do that," the boy said quickly.

"Don't answer so fast," said John. "I think you'd make a good salesman. I'm going to speak to the front office about switching you to another job."

The boy was upset. It made him feel insecure. He was used to sticking on labels. But John had his way and in a few

lays the boy was out of his blue denims and into a smart
suit, reporting for instructions.

"What do you want me to do?" said the boy. "I couldn't
possibly sell anything."

"Well now, the first thing I want you to do is to take a
good look at that door over there." The boy looked. On the
glass panel were the words "Sales Manager," and under it
was the name of the present sales manager, an older man
who was scheduled to retire in a few years.

"Now," said our business doctor, "I want you to photo-
graph mentally a picture of that door. Only I want you to
substitute your own name for the name you see there now.
Close your eyes. Can you mentally see that door? Can you
see your own name on it?" The boy nodded yes. "All right,
then. Here's what you do. Hold that picture firmly in your
mind; then work hard, study hard all the time, believe that
your name will eventually be on that door, and I know that
it will."

"And was it?" I asked.

"What do *you* think? I never saw anyone work so hard and
so long and so persistently. When I thought he was ready to
go out and sell I went with him on his first trip. I left him at
Wheeling, West Virginia. The boy looked at me and said,
'When you leave me I'm all alone, but I'll do my best.' "

"But I reminded him, 'You're not alone. Just remember
that; and remember also, you know how to sell. And that
Partner who is with you will help you.' "

A look of satisfaction came over John's face. "He turned
out great, that boy, and finally became the best sales manager
that company has ever had."

The manner in which you precondition your mind is extremely important because, whether good or bad, strong or
weak, that preconditioning tends to become a reality. Whatever you picture about yourself either as a success or a failure
will likely come to pass. "There is a deep tendency in human
nature," said a psychologist, "to become precisely like that
which we habitually imagine ourselves to be." Now imagination isn't fantasy. Imagination is the art or science of the
projected image. You might call it image-ing. And the sort
of image of yourself that you hold is very important—for
that image may become fact.

The thought is ancestor of the deed. If you precondition
your mind with thoughts of success, the deeds of success
naturally tend to follow. But, notice that an important in-

gredient of this pattern is to ask for God's help. Let me just say that again: A very important part of the secret of using positive thinking in any form is to include the active participation of God. This is borne out time and again in our mail.

I ordered *The Power of Positive Thinking* from Montgomery Ward at Fort Worth. At that time I was out of work. I called all over the country to find work. Everything looked very black for me and my family, then one day I just happened to see this book. Well, I didn't tell anyone about it but just ordered it and when it came I got busy reading it.

In a few days I began to get some confidence in myself, which I didn't have before, and God gave me courage. So one night I read where you could take God as a partner in your business so I asked him to be my partner. I got me a welding machine for I am a welder; and then I got a contract to build some cattle guards for the county. I kept asking God to be my partner so I finally got me a truck and put my stuff on, welding machine and equipment. Everything on credit. Didn't know how I was going to come out, just kept on fighting, having faith in God and praying.

All of a sudden my prayers began to be answered. I got some oil field welding pipe and got a pipeline contract that really gave me a push. He liked my work and gave me another line.

I could write about many things, but it is getting late. I can say one thing, through this book I got to know God more and the way you can have joy out of life that I didn't know before. Now I know what you can do with faith in God. Thank God, and you, for sending me on my way to success.

And then in a completely different vein, there is this letter from a woman who faced a terrible ordeal, but who preconditioned her mind to a successful adjustment. Here, too, note the important role God played in her success.

During the last year I have had three operations for cancer, the last one involving the amputation of my right arm and shoulder. I have been so thankful for God's presence during this time.

I had quite a struggle deciding whether to let the doctors do the extensive surgery they felt was necessary. I read the chapter "How To Use Faith in Healing" in *The Power of Positive Thinking* several times and prayed for guidance. I came to the conclusion that the best thing to do was to let the doctors do all they could and trust God for the rest. Once I was able to put myself completely in His hands I found peace and was able to go to the operating room without fear.

I made a very rapid recovery and now, eight weeks after surgery, am making preparations to be fitted with an artificial arm. I have been amazed at the way I have been able to accept this handicap without bitterness and depression.

Taking the power of God into your life is one of the most essential steps in preconditioning your mind to success. Forecast that you are going to achieve a certain goal, and then move steadily toward that goal. But if you have given yourself a really difficult assignment, you cannot achieve it by yourself. You need the help of God. The pathetic fact is that many of us do not live as people who have the Kingdom of God within us. We do not really use the great forces that Almighty God has put into us. Draw fully and confidently upon the power of God that He placed within you when He created you.

These are the powers that are available to all of us on our road to success. They are available, but they are of no use unless we take advantage of them. Far too often people spend their whole lives close to these riches without ever tapping them. They are like an old man I once heard about down in Texas. He had a small ranch which never amounted to much. All his life he had scrimped for a living and eventually he grew old and died.

The property was sold. The new owner drilled a well and struck a rich deposit of oil. Of course, the oil was there all the time waiting to gush forth. Many of us are living like that: we are sitting right on top of the richest sources of power that can be imagined, and we do nothing about it at all. It is there, waiting to be tapped. But the exploitation of these resources is up to you. Precondition your thinking to this truth and successful living can be yours.

It doesn't matter who you are or how often you've failed. Neither does it matter how old you are. Successful living can always be yours. I received a letter from a woman in Georgia describing the amazing transformation in the success-pattern of her father after he discovered what God could really do with his life. Before he tapped the powers of the Almighty, this lady told me, her father was a very unsuccessful person. He lost all his money in the market and after that he became bitter and resentful. He changed his work and tried to make the climb back, by himself, but failed again. But read the daughter's letter:

. . . he was terribly unhappy. He had no belief. He didn't believe in God, he didn't even believe in himself. He shut out all friendships, and did nothing but criticize people. You can imagine the effect this had on his children. I don't remember ever having a peaceful meal at home. None of us could gain any weight because we were so tense all the time.

About eighteen months ago my mother and father moved to Florida. He wanted to start all over again. Well, as you can probably guess things didn't work out well, and he became more unbearable than he was back in the dark days. He finally became so despondent that last September he had a serious heart attack. Later it was decided that he would have to have an operation.

It was while he was waiting for the operation that God came in. First of all, God told my sister and me at exactly the same time to send Dad some material about positive thinking. Dad read it and took God into his life.

Well now, here is your miracle, Dr. Peale. I was in Florida in February and my father looks twenty years younger. He is full of health and vitality. He keeps a Bible by his chair all the time. He loves everybody now, and he made three big sales in one day just while I was there. He constantly talks unashamedly of God and after witnessing this metamorphosis I am convinced that nothing, absolutely nothing, is impossible in this world as long as God is given half a chance.

Success is available to all of us if we will follow the basic principles of positive thinking.

You must never conclude, even though everything goes wrong, that you cannot succeed. Even at the worst there is a way out, a hidden secret that can turn failure into success and despair into happiness. No situation is so dark that there is not a ray of light. So if you face circumstances that you think are extremely difficult, if not utterly hopeless, I urge you to read and ponder the experience of Mr. and Mrs. J. P. Lingle of Missouri.

A couple of years ago Mrs. Lingle wrote me after reading *The Power of Positive Thinking* as follows:

Three years ago, after fourteen years with a national chain variety store, my husband and I had an opportunity to open a store of our own. We were quite undecided, and turned the decision over to God, asking that, if it were His will to please provide the money we would need to get started; and if it were not His will, to keep us from getting it.

Well, friends and relatives actually came and offered money to help us, and we felt that was our answer.

But it seemed to have been wrong from the beginning—we could never make ends meet and were constantly, for two and one-half years threatened with lawsuits, telegrams demanding payment, etc.

We are $10,000 in debt, and have no material assets other than a seven-year-old car and our furniture. My husband is making $310.00 a month after taxes, so that doesn't leave much to pay off debts. We refused to go into bankruptcy as too many people would have been cheated out of what we rightfully owe them, and we felt God wouldn't want us to do it that way, even though we could have, legally. It's especially hard to keep faith when we get a nasty letter from a creditor or I look at the staggering debts compared with the miniature salary.

If you would just send me a word that will help me through this, I would be deeply grateful. I'm not experienced enough to know how to handle my spiritual thinking at a time like this.

Well, I wrote the Lingles describing some steps which I thought might be helpful. But I thought that the *most* helpful thing I could do was to put them in touch with a successful positive thinker who lived near them. I asked him to talk with them. I am going to call this man simply "Mr. S." because Mr. S. believes in keeping his good works secret. He follows the spiritual principle of not letting the right hand know what the left hand is doing.

Mr. S., I knew, believed strongly in the spiritual principle of sharing, not only as a means of maintaining a successful way of life, but also as a means of obtaining it in the first place. He promptly went to see the Lingles and found that they were so deeply engrossed with their problem that they could talk of nothing but their $10,000 debt. He told them that the first step in solving their problem was to start sharing, to begin at once to give away at least 10 per cent of the little that was coming in.

"But," they protested, "we are $10,000 in debt!"

"So what," Mr. S. replied. "My wife and I went broke back in 1933. We were in your very same situation—only we were $63,000 in debt. And we tithed our way out." He explained the principle of sharing, how it stimulates and maintains success. He pointed out one of the most subtle rules of successful living; namely, that unselfish giving makes real receiving possible.

Mr. S. prayed with this couple and together they surrendered the problem into the Lord's hands, promising to follow

His guidance as it would be revealed to them. They broke with their self-pity, worry and tension. They let the problem go into God's hands; they let God take over. Then they were ready to start doing business on a creative and positive spiritual level. And incidentally, as they found, this is where being practical begins. They began to tithe their time, money and effort—in other words, they began to share themselves.

The first result to be recorded was in a letter from Mrs. Lingle in August, about four months after she wrote me the first time.

I wanted to let you know that I haven't had a single worry day. I even received a letter from a creditor and it didn't upset me in the least, which is a remarkable change in itself.

And a little later there was another report from the Lingles on the effects of tithing:

Have you time for an "inspiration story?" I have one. Two weeks ago, we received a notice from the State Tax Department informing us we were being assessed for $90. In addition the points were worn out in our car, and our liability insurance on the car had expired.

We had no more than received the assessment notice, (and had no idea where the money was to come from) when the Monroe Calculator office man here called and said he could sell our calculator (we've been trying to sell it for five months) at a price which would cover the tax, the auto repairs and buy the necessary insurance! Isn't that wonderful? But there's more to come!

I hadn't had any luck finding work that would allow me to be home with Skippy (our little boy). But, following the principles of tithing one's self, on an impulse, I stopped by the church here and went to the office, introduced myself and told them I had a typewriter at home; and if they ever had extra work to do, I would like to take it home and do it in an effort to give some of my time to the church.

Well, they were almost stricken dumb! They explained they had lost a secretary, and were so snowed under, my offer was truly an answer to prayer! So I brought several stencils home and cut them; and then the next day ran them, and lots more, off on the mimeo for them.

That night I received a phone call from an office I had called two months ago about work and had almost forgotten about. They wondered if I would be interested in doing extra work—*cutting stencils*—at $1.25 per hour to start. There wouldn't be any regular hours for me, I could come in each day whenever I wanted and go home whenever I wanted! Don't you find that inspiring?

And so it went, blessing after blessing, guidance after guidance to these happy people. They prayed, they trusted, they gave, and they got right up on top of their difficulties. Mr. Lingle made a new business connection as a store manager and he did all right, too, as the following happy letter from Mrs. Lingle, written two years later, indicates:

I just can't wait any longer!

Here is another story for you of how God is looking after us. It happened after your last visit.

You remember we had been looking for a car since last October, when our seven-year-old Studebaker started giving us fits. We found the one we wanted then, in October, a second-hand Buick, but we felt that we didn't need such a fine one. So Jim kept looking and looking, but none came up to the Buick in price, mileage, cleanness and all things considered.

So one day he said, "Well, we know we don't need that nice a car; we know we don't have the down payment, but if that's the car we're supposed to have, the down payment will come to us, and the car will still be on the lot waiting when it does."

You know, in Jim's business, he gets a percentage on any profit made during the year, but we were only open two months in 1958 and, of course, the profit the store made was eaten up by the opening expenses.

So imagine our surprise when Jim got a note from the office saying they were going to pay him a bonus on his profit, just as if there had been no opening expenses, but they felt he had worked hard and deserved it. They just don't do things like that! And instead of the usual 10 per cent, it was 15 per cent! So there was our down payment! And after four months of waiting, the car was still there!

Remember you asked how much we had been able to repay on our $10,000 debt when we talked on the phone? Well, next month, it will have been two years and we have repaid $4,000 since then! Well, four down and six to go. What a challenge!

And here is the last report to date from the Lingles. Note in it how the Lingles have now completely absorbed the principle of sharing:

This will tell how we are doing at the present time. We are far from being out of debt, but far from out of faith, too.

As for some of the spiritual principles which have helped us, there is no doubt that *helping others who are in need* stands at the top of the list. I'm enclosing a copy of the type of note we send when we discover someone who could use a little boost. In so doing, I'm letting out our secret, but perhaps, Dr. Peale, if you desire to use the idea, other people will pick it up and it's the sort of thing that can snowball into something wonderful. Here is the note which we send:

Dear Friends:

Every week Jim and I put back an offering in a little envelope we have for "others." Then when we learn of someone who could use a little boost—as we often have—we send something to them with a note like this.

We know Stan has a job now, but Saturday you said you only had a dollar, so maybe this will help out with his lunches and carfare until his first pay check comes in.

We don't want it back for ourselves, but there are two things we would like you to do—don't tell anyone about it, and when you begin to get on your feet again, find someone who could use it, and repay us by giving it to them under the same conditions.

No one knows we do this, and it must be kept just between God and you and us. And if you want to know our reasons, I'll give you a clue. Read Matthew 6:1-4.

Well, let's run down the list of principles of successful living that we have been talking about in this chapter.

First, it is important to define what success means to you. Define your goal clearly, pinpoint it. Be sure that your goal is in harmony with God's desires for you. For example, don't make the mistake of having only material success as your goal: God wants a lot more for you than superficial material wealth. He wants real wealth for you, the wealth of life that is successful in all its aspects: economic, social, spiritual, intellectual, physical. It is His desire to give you real riches. Don't underestimate the good things that God wants for you and will give you if you will only learn to receive.

Second, study until you really grasp the life-changing power of the truth that you can precondition your own success. Paint a picture of yourself as succeeding, hold that picture ever before you, and it will materialize. With positive thinking you can actually change the conditions of your life.

Third, bring God into a central place in your thought pattern. Pray, seek His guidance, strive to bring your effort into harmony with His teachings.

Fourth, to maintain your success with poise and without

tension, learn to share. Share your success liberally with others. Teach others how to think positively, how to achieve the same results with their lives that you do with yours. In this way you will be guaranteeing the continued flow of creative ideas in and around you: you will be paying the premiums on an insurance policy protecting the success you have achieved.

Use these four principles steadily and regularly in your life, and success—the true success of bountiful living—will be yours. Start now to precondition your mind to success.

Chapter III

No More Failure for You

HIS NAME was Bob. He was a big man, but shy. He was a salesman. But Bob's record was perilously near the bottom.

Yet, only a year after his superiors had decided to give Bob one last chance, he passed every other salesman to become the company's top producer. At the annual sales meeting, the manager called Bob to the platform to receive the prize as top man for the year. As the manager handed him a check he said: "Bob, you're a mystery. You've never been anywhere near the top in sales before, but now you've reached it. Besides, you came up from near the bottom. How did you do it? Tell the boys here."

Bob was embarrassed. He shifted from one foot to the other and his face turned red. "There's nothing I can tell them," he said. "I just got hold of something that changed me into a new man."

"What was that?" the manager asked curiously.

"Well, I simply found thirteen words—and those words changed everything. You see, when I was told you'd have to let me go if I didn't improve, I got to thinking. I went home that night and sat in my chair thinking some pretty honest thoughts with myself.

"Well, after a while, I happened to see an old Bible my mother had given me but which I hadn't looked at very often. She told me if I ever got into trouble I'd find an answer in that Book. Well, I was in real trouble. Maybe this was the time. Anyway, I took it from the shelf, blew the dust off it, and began to leaf through. But it wasn't until I was almost going to close it that I found exactly what I needed."

He hesitated in some embarrassment. Talking religion wasn't his line, but he continued doggedly. "I found these thirteen words: 'Behold, I make all things new . . . He that overcometh shall inherit all things.'

"Well, those words hit me like a ton of bricks. If anyone needed to be made new it was I.

"Right there I prayed to God to make me a new man, to

44

help me stop being such a flop. I meant this too, and I felt much better. I had the best sleep in weeks. I felt a little confidence for the first time.

"Next morning, I said those thirteen words to myself several times. And because I made up my mind to change everything about me and make it all new like the words I said, I went downtown and shot some of my last few bucks for a new suit and tie and took them home. I undressed, got into the tub and scrubbed myself hard. It seemed like I wanted to wash all the failure off of me. Then I dressed, and before going out, knelt down and prayed to God to help me. I looked in the mirror and, believe it or not, I actually looked like a new man. I know that sounds crazy, but it's the way I felt, too.

"I said, 'God, I'm going out now to make calls and I'm a new man. I'll do better with Your help. I found myself taking a lot more interest in the prospects I called on. I was more enthusiastic. I began to sell. I was enjoying myself, too. Everything went better. I guess that's all there is to it."

The man who told me this story said, "You could hear a pin drop. Then the boys tore off the lid with cheering like you'd never heard at a sales meeting." And why not, for they had seen actual proof that a man, with God's help, can make himself over, despite all failures.

So you do not need to put up with continued failure. I know this to be a fact and not theory. My reason for being so certain is because of the many people who have convincingly demonstrated the power to change from failure to success. Such change may not come easily, but it can and does come and that is the main thing. When you decide, really decide, that there shall be no more failure for you, and carry out the principles outlined in this chapter and book, there is no doubt there need be no more failure for you.

I base this assertion upon the many amazing results which have been reported to me by those who have practiced positive thinking.

For example, in a western state I stayed in a large and beautiful hotel. When I checked out, the manager came over to say good-bye.

"A fine hotel you have here," I said in thanking him for a pleasant stay.

He smiled and said quietly, "I owe it all to God and the help I received from positive thinking." Later he wrote me a sincere and moving statement of his dynamic change.

I used to be the biggest worry and fear man alive. When I had nothing to worry over, I would dream one up to stay in step with all the confusion and upheaval I lived in. This was a condition dating back from early childhood.

Five years ago this coming September, I came across some of your writing about positive thinking. This article aroused a tremendous amount of interest, and I knew immediately that here I had found something which could help me. I began to collect all the material you had written and listened to your Sunday radio broadcasts.

Dr. Peale, it is not easy to shake off long established habits, but the one thing which helped me most was that I began to read the Bible, and in very short order I realized that I wanted God to help me, and I received Jesus Christ.

I came across in your writing where you suggested draining out all your bad thoughts, like water out of a faucet, and replacing them with clean, healthy thoughts. I did this and had a real brain washing. Gone are the worries, fears and emotions. I might also like to mention that I gave up drinking.

Today, I am happy. I love everything I come in contact with and have acquired your habit of staying on top of every situation.

The principles of positive thinking work when applied with the honesty and sincerity this man used. Let me suggest an experiment. Take a pencil and paper and list your three chief failure areas; three points at which you are currently failing, or at least not doing as well as you desire.

It may be you do not get along too well with other people. Perhaps you are having trouble controlling desire. Is it for alcohol, sex, tobacco, or perhaps simply too much fattening food? Could be you simply cannot seem to master efficiency. Maybe you are easily discouraged, or negative. Whatever they are, big or little, list your failure areas in the order of their importance. Then let's see what to do about turning these failures into successes.

The first thing is to get an answer to that basic question, "Why do you have these failure points?"

That may be difficult to determine, and you may even require professional help to ferret out the real reasons for your failure. But actually, more often the place to look is within ourselves. And here we come upon some strange and complex facts. For one thing, psychologists tell us that there is even such a quirk as a failure wish. Success, for some psychological reason, seems too dangerous for many people. They cleverly find ways to avoid it, unconsciously, of course. They do not really want to succeed. So, when you give the reason for your failure, be sure it's the true reason.

But let us suppose that you really want to do something about failure. What corrective formula can you use? There is one simple formula that I have known to produce amazing results. It is a definite one, two, three positive-thinking procedure. If applied with maximum effort, it will almost certainly result in no more failure for you. Here's the formula:

> Try, really try.
> Think, really think.
> Believe, really believe.

Let's take that first point; *Try, really try.* Probably this doesn't have too much appeal, because trying can be very hard, so hard, in fact, that few people will actually attempt it. Or they may attempt it, but do not have what it takes to keep on trying. Let's face it, when was the last time you tackled one of the failures on your list with the determined attitude that you were going to get in there and try, *really* try? Most failure is simply due to the fact that we take the line of least "persistence." We do not make a prodigious effort to succeed.

Eddie Arcaro, the famous jockey, says that only a few horses really try. "Seventy per cent of them don't want to win," he declares, and he ought to know. In this respect it would seem that we are like race horses; we too seldom try, really try, to win.

William James, the famous psychologist, recognized the difficulty of making a great effort. He speaks of "the first layer of fatigue." This is the tiredness that comes after a little unusual effort. You try for a short while, become fatigued then simply quit. But God built an enormous reservoir of reserve energy into your system, which is available if you will just push down to it—just give a little more effort. It is like the accelerators on some automobiles which produce a sudden burst of added energy and power whenever needed by simply pressing down harder. Personality is constructed in much the same way. Push down hard on our personality accelerator and this extra power will come surging forth. We seldom give ourselves the extra push that penetrates below the first layer of fatigue to where vast untapped power lies. But when you do, you get amazing results.

The secret is in putting your *whole* mind to it. Actually we seldom use our full mental power—certainly not our full spiritual potential. We might as well admit we do not give a problem all we've got; only in the rarest instances or in the greatest crises. If you put your whole mind to a difficulty you will be astonished at your own power over it.

Do you really want power over your failures? Do you want it enough to try, really try? You can have it if you do. This applies in any failure area. A remarkable example of the victory-producing power over sheer, dogged effort, plus faith, is described in the following letter from a reader in New York. The writer herself says she hasn't much education. Indeed, the lack of punctuation adds to the letter's charm, so I am going to copy it just as it is written.

I'm a little old lady in my late 60's, and I would like to tell you all the ones that have no faith that with the power of faith one can achieve miracles. I'm sorry I have no education and can't even spell right, but I'm going to try and relate to you my first great problem of my life and how I did draw on the power of faith.

I was born a cripple with dislocation of both my hips and doctors said I would never walk but as I grew up and looked at others walk I said to myself please God help me. I know you love me, I was six years old and my heart was broke and so one day I tryed to stand up between two chairs and down I would go but I didn't give up. Every day I'd speak to God and tryed again and again until I held myself up for a few seconds and I can't describe to you the joy in my heart being able to stand on my feet. I gave one scream to mamma. I'm up. I can walk!

Then I went down again. I can't never forget the joy of my parents and when I tryed again my mother handed me the end of a broom stick while she held the other end and said, Give one step forward with one foot and then another and that is how my faith helped me to walk the duck walk thats what the doctors calls it but I have been so grateful ever since then.

Three years ago I had an accident and I broke my left ankle and was in the hospital and they took exrays of my legs. Then the doctors came to me and said lady how did you walk? And I said God was my doctor and they said its a miracle you have no socketts and no joints on your hips how did you stand up? And memories came back to me and I have waited 60 years to find out that I have no socketts and no joints for I never knew why.

Then the doctors were afraid that with the accident and broken ankle and my age I would not walk again but God

came to my rescue again and to the surprise of all I'm walking again, and still holding my job of taking care of four
children of a widow mother while she works. I'm a widow too
and had to work very hard to grow my children. My husband
died with the spanish flu in 1919. I had two little girls and a
son was born two month later. I scrubbed floors on my knees
for 17 years and never was sick in life. I don't know what
an headache is.

Now here is a person who knows what it is to try, really
try. "Every day I'd speak to God and tryed again and again
until I held myself up," she said. And I like that advice of her
mother, too: "Give one step forward with one foot and then
another." That's what trying means. It means being willing
to keep at your problems until they are solved. Keep at it,
try, keep at it; that constant attack attitude will ultimately
overcome any failure.

So with regard to your own problem area, or your own
failure area, are you tackling it well, only half-well, or just
well enough to get by? Are you putting an honest, all-out
effort into the solution? The fact cannot be repeated too
often, namely: You can eliminate your failure pattern by
learning to try, really try.

Difficulties should act as a spur. Charles de Gaulle once
said, "Difficulty attracts the man of character because it is
in embracing it that he realizes himself." That's real stuff.
Try and try and keep on trying and God will come to your
aid. God is always with the man who is willing to make a
gallant and repetitive effort.

I witnessed the Millrose Games in Madison Square Garden.
These are great games in which the finest athletes in the
country compete in various track events: running races, pole
vaulting, high jumping. And I saw something that was truly
wonderful, the breaking of the world's indoor high jump
record by John Thomas, a seventeen-year-old freshmen from
Boston University.

I saw John Thomas become the champion high jumper of
the world. One month before the Millrose Games, he jumped
6'9"; two weeks before the games, he jumped 6'11¾".
On the night of the games themselves, before a hushed
fifteen thousand people, he broke the world's record. To quote
one sports writer: "In one of the greatest moments of sports,
he took off toward the ceiling and topped the bar at seven
feet."

Only seventeen years old and world's champion indoor high

jumper! The crowd went wild. John was immediately be-
sieged by photographers, reporters, people hugging him and
shaking his hand. But he paid scant attention to them. In
fact, he waved them aside. He wasn't through trying yet. He
had made one world's record. He could have rested on his
laurels, but he was a boy who knows what it is to keep trying,
and there was another record he wanted that night. He
wanted to go after the outdoor record too. That was 7'1.2".
It was a record held by a Russian. John told the officials to
put the bar at 7'1.25". And once again fifteen thousand
people dropped into a deep silence. One time John failed.
Twice, he failed. A third time . . . he failed.

Now, I had a curious reaction to all this. At first I said to
myself that John Thomas had made a mistake. He had taken
the edge off his victory. But then I was ashamed of myself.
When I got to thinking about what that boy had done, I
saw that he was not out for the glory; he was driven by some
godlike impulse to try for something always just a little bit
out of his reach. Something greater.

They wouldn't let him try further that night. But I came
away with the feeling that I had been watching one of the
greatest athletes of all time in the making, because he knew
what it was to reach up and try, and even when he had
won, to try again for a higher goal. And this feeling proved
itself three weeks later when, in the same Madison Square
Garden, John "took off toward the ceiling" again, and this
time topped the bar at 7'1.25", thus becoming the world's
champion for both the indoor and the outdoor jump. He
tried, really tried. And it paid off in victory.

How about your own efforts? Are you willing to stretch
yourself? Have you honestly given your problem that big
extra try and done it more than once? Once isn't enough. It
takes many tries. And you will be surprised at what real trying will release in you. For so many people failure is simply
a matter of not making the expenditure of physical and mental effort that is needed for victory. Look over your failure
list. Can you say that each of these failures has been
probed with an honest, all-out effort, the kind of trying that
makes champions? If not, test the theory of trying, and
trying some more, and see what happens.

The second part of the formula for overcoming the failure
pattern is to think, really think . . . positively. I believe that
the power of positive thought is so great that you can think

yourself through any failure. You can think yourself out of any problem.

An illustration is the fourteen-year-old boy who read a want ad in the newspaper in which a job for a boy of his age was offered. When he arrived next morning at the appointed place, on time, he found twenty boys already in line.

This would have stumped a less forceful and resourceful boy, but this lad had what it takes to handle a situation. He thought. He made use of his head, which is a thinking machine designed by the Creator to help a person solve problems. His mind was not negative. He could think, really think, and so an idea was born. What a wonderful thing a thought-out idea is. It's powerful.

Taking a piece of paper he wrote a few lines; then, stepping out of line and asking the boy behind him to hold his place, he went over to the secretary of the man doing the hiring and said politely, "Please, Miss, will you kindly hand this note to your boss? It's important. Thank you very much."

The secretary was impressed by the boy; he was courteous, pleasant and forceful. A lesser boy she would no doubt have brushed aside, but this youngster was different. He had that attractive, indefinable quality called force. So she complied with his request and took the note in to her employer.

He read it, grinned, and handed it back to her. She read it and laughed. This is what it said:

"Dear Sir, I am the twenty-first kid in line. Please don't do anything until you see me."

Did he get the job? What do you think? A boy like that will inevitably go places and do things. He knew, though young in years, how to think, really think. He had already developed the ability to size up a problem quickly, attack it forcefully, and do the very best about it.

If the problem happens to be yourself, as actually a great many of life's problems are, solutions come more surely and even more easily when you think, really think. The *Saturday Evening Post* carried an interesting article about Tommy Bolt, who won the National Open Golf Championship in 1958. The subtitle of this article read, "It was clean, positive thinking that changed my life." It is a story of how a champion was made by positive thinking.

It seems that Mr. Bolt used to be called the "terrible tempered Mr. Bolt." He missed the championship a couple of times, due to his terrible temper. On one occasion, in a rage because he had missed a putt, he deliberately broke all of his clubs. Frequently he broke his five iron. To use his own colloquial phrase, he would just "wrap the five iron around a tree." Gradually the fans got onto this. Spectators followed Tommy Bolt around the course, and they would congregate at the greens and chant, "Miss it, miss it!" And he would accommodate them by missing. Then he would go into one of his rages, and the spectators were delighted. Mr. Bolt, not knowing how to think properly, was emotionally unstable. Wrong thinking, expressed in temper, resulted in failure to reach his goals.

Finally Tommy Bolt read a couple of books which straightened out his thinking. One of these was by Bishop Fulton J. Sheen. Another, as I was pleasantly surprised to learn, was one of my own books. And here is some of Tommy Bolt's testimony about his experience.

"I reformed my thinking," he said. "I reconditioned my attitudes, I strengthened my faith and put my trust in Someone bigger than I was, and it worked. My new positive attitude never wavered once I started. Clean positive thinking changed my life. I wanted to keep my thinking clear and straight. The things I read put a safety valve on my temper and formed a sort of protective coating against outside influences and distractions." The last sentence is a classic, but now comes one that is even more so: "I promised the Lord I would help Him help me." That's a tremendous idea, for God needs your help with you. Tommy Bolt used his failures to spur him on to success. Failure, for him, became a challenge, and that of course is what failure should always be.

It is absolutely vital to learn to think positively if failure patterns are to be overcome. You must recondition your attitudes until you have turned negativism into positivism. In this I am always reminded of a dynamic and unforgettable schoolteacher I had when I was a boy. All of a sudden, for no apparent reason, he would stop the class, walk up to the blackboard and write in big bold letters the word, CAN'T. And then he would turn to the class and smile and chant to them:

"What do I do?"

And the kids would laugh and chant back to him, "Knock the T off the CAN'T!!!"

He whisked an eraser over the "t" and the word became CAN. That's the kind of teaching we need to give ourselves. Knock the T off the Can't, and make it Can. This is the way to think, really think yourself away from your failures. If the word Can't ever gets firmly embedded in your mind it will cause all sorts of trouble.

It is astonishing how even successful enterprises can go badly when you take on the can't attitude. Years ago I knew an old gentleman who ran a lunch counter along the highway. It was a time of depression in business. The old man was fortunate enough to be a little blind and deaf. I say fortunate, because he didn't have to read about the depression or hear the negative conversation of his friends. So, not knowing there was a depression, he had a remarkably successful business. He painted his stand, he delivered a good article; he put up bright signs along the road which almost conveyed the aroma of his sandwiches. He made his merchandise so delicious that people who "had no money," would stop and buy his food.

The old man worked hard and sent his boy to college. There the boy took courses in economics and learned how bad things were. When he came home for Christmas and noticed the thriving business, he went to his father and said, "Pop, something's wrong around here. You shouldn't be as successful as you are. Why, you act as if you didn't know there was a depression on!"

And he told his father all about the depression, and how people were retrenching everywhere. As the father began to think it over and look around him, and listen to the negative thoughts, he said to himself: "Maybe I'd better not repaint my stand this year. I'd better save my money because there's a depression. And I'd better cut down on the amount of hamburger I put in these sandwiches. And what's the use of putting out signs if nobody has any money." And so he stopped all positive efforts. The result: business soon fell off. When the boy came back for the Easter vacation the father told him, "Son, I want to thank you for the information you gave me about the depression. It's absolutely true. I feel it in my business. A college education, son, is a wonderful thing."

That is what happens when negative thinking gets lodged in our minds. Such thoughts should be drained out constantly. Dr. Sara Jordan, co-founder of Boston's Lahey Clinic, has a wonderful way of putting it. "Every day give your brain a shampoo." What a thought! Get rid of all the dust and dirt and grime of negative thinking. Start off every day with clean, sparkling thoughts that will have nothing in them to impede the flow of success to you.

Give your brain a shampoo every morning. Get your day started right mentally and it will continue right. One winter morning I had occasion to get up very early. I went into the living room and looked out at the glorious morning sky. It suddenly occurred to me that Emerson was right when he said that ". . . The sky is the daily bread of the soul." Our apartment faces west, overlooking Central Park, an area in the heart of the city, four miles long and one-half mile wide. The sky that morning was like a gigantic fireplace, with flames shooting up over the city. There was a soft blanket of broken clouds overhead and, across the park, windows were golden as they reflected the rising sun. The whole city was as still as an etching. The air was clear as crystal. The snow was clean and fresh. Suddenly I felt a strong instinct to pray and the prayer became one of joy and exhilaration. It was an unforgettable experience.

That day was a wonderful day. There were no failures in it, and I am sure it was because I had washed my mind clean before the day ever began. I felt stimulated and on a higher level of energy all day long. There is an anonymous poem that describes this type of experience graphically:

> Every morning, lean thine arms awhile
> Upon the window-sill of Heaven,
> And gaze upon the Lord . . .
> Then, with that vision in thy heart,
> Turn strong to meet the day.

I have made this a kind of morning habit and can assure you of the amazing value of this technique for starting off a day—"lean upon the window-sill of heaven," leave off looking so hard at your difficulties, and instead, "gaze upon the Lord." In so doing you will have strength and peace and power. This practice has powerful revitalizing potential.

What are the things that you may wash out of your mind by a daily mental and spiritual shampoo? Resentments, of course, and fears and hatreds; also, the negative and selfish thoughts that impede the flow of power through your personality are flushed out. Such daily mental shampoo or thought cleansing re-establishes the perspective that leads to successful action.

Some years ago I was in Hollywood as technical advisor

for a motion picture called "One Foot in Heaven." One of the character actors working in this picture was a man named Harry Davenport. Harry told me a story about an experience he had with right-thinking a few years earlier. It seems that, at one time, he had been in a profession slump.

"I was actually a failure," said Harry. "And when I began to analyze what had happened to me, I saw that my motives had been all wrong. Performing before an audience I would think about how great I was, and had no special interest in the people of the audience. Well, it didn't take long for that kind of self-centered thinking to transmit itself to the audience, and ultimately it threatened my whole career. For if you think only of yourself, people pick it up and don't like you. I wasn't getting good jobs. After a while I became really disturbed and began to pray about it, and the answer I got was this: Project an attitude of love to your audience and see what happens.

"I thought that was a strange idea, but I was in such desperate straits that I would have tried anything. A few days later I received a call to play a part; it was not an important role, but I took it. Before the play started, I stood off stage in the wings and looked out over the audience. I saw a business man out front who seemed very unhappy. He looked like he had been dragged there by his wife, and wanted to be elsewhere. 'Well, I will try making you happy tonight,' I said silently. 'I will project love to you, and try to give you a pleasant evening.' And do you know I have never had a better performance or felt greater happiness in my work. It was the turning point in my career. Today I wouldn't dare give a performance without first seeing to it that my thinking is in proper order."

This conversation was one of the most determinative of my own life. I decided then and there never to go on the platform to make a speech or into the pulpit to deliver a sermon without sending out genuine love thoughts to my audience or congregation. I look out at the people present and pray that through me, as a medium, God may help each one. I wouldn't think of attempting a speech without carrying through this formula.

The same principle and procedure applies to anyone in any kind of work. Jim Johnson, my friend who operates a big hotel in Harrisburg, Pennsylvania, spends a definite period each day sending out such thoughts to his employees, and has created a wonderful spirit in his organization. At night when he leaves for his home, he stops his car across the river and looks back at the towering hotel. From there he sends out thoughts of good will and prayer to all the guests behind those windows and to all the workers who staff the hotel throughout the night. As you might suspect, this kind of thinking gives one a positive and wise attitude toward life. Jim once said something I never forgot. "I never knew a storm that didn't blow itself out."

And, last of all, believe, really believe. Believe in whom? In God, in Jesus Christ, and, with real humility, believe in yourself. Believe that you are going to be victorious and that very belief will go far toward bringing you the victory you believe in. Why does the Bible talk about faith so much? Because if you really believe, you can do tremendous things. You can if you believe you can. Believing opens the channels of creative, dynamic good. It sets power to flowing in even the most difficult circumstances.

One of the world's most accomplished positive thinkers is Casey Stengel, pilot of the New York Yankees. During one World Series, when the Yankees were fighting it out with the Milwaukee Braves, positive thought power brought really spectacular results. The Yankees had had an easy year of it in the American League. They had no real competition at all, and they won the pennant so early that it worked to their disadvantage, for they played rather colorless ball toward the end of the season. The Yankee players were not really on their toes by the time the World Series started. The Yankees lost three out of the first four games. It looked like an ignominious defeat for Casey Stengel and his team. He had to win the next three games in a row if he was going to take the Series.

And that is exactly what Casey did. He got his players fired up to the point where they played super-human baseball. It was one of the most thrilling exploits I have ever witnessed, and at the time I found myself wondering what magic Casey used to turn such defeat into victory. Later I found the answer. I read an article in *Sports Illustrated* about Mr. Stengel, and in this article were two sentences that describe him perfectly. I copied them and memorized them, because to me they are really powerful sentences. "Defeat does not awe Casey, and he is on good terms with hope." And the other was, "In the worst moment of defeat, he was looking for victory."

There you have it. Casey Stengel never once believed in

defeat. He believed in victory. He "knew" he was going to win that Series, and he managed by some peculiar alchemy to transmit this belief to the Yankee ball team. And, of course, with that kind of certainty behind them, they were invincible.

I am going to close this chapter with a deeply moving letter that I received from a young mother. If you have any doubts as to the amazing results of positive thinking, you will surely lose them after reading this letter. We get thousands of letters in my office, from people in all kinds of circumstances. Some are enough to break your heart. They are filled with stories of pain, suffering, heartache, disappointment—it is most pathetic, all the troubles people have to deal with in life. But it is also inspiring to read about how tremendous people become when they develop that magic ingredient of belief. You can believe yourself to victory over the greatest obstacles in the world, as did Mrs. Harry Fike of Bexley, Ohio, who writes:

Dear Dr. Peale:

On October 30 of last year when I was pregnant five and one-half months I had an unfortunate accident—a rupture of the membrane enclosing the baby. This had happened to me in two previous pregnancies with the resulting loss of the baby. On the first two occasions the doctors told me such an accident was absolutely hopeless and I accepted their decision. I remember going to the hospital and saying on the delivery table, "It is hopeless. My baby is too small and will die," and that is what happened, exactly.

This time another doctor told me, "It's up to you and God." At first I panicked, but soon got hold of myself. My instructions were not to move. So I propped myself in an upright position in bed and vowed I would not move for at least a month—which I did not. With a four-year-old and a two-year-old this was easier to say than to do. But with the help of my husband I stayed there one month to the day, never lying down or turning to the side. Whenever the situation seemed threatening I would thank God that the baby was going to be all right. I prayed constantly for myself, but most of the time I thanked God for His blessings.

Every time someone talked discouragingly to me I simply told them that everything would be all right. One month later I went into labor, but I was not afraid. Even the resident doctor in the labor room told me that my baby would be too small. I heard him on the hall telephone telling my doctor that I thought the baby would be large enough but it was

wishful thinking. I watched the baby's birth and when I saw
him I almost panicked again seeing how tiny he was. But his
eyes were open and he was struggling for breath. He was also
deep purple. He weighed 2 lbs. 9 ozs.

My pediatrician arrived at the hospital and met me coming
out of the delivery room. While all others shook their heads
he smiled and said, "It is possible for him to survive." He
didn't spout the discouraging statistics to me as most of the
others did. On the fourth day my obstetrician came in and
told me the baby was barely breathing, but I can remember
saying, "But he *is* breathing." I called my pediatrician and he
said the next time the obstetrician comes in and talks that way,
tell him to jump out the window. So I hung on and thanked
God over and over again.

After seven weeks my baby was discharged weighing 5 lbs.
3¾ ozs. He has been home a week, has a wonderful appetite
and weighs 6 lbs. In four days he will be two months old
and he wasn't even due until February 8th. No one will ever
discourage me in believing the power of faith.

How about that for a human experience of faith over defeat? She simply determined that, with God's help she would
not fail. I sent the letter back to that mother to save for her
baby when he grows up. What a priceless and inspiring possession it will be to him.

So, take another look at your failures in the light of these
three principles: *Try, really try. Think, really think. Believe,
really believe.* Put these powerful principles to work on your
failures, and they can be overcome. As you work with positive and creative ideas you can so develop yourself that
there will be no more failure for you.

Chapter IV

THE KIND OF PEOPLE PEOPLE LIKE

YOU WANT to be liked. So do I. To be liked and appreciated is a deep-seated human desire. That is why Dale Carnegie sold several million copies of his book *How to Win Friends and Influence People*. That is why tooth paste and gargles and deodorants are sold by the millions from ads which promise popularity for fifty-nine cents. In poll after poll the personal wish that comes up strongest is the desire to be well liked.

And so the problem of getting along well with others is no trifling matter; it is an important skill which must be mastered if we are to be effective and happy. And how is it done?

A first answer is a simple one, but one that is extremely vital, as experts will testify. I was having lunch with two good friends of mine, C. K. Woodbridge and Carol Lyttle, Chairman of the Board and Vice President of the Dictaphone Corporation, respectively. Our conversation was concerned mainly with the techniques of effective living. Since these two men are outstanding in sales work, I asked what, in their opinion, was the basic requirement of a successful salesman. Mr. Woodbridge answered me quickly. "It's to like people. Of course a man must believe in and know his product. He must be a hard worker and a positive thinker. But first of all he must like people."

I think that is the basic ingredient of popularity, too. Essentially, popularity is a form of salesmanship in that you "sell" yourself, if I may use that concept. When a man genuinely likes other people, he himself is quite certain to be liked in return. So, a primary step in being well liked is simply to like other people and like them sincerely, not for a purpose.

Of course, this is not always easy. Some people are more difficult to like than others. But the more you practice liking people, the easier it becomes. This is not done by blithely saying, I am now going to like everybody. While, as I said, it is simple, it is not that simple. Liking other people is the *result* of a way of life. It is the result of certain disciplined thought patterns. And one of the principal thought patterns for liking other people is positive thinking. It is taking a positive and not a negative attitude toward everyone.

It amazes me how often I hear the phrase, "I began to love everybody," when people are telling about the results of positive thinking in their lives. Here are a few examples culled from letters that come from Oshkosh, Fort Worth, San Diego and Louisville.

    . . . and then I just began to love everybody.
    . . . so that is the way things stand now. I like everybody and get along fine with them.
    . . . Then a strange thing began to happen to me. I began loving everybody.
    . . . Before I read *Positive Thinking*, frankly, I loved only myself; but then I went beyond myself. Now I actually like everyone. I can in all honesty say that.

It's not hard to understand why this is true. When people get rid of fear, anxiety and self-centeredness they develop a kind of ecstatic joy and delight in living. The world seems so different and newly wonderful that they tend to love everybody and everything. And they become so warm-hearted and delightful that people take a real liking to them. They change from withdrawn, worrying persons to ones with vitality and charm. They become "out-flowing" personalities; that is, personalities which now flow outward toward others in kindness and helpfulness.

If you are primarily concerned with yourself, you really haven't much chance of being one of the people people like. To become of that enviable type you'll just have to shift your primary attention away from yourself to other people. William James said, "The deepest drive in human nature is the desire to be appreciated." That also goes for the other person; he, too, wants to be appreciated by you. If you are abnormally concerned with yourself, craving attention, but absorbed in yourself, you will have no time to appreciate others and no inclination to do so, for that matter. And the other fellow wanting attention and regard, failing to get it from you, isn't going to be too enthusiastic about you.

I have a friend who is a natural-born positive thinker, and that's a blessing, for most people have to cultivate it. His

name is Charles Heydt. Charlie is one of the great "appreci-
ators" of this world. And as a result he is very well liked by
everyone. When my secretary buzzes and tells me that Charlie Heydt is on the line, my face always brightens. I am
delighted to talk to him, because Charlie is a builder-upper.
If he sees an article that I have written for some magazine,
he will take time out to call, or even to write a letter. "Dear
Norman: By golly that was a good article. Something that
needed to be said, too. You sure came up with a ringer."

It is not surprising, of course, that Charlie Heydt is one of
the people people like. Being a builder-upper is essentially a
question of paying attention to the other person's needs and
the inevitable result of this is that the builder-upper himself
becomes a beloved person.

If you want to be liked and respected, get to loving other
people. Really put yourself out in interest and love for them,
and stimulate them to bring out their best. Then, like bread
on the waters, interest and love will come back to you a
hundredfold.

One of my readers told me a story about Henry Ford
which I like very much. He and this friend were lunching
together when suddenly Henry Ford asked this question.
"Who is your best friend?"

His companion named several persons, but Ford took a
pencil and wrote these words on the tablecloth: "Your best
friend is he who brings out the best that is within you."

Look behind actions and see the real person. If you try to
help him be his best self, you will win esteem and confidence. If, in trying situations, you show a deep understanding and patience for a person, not only he, but others also
will like you very much indeed.

I received a letter from a woman in Philadelphia who
works on this principle. She had a difficult office manager
to deal with:

    . . . the day the office manager opened up a tirade against
  me, I wanted to quit. Actually I started to look for another
  job. Then, what I had been reading about positive thinking
  caught up with me. Now was the time for me to put it to
  work.
    So I took a chance. I wrote the boss a letter and told him
  I was very appreciative of his giving me a job and an opportunity of working in his business, but I felt that he could
  double his business if the atmosphere around the place was
  more amiable.

Did he realize that every time he called his office manager, the man became paralyzed? His brain went numb, he dropped whatever was in his hand on the nearest desk; that when he lit into the office manager he, in retaliation, lit into the people in the office? I told him I wanted to be a Christian. Why can't we all start loving one another around this place?

That was some weeks ago and to date I haven't been fired. The conditions are 90 per cent improved and everybody is happier. I know the boss came up the hard way and I feel sorry for him, so I am going to redouble my efforts to help him all I can.

This woman, thinking positive, reacted to a difficult situation, not emotionally, but intelligently. She looked behind the "crippled condition" of the frightened office manager and had the keen insight to see that he acted as he did because he was insecure. She lifted the situation to a higher level of understanding because she was looking behind actions to the people themselves. Naturally she was a well liked and respected person in that office. She had learned to listen with understanding to a person's troubles even when he communicated through odd behavior rather than words. She knew that behavior often speaks as plainly as words, sometimes even more plainly. Many of us listen to words, but not to the harsher language of behavior, and therefore are blundering in our human relations.

And many of us, unfortunately, do not even know how to listen to words. The art of listening is certainly one of the great secrets of being well liked. Most of us tend to talk too much when people come to us with a problem. We try to give advice, whereas more often the thing that is needed is silence and the ability to transmit to the other person the sense of patient, understanding love.

My friend Arthur Gordon, the writer, tells a poignant story about a newspaper editor in a small town. He was often at his desk until late at night writing editorials and doing other work. One night about midnight there was a rap on his door. "Come in," he called. The door opened and there before him was the haggard face of a neighbor, a man whose little boy had recently been drowned. The editor knew the story. This man had taken his wife and son out canoeing. The canoe had overturned; the wife was saved, but the child had drowned. Ever since the tragedy the father had been beside himself. Apparently he had been walking the streets in a daze and had been drawn by the editor's light—perhaps by the editor's understanding and kindness.

"Here, Bill," said the newspaperman. "Sit down and rest yourself a while."

The broken-hearted father sat down, then slumped forward in utter dejection and silence. And here the editor did an interesting thing. Instead of filling the void with a lot of talk, he simply went back to work. He was not upset by the other man's silence. After awhile he asked, "Would you like to have a cup of coffee, Bill?" He poured Bill a steaming cupful. "Drink that, old boy. The heat inside you will do you good." They sipped their coffee. Still there was no conversation.

After quite awhile the neighbor said, "I'm not ready to talk yet, Jack."

"That's OK. Just sit there as long as you want. I'll keep on with my work."

Much later Bill said, "I'm ready to talk." Then for a solid hour he poured it all out, while Jack listened. Bill went over the tragedy in meticulous, minute detail—what actually happened, what would have happened had he done this, what would not have happened had he done that, blaming himself for everything. He talked on and on until about three o'clock in the morning. Finally he stopped talking and said, "That's all I want to say tonight."

The editor came over, put his arm around his shoulder and said, "Go home, Bill, and get some sleep."

"May I come and talk to you again?"

"Any time," the editor told him. "Whenever you want to, day or night. God bless you."

That was all the editor did; he listened quietly, sympathetically and with love in his heart. And he was beloved by everybody in his community because he had this ability to listen creatively. He stimulated people to talk out their problems and find their own solutions. They all liked him for that.

Out in Ottumwa, Iowa, there is a man by the name of Al Stevens, a good friend of mine, who also knows how to listen creatively. Al Stevens is in a business that often stirs up a good deal of ill will; he is a bill collector. He owns the Wapello Adjustment Bureau. Businessmen pay him to collect bad debts. For years Al's was like any other collection agency. He made his calls, cajoled, pleaded, and sometimes he had to be rather firm. But then one day he came across the principles of positive thinking and he decided to run his business along those lines.

"Suppose," he said to himself, "that I take a more positive approach. Suppose I try to see each of these debtors as people who are faced with serious problems that are getting them into debt. Suppose I try to help them solve their problems . . ."

So Al Stevens turned his collection agency into a human service bureau aimed at helping other people. On his first interview after he had made his decision, he met a twenty-seven-year-old housewife who owed a seven months old bill to a local merchant. Al didn't ask for money right away. Instead he said, "I know you have a problem or you wouldn't be in debt. I'm confident that we can work it out. Let's see if there isn't some solution." The kindly yet positive tone in which he spoke inspired a spirit of confidence.

He learned that a series of medical bills had consumed all the family's savings. Heavy debts had followed. Depression set in. The husband couldn't seem to hold a job and soon he and the wife were fighting all the time. Al figured out that the basic problem these people faced was the lack of a sense of organization. They couldn't seem to conquer their debts, no matter what they did. Al saw his job—he had to restore these people's confidence by showing them how to organize their way out of their difficulties. Then and there he had the young housewife write down all her family's debts in one column, and in another column, all their assets. Then, together, they worked a system of rotating payments.

"For eighty-five cents a day you can have all of your debts paid within a year. Can you manage that?" Al asked. The young woman was now sure that she could . . . and she did. Nine months later she was completely debt free, the husband had a good job, and their marital relations were on a much better footing.

Is it any wonder that Al Stevens is known as the Debt Doctor around Ottumwa? He is so beloved in his town that many of his customers send him Christmas cards. People go out of their way to cross the street and wish him a Happy New Year. Imagine that—sending cards and good wishes to your bill collector! When you start to think positively about your relations with other people, when you start to see their behavior as the result of problems which they are not handling successfully, you quickly become one of the people people like.

There is another quality that is possessed by an astounding percentage of sought-after people and it is this: they seem to know how to help their friends to accept themselves. Anyone who can do that will always gain affection. It is amazing how self-conscious people are, and it makes them most unhappy.

Self-conscious people are often those who have never learned to accept themselves. It's a very misery-producing state of mind, and self-defeating, too. Because the individual is suffering inwardly, other people unconsciously pick up tension and rigidity from his attitude and he never quite makes the grade with them. At least he thinks he doesn't and, in thinking it, he helps to create unsatisfactory relationships.

One of my readers is a writer of note and a popular public speaker. He is about 5'8" in height, which is only a shade below average. But he was very self-conscious about his height. He would never allow himself to be pictured with a group of men lest he appear dwarfed by them. He became shrinking and retiring and avoided social contacts as much as possible. He happened to read in one of my books about an old friend of mine, a rugged character who had a formula which he often gave to those who were having trouble, either with themselves or with circumstances, and it was this: Think big, pray big, believe big, act big and you'll be big.

That formula really took hold with this man and he began practicing it. It started him on the study and practice of positive thinking which led ultimately to a normalizing of his attitudes toward himself. He accepted himself. Now he has no self-consciousness at all about his height. I have heard him say that height isn't measured by the length of a man's legs or the size of his frame, but it's how tall he is above his ears that counts. Now, big men look up to him even though they have to glance down to do it. He learned to accept himself and his height and, in so doing, found his real size—which is plenty big. He often tells me that he loves me because he feels that I helped him accept himself. And I feel the same toward those who helped me accept myself.

I used to be very self-conscious of my speech because I felt that I never could get just the right words. Oftentimes I would grow hot and almost blush because of my awkwardness of expression, especially in small groups in personal conversation. Strangely enough, I was not bothered by this before an audience. If a person from a university background was present, for example, one whose use of words was exceptionally cultivated, it gave me an enormous inferiority complex and tended to cause me to close up and retreat. The inhibitions and inferiority feelings caused by this self-consciousness was one of my most painful struggles.

The man who together with the never failing support of my mother helped me conquer this sensitivity was Professor Hugh M. Tilroe, Dean of the College of Public Speaking of Syracuse University. He taught me the importance of being myself, of not trying to be like any other person or following any style or mode of speech. "Use plain, simple, every day English," he said, "words everyone understands. And just talk like yourself; you sound all right to me."

Professor Tilroe was a member of my church and I was very young. I asked him if he would criticize my sermons from the standpoint of technique. "Not on your life," he responded. "If you want instruction in public speaking, register at the University and pay your bills and I'll teach you in class. But when I come to church, you are the teacher and I am the pupil in the great school of Christ. You just be yourself and speak out of your heart."

To this day and until the end of my days, I shall love this man, for he helped me to accept myself and be myself.

If you always have a genuine interest in people and always think of them as important, if you are concerned about them, it will vastly add to your success and happiness and they will like you in return. This requires having something constructive to give to others and a skill in communicating it. Knowing how to help people is an art and the person who knows how to do it can always know that he will have the lasting affection of many.

One of my readers runs a clothing store in upstate New York. This man's business was in a run-down condition a few years ago. The store was drab and dark and unattractive. Merchandise lay on the tables in sloppy piles. The owner himself was in a state of gloom and negativism which paralleled the physical condition of his store.

One day an old friend, who was concerned about the storekeeper, came in to see him. "How's business?" the friend asked.

"Awful," was the answer. "Simply terrible."

The friend walked around studying the situation and he said, "Really, I'm not surprised. Just take a look at the condition of this place. What's eating you, Fred? You used to have the snappiest store in town."

The storekeeper said, "The trouble is I haven't enough money to freshen things up. I know how everything looks. If I could just collect my outstanding accounts I'd have enough to start fixing things the way they once were."

"You can't collect any of your debts?" asked the friend. "That's strange. Maybe I can help you. Let's just take a look. Would you mind showing me the names of those who are behind in payments?"

The storekeeper brought out his accounts and pointed to a list of some ninety-six customers who owed him money. The friend took out a pencil and pointed at random to a name. "Tell me something about this person," he said.

The storekeeper looked at him in surprise. "What do you mean?"

"You don't know this customer—anything about him, his family, his problems, his needs?"

The storekeeper was astonished. "Of course not. I haven't time for that kind of stuff. He's just an account to me and one who doesn't pay, at that."

The friend chose another name. "What about this one?" The story was the same. The storekeeper had to admit that he did not know, personally, more than ten of the ninety-six people he carried on his books as bad debts.

"All right now," the friend said, "will you try an experiment? Send out all of these bills as usual, but this time say a prayer for the person who will be receiving it. In your prayer express the desire that each person have a happy and prosperous use of the clothing which you have sold him. Pray that things will go well with him. Then at the bottom of the bill add a word of personal interest. I do not care what it is. Simply, 'I hope you are enjoying the sweater,' or 'If there is any problem with this pair of shoes, be sure to bring them in and we will see what we can do about it.' Then add a cheery word like 'Lots of luck,' or 'Hope the family is all well.'

"Then, at the first opportunity, learn something personal about each one of these people. When this customer comes to you again think of him not as a sale, but as a person you are going to help. These are not accounts—they are people. Your job is to serve human beings through your store, helping them to the best of your ability."

Well, the storekeeper was not sure this was a very businesslike approach, but he was at the point where he was willing to try anything. So, to please his friend and with a new feeling of faith, he decided to try the experiment of praying for each of the persons he was billing and adding the personal note.

And then was he surprised. Right away an amazing thing happened. Of the ninety-six people, over half promptly remitted in whole or in part. Others wrote back that they were sorry to be slow in their payments and asked if it would be all right if they paid next month. Some few even came by personally to pay their bill. The storekeeper was so impressed with the first success of the experiment that he decided to double his efforts. From that day his philosophy of business changed and today he is a very greatly liked and sought after member of his community. People think of him first as a friend and then as the man from whom they buy their clothes. Being liked is so simple; just be concerned in a helpful way about people.

I would like to mention another characteristic that almost all popular people have. It is a kind of urbane imperturbability. They are not easily irritated or annoyed. Some people seem to be able to rise above their irritations and they are fun to be with because they are poised and even-tempered. They seem to live on an upper level emotionally and are not easily riled up. They keep in a good humor and spirit.

In California I met Mrs. Sadie Bunker, a remarkable lady now over sixty-five who has come to be known as the "flying grandmother." Three years before, she had decided she would be a licensed pilot. She studied, practiced, got her license and now flies her own plane all the time. Recently she passed all the tests necessary to go on a sound-breaking flight. She told me she thought everybody ought to have a plane. When things get on her nerves she just goes to the airport, takes her plane seven thousand feet up in the air and right away everything seems different. "You look down on the earth and it looks like an awfully nice place; and the people, too, seem different from up above," she explained.

While you and I may not be able to get into a plane whenever we get irritated and go up to a higher altitude in the physical sense, anyone can, by positive thinking, take altitude in his mind and spirit. The higher your spiritual altitude the less irritated you will be and the more fun you will be as a companion. Just be sure you always stay on top of things.

Suppose, for instance, that you are being criticized. Does criticism get under your skin, hurt your feelings, make you irritable and therefore unpleasant to be around? Or are you able to handle criticism in such a way that you gain friends? Anyone can handle criticism if he tries. And the secret is to keep your thinking positive. Note the following letter:

I am a member of our City Council. At a recent meeting one Councilman became incensed when the rest of us disagreed with him over a bill. He stalked out of the chambers in wrath and into the arms of reporters.

The next day the newspapers quoted him as berating each of us for attempts to block progress. In his anger he attempted to cause sectional bitterness.

Fortunately, before the news reporters interviewed me I had been doing some reading in positive thinking. I shall always be grateful for the thoughts on this subject because it gave me the power to make the right kind of reply. I answered softly and constructively. That was several weeks ago and I am still hearing approval of my kindly feelings toward the angry councilman.

People who are able to turn criticism into a positive situation are going to attract friends. One of the most beloved public figures in this country was former President Herbert Hoover. Some time ago I had a good visit with Mr. Hoover and asked him this question. "At one time," I said, "you were probably the most criticized man in the United States. Nearly everybody seemed to be against you. It was customary to sneer at you. Nowadays, of course, you are America's grand old man and everybody on both sides of the political fence admires you. But when you were being so criticized, didn't it ever get inside you and bother you?"

Mr. Hoover looked at me with genuine surprise in his penetrating eyes and said, "Of course not."

Rather amazed, I asked, "But how come?"

"All you have to do in life," he said, "is to use your head. That is what you have it for—to use. When I decided to go into politics I sat down and figured out what it would mean. I weighed the cost. One thing was sure, I would get some very hard criticism. But in spite of that I went ahead. So when I got the criticism, I wasn't surprised. I had expected it and there it was. I was, therefore, better able to handle it. You see," he smiled, "I'm a positive thinker."

He looked at me for a moment. "But that is not the whole

answer. I am a Quaker." He did not amplify that remark, for he knew that I would understand. Quakers cultivate peace at the center. Irritation is simply absorbed in a deep spiritual peace in the mind and heart.

And so, being able to handle criticism, Mr. Hoover was destined to outlive the slurs of political life and become one of our best liked Americans. His philosophy is one that all of us could well follow, whether in public or private life. We are going to be criticized; you can count on that all right. This is one of the facts of living. By urbanely recognizing that fact we can develop the right spiritual attitude for handling criticism creatively. And it won't get you down when it comes if you are mentally and spiritually prepared for it.

Senator Paul Douglas of Illinois tells of a Quaker meeting where he learned a great lesson in handling criticism. As you know, the Quakers practice silence in their worship. Sometimes they sit for a long time without anybody saying anything. At this particular meeting the only person who spoke was an old man who rose and made this statement:

"Whenever a man differs with you or criticizes you, try to show him by every look, by your demeanor, and by your actions that you love him."

That was all the old man said, but Senator Douglas instantly knew that, as the Quakers phrase it, this man had "spoken to his condition."

One of the most practical anti-criticism formulas ever outlined is this: "Love your enemies, bless them that curse you, do good to them that hate you, and pray for them which despitefully use you, and persecute you." (Matthew 5:44) This is wonderful teaching when put into action, for it enables you to remain poised and confident in the face of the hostile words and actions of others. And those who watch you handling criticism in this way will instinctively be drawn to you. You will be the kind of person other persons like. As a matter of fact, people tend to like a criticized person (providing he is criticized a great deal by a great many) on the basis of the kicked dog psychology. And if the criticized person takes it quietly without rancor, not striking back but constantly loving, he will gather in friends faster than his critics can manufacture enemies.

That Scripture verse about loving enemies and treating people kindly is actually the subtlest technique ever devised for getting the love of everyone. It proves once again, if proof is needed, that Jesus Christ is the wisest of all teachers of the skill of living.

It is so easy to hate, so easy to be negative, so easy to accept defeat and live on a low level. It is easy, but it is also frustration and misery, because we never can be happy, deep in our souls, until we live according to what we are; namely, sons of God with the Kingdom of God within us.

In my correspondence with those who are working with the principles of positive thinking, I have noticed something else about the kind of people people like. And it is this; those who have what you might call up-beat personalities, who inspire others, who supply courage, strength and hope are deeply appreciated. All of us need courage, we need strength and hope, sometimes we need these qualities desperately. So, when people are able to draw this strong spirit from you, the natural result is that you become important to them. You gain a place in their hearts.

I know full well the effect of such people on me, and many others also testify to the effect upon them of the inspirational personality. The man who believes in something, who has some real convictions, who lives by a strong and sturdy faith and shares it freely becomes an influence in men's lives.

For example, one of my esteemed friends, George E. Sokolsky, the famous newspaper columnist, is a strong positive thinker and the word defeat is not in his vocabulary. He experienced several illnesses and I saw little of him for quite a while as he restricted his activity. But a few days ago he telephoned me about helping some people and I noted the old time vigor and verve in his voice.

"You seem on top of things, George," I commented.

"Sure thing," he replied. "We're supposed to be on top of things."

"But you've been through so much, what is your secret?"

"Secret! It's no secret. We have Someone with us, haven't we?"

He went on to tell about going into the hospital for examination. Then the doctors came in and put the X-ray pictures up against the window. "Know how to read an X-ray?" they asked.

George took a long look and said, "Sure, I've got cancer ... let's cut it out."

"They told me," he explained, "because they knew I could take it."

His heart doctor called to check his heart, to determine whether it could take an operation since he had experienced a coronary. He was amazed at Sokolsky's calmness. "You astonish me by your composure," the doctor said. "If I had your attitude I would live ten years longer."

"But," said George, "I have faith so I'm completely at ease. I'm in God's hands."

Following nearly five hours on the operating table, upon Sokolsky's return to consciousness, the surgeon said, "Well, you're alive."

"How do you know I'm alive?" returned his vigorous patient. "There's only one way I can know I'm alive—can I do my work. If I can't work, I am dead. Bring me a pad and pencil and I'll try writing a column. Then I'll know whether I'm alive."

The column was one of the best of his entire career.

Another up-beat personality is Colonel Frank Moore, head usher in my church in New York. Frank is a positive thinker who takes his Christian faith into business activity as well as into personal life.

In his office is a large conference table around which his executive staff of seven persons gathers regularly for important conferences. The table accommodates eight chairs. Colonel Moore at the beginning of his service in this organization commented to his staff upon the importance of the decisions they would reach in conferences and referred to the necessity for Divine guidance. In view of the fact that there was normally a vacant chair at the table, he wondered if it might not be a good idea always to leave the chair at the head of the table vacant to remind each person of a Presence who would always guide in decisions.

Slowly at first, but with growing appreciation for what it did to the meetings, the suggestion was accepted. The information regarding the vacant chair got around through the other offices and when joint meetings were held that chair was never occupied. The news spread outside the organization and a quiet but definite influence seemed to be derived.

Back of the table on the wall a prayer was reproduced on a framed mat 18 x 24 inches. It so impressed buyers and others that in one year alone over two thousand copies were requested and given away. This is the prayer:

O Lord, grant that each one who has to do with me today

may be happier for it. Let it be given me each hour today what I shall say, and grant me the wisdom of a loving heart that I may say the right thing rightly. Help me to enter into the mind of everyone who talks with me, and keep me alive to the feelings of each one present. Give me a quick eye for little kindnesses that I may be ready in doing them and gracious in receiving them. Give me a quick perception of the feelings and needs of others, and make me eager hearted in helping them. Amen.

Want to be liked? Lift people's spirit. Give them a little extra inspiration. Help build up their strength. They will like you for it. You'll have a warm place in their hearts for always.

So let's review some of the things we have been talking about in this chapter. What are the secrets of popularity? How do we go about becoming the kind of people people like?

1. In the first place, start now to like other people. How do you do this? One of the most successful ways is through positive thinking. Positive thinkers become out-flowing personalities, they cease to be obsessively concerned about themselves, and they begin to be concerned for others. They "love everybody" as is evidenced by the many times this phrase has cropped up in the letters people write me about the results of positive thinking. Once they begin to "love everybody," they themselves become lovable. They are sought out, needed personalities.

2. Always try to bring out the best in other people and you will be welcomed wherever you go. Learn to "listen" to behavior as well as to words that are spoken. People are often trying to communicate with you, for good or bad, through the way they act as well as by what they say. When you learn to listen to the problems people have, you are in a position to help them bring out the best that is within themselves.

3. Make your friends feel comfortable with themselves. People have a hard time accepting themselves. Help them do that and everyone will enjoy having you around.

4. Be calm, poised and cheerful. Learn how to rise above the irritations that life holds for us all. Develop an ability to fly to higher "spiritual altitudes," so that criticisms and petty unpleasantnesses will no longer ruffle you. Take for its full meaning the Biblical injunction, "Love your enemies, bless them that curse you, do good to them that hate you,

and pray for them which despitefully use you, and persecute you."

5. Be an up-beat personality so that people may receive inspirational support from you. You'll become very important to their lives.

Practice these principles in your daily life, and it will follow automatically that you will become one of the people people like.

Chapter V

There Can Be Lots of Fun in Life

HOW GOOD it is to be alive! What a glorious morning! I've really never felt better. This promises to be a wonderful day.

This may sound a bit exuberant but it's the way I feel this morning. I'm happy, I feel good. I'm getting ready to have a lot of fun today. When I walk down the street wouldn't be surprised if I whistled, just like when I was a youngster.

Come to think of it, it's been a long time since I heard anyone whistling on the street in New York City. And this isn't just an observation of my own. I was talking to Bill Arthur, the other day. Bill is managing editor of *Look* magazine. "Have you noticed that no one ever walks down Madison Avenue whistling?" he asked. Bill was raised in Louisville, Kentucky and he remembers his childhood days as a time when people seemingly knew how to get more fun from life than they do today.

Why is this? If it is true of you, what can you do to bring the want-to-whistle back into your attitude-of-living? What can you do to gain the natural, unaffected kind of joy that comes from deep down inside? I heard recently about a well-known psychiatrist who is working on a program called Positive Mental Health. Whenever he describes the results he hopes to obtain, he talks about his dog. "I come home from work and my dog greets me with a bound and a yelp and a kind of frenzy of joy. What a contrast this is to the gloom and depression I see on human faces during the day. This animal has the secret of deep fun. *This* is the way we should be able to react to life."

Now I'm not suggesting that we start bounding all over the place. We've all known people who make themselves a little ridiculous by overdoing this kind of enthusiastic happiness. I've often suspected that such people are only feigning happiness. But all of us have also known the rare and wonderful individual who is full of *deep* fun. There's the key. It's a fun that is not on the surface, nor light or superficial but one that derives from a deep sense of happiness at being what you are and where you are and doing what you are doing. Catch such a completely well adjusted person unawares, and you are apt to find him singing or whistling.

Let me repeat. I really feel happy today. And I think I can spot the origin of this good feeling, too. Yesterday afternoon it was a bright Sunday, and my wife Ruth and I took a walk with our young daughter, Lizzie. (I can't break myself of the habit of calling her Lizzie, although her mother would much prefer Elizabeth.) We had a lot of fun together. We walked up Fifth Avenue along the park, stepping out briskly, with our heads held high and our spirits held high, too. "It's fun to walk tall," Lizzie and Ruth and I agreed.

We walked a mile or more, all of us feeling dynamic, gay and enjoying life. We passed the Frank Lloyd Wright building, the Guggenheim Museum, on upper Fifth Avenue. "Isn't that beautiful!" said Lizzie. Well, I had never thought of that building as being particularly beautiful, but through her eyes I took a second look. (I was thinking a little taller, perhaps.) And when I looked that second time, I sensed the joy that the great architect had built into this structure. It spirals upward. It really transmits an emotion of enthusiasm and happiness and vigor. For the first time I began liking that building. Perhaps it was just the way I was feeling.

But that's the point. When you feel right, you tend to be joyful, you tend to have a sense of deep fun and your appreciation of everything expands. Dr. Henry C. Link, the psychologist, would never see a patient who was in a state of depression without first sending him for a vigorous turn around the block. "Walk rapidly around the block ten times," Dr. Link would say. "This will exercise the motor centers of the brain, and the blood will flow away from the emotional-activity centers. When you come back, you will be much more rational and receptive to positive thoughts."

Your physical condition has a lot to do with your ability to enjoy life. When you are refreshed and rejuvenated, life takes on new meaning. Proper exercise and proper rest are essential ingredients of joyful emotions. Some scientists, according to an account I read, recently made some experiments with what they call "massive doses of sleep."

Using drugs, they induced sleep in people who were tired and aging, and they reported a regeneration of tissues, a prolonging of life, the disappearance of disease and of course with this, the appearance of a new vitality and joy in living.

So, the first step in attaining this wonderful sense of the deep fun of life is to feel right. And treat your body right if you want your feelings to be right.

And the second step is to think right. Treat your mind right. Think positively. The positive thinker trains himself in the attitude of joy. He expects it, and then he finds it. What you look for, you will find—that is a basic law of life. Start looking for joy and you'll find it. For when you look for it, you will be able to see and recognize it. Some good friends of mine, Elsie and Otto Palmer, who live in Brooklyn, N.Y. looked for it and found it. They wrote:

> It is extremely difficult to give expression to one's innermost feelings; but since we have been learning about positive thinking, we feel you should know that we, too, are experiencing that wonderful something within that makes us want to sing for joy and tell the world about it.
>
> The application of your techniques has revolutionized our lives. While we have been brought up in a religious home, we never before understood how helpful and practical religion could and should be. It has given us a completely new and happy outlook on life to the extent that each day is begun with great expectancy and joy.
>
> I have made it a habit to expect a pleasant surprise each day and it has never failed to come to pass with one exception; and that is, the degree of the surprise depends on the degree of faith I put into my expectancy. If I am very sure, lukewarm, or cool—to that degree will the surprise come to pass.

I like the paragraph in this letter that speaks about expecting a pleasant surprise each day. This is first-rate positive thinking. The people who look forward into the future expecting to see great things are people who are going to be happy.

The other night I was driving up Park Avenue with a wonderful man, Dr. Arthur Judson Brown. Dr. Brown is 101 years old, and he has the spirit and verve of a teenager. "Just look at that skyline," he said. "New buildings everywhere. I think it's just great the way this town is always changing, always improving itself."

That's the way a *young* person thinks. I asked Dr. Brown what he thinks of modern young people. "I thank God for them," he said. "They are really great, these youngsters. They're so much wiser and better than I was at their age. They're going to create a new world for us. There is a new day on the way, and I'm looking forward to it."

At 101 years of age, he's looking forward to a great new day! I apologized to Dr. Brown for keeping him out so late at night. It was nearly eleven, and I thought he would normally be in bed at that hour. "Oh, not at all," he said. "I'm often up until midnight. But I'll get my rest tomorrow. I've learned, long ago, not to push myself too much. You ought to learn that too, you youngsters. Tomorrow I'll get up and have a leisurely breakfast and read the paper; and if I don't see my name in the obituary column, I'll go back to bed for some extra sleep."

The thing that determines whether or not a person is happy is an *inward* state or condition. It is what goes on in the mind that tells the story of whether you are happy and positive or sad and negative. Marcus Aurelius Antonius said, "No man is happy who does not think himself so." William Lyon Phelps remarked, "The happiest person is he who thinks the most interesting thoughts."

So, if you're not happy, you can experience this deep fun in life by doing a constructive job on your thoughts. If your mind is filled with grudges, hate, selfishness or off-color thoughts, why naturally the clear light of joy cannot filter through. You'll need to shift to a different mental life, and up-beat attitude, if you want a lot of fun out of life.

A reader I have known for some years was originally one of my "miserable" friends. A miserable friend is a person who makes everybody around him unhappy because he is unhappy himself. You might come into the presence of this man in a more or less jaunty frame of mind but he was a jauntiness-extractor. In no time at all he would take the jauntiness out of you.

In the course of time this man moved away, though he remained on my mailing list for positive thinking material. Then, three or four years later, I saw him again. He was so changed it was as though he had been reborn, which is exactly what had happened to him. He had been mentally reborn and spiritually, too. He was definitely a different person. I was so impressed by his change that I asked how he had managed it.

"I went on a seven day mental diet," he replied. He explained that he had become interested in a pamphlet by Emmet Fox called, "The Seven Day Mental Diet," which I had recommended to my readers. Observing that Americans are physically diet conscious, Dr. Fox urged people to undertake a mental diet as well. He made the point that a man becomes what he thinks.

And what is the seven day mental diet? It is this: you resolve that from a given minute you will, for seven days thereafter, watch your every word. You will not say a single negative thing, or a mean thing, or a dishonest thing. You will not make a depressing remark for seven days.

Now that is, of course, a big undertaking. "I tried it one day and failed," my friend said. "I tried it again, and went two days this time before I slipped. I tried again, unsuccessfully, and then again." But this is the kind of man who, when he goes out for anything, goes all out. "I asked God to help me, for I knew I just had to change myself or else! Then finally, for a whole week I succeeded. Not once, for seven days, did I fail. Then I thought I would ease off and just slump back a little into the old ways. But do you know, I found that there was a difference within myself. Actually, I could not slip back. I was changed, not completely of course; but I was not the same person. Since then life has become different. Now my mind is free of negative thoughts and I get real fun out of living." This is one of those sound new angles on positive thinking that readers pass along.

The two most important moments in the day are when you first open your eyes, and the moment when you drop off to sleep. These are the brackets of your conscious day. If those moments are packed full of positive, joyful thoughts, your day will be full of positive, joyful living. Elbert Hubbard said, "Be pleasant until ten o'clock in the morning and the rest of the day will take care of itself." Henry David Thoreau used to give himself good news first thing in the morning. He would tell himself how lucky he was to have been born. If he had never been born, he'd never have known the crunch of snow underfoot, or the glint of starlight; he'd never have smelled the fragrance of a wood fire nor would he have seen the love light in human eyes. He started off each day with thanksgiving.

My old friend from college days, Judson S. Sayre, President of the Norge Corporation, gets up every morning, looks in the mirror and says, "I am going to make good things happen today." And sometimes when he tends to become discouraged, he stops everything and thinks of some of the happiest experiences of his life. His spirit rises again. During the forty years I've known him, I've never seen him when he didn't radiate optimism and joy.

An excellent go-to-sleep technique is suggested by J. Harvey Howells in *This Week* magazine. "When the last good night has been said and the head is on the pillow, the soul is utterly alone with its thoughts. It is then that I ask myself, 'What was the happiest thing that happened today?' "

This has a great effect not only in setting the tone for a deep and peaceful night's sleep, but also in conditioning the mind to anticipate the new day soon to dawn.

This happiest thing may be only a little experience like the aroma of a flower, golden sunlight through a soft glass curtain, a chance word of friendship, a little kindness done, a fragment of melody. But to go mentally searching through the activities and fleeting impressions of the day for that one happiest thing; this is a most rewarding adventure on the borderline of sleep.

And Emerson used to end his day in a wonderful way. He would see to it that he finished it, completely. "Finish each day and be done with it," he advised. "You have done what you could. Some blunders and absurdities no doubt crept in; forget them as soon as you can. Tomorrow is a new day; begin it well and serenely and with too high a spirit to be cumbered with your old nonsense."

He knew better than to let his day end with regrets. Emerson was a door shutter. He shut the door on the day, and forgot it. He was like Lloyd George who, one day, was taking a walk with a friend and was carefully closing every gate after him. "You don't need to close those gates," said the friend.

"Oh yes," said Lloyd George. "I've spent my life shutting gates behind me. It's necessary, you know. You shut the gate behind you and the past is held there. Then you can start again."

In becoming a joyful person, it is extremely important to clean up mistakes, sins, errors; then forget them and go forward. "Forgetting those things which are behind, and reaching forth unto those things which are before." (Philippians 3:13) This is to be smart and wise.

The kind of people to whom life with Christ has become a

personal friendship are as natural as they can be in their enjoyment of religion. My friend Floyd McElroy, for example, is one. He and his wife Edith invited us to dinner with some other friends in their apartment on Fifth Avenue overlooking Central Park.

When we sat down to dinner Floyd did not call on me, his pastor, to offer thanks. I loved what he did. He offered the blessing himself and I thought it was one of the best I ever heard. Floyd said in his humble and unaffected manner, "Lord we thank You for our friends and we are happy that they are with us tonight. You have been so good to all of us and we are grateful. And now give us a gay and jovial evening in Jesus' name. Amen."

This kind of religion, in my judgment, is the real thing and it is a big natural part of life. Why do people insist upon making religion stilted and unnatural, and above all, getting pained looks on their faces when it is mentioned. When you've got the real article, you can hardly contain yourself, you're so happy. You are walking toward the sun.

The McElroys are people that I like to call "shadow leaders" rather than "shadow pushers." And what might that be? One sunny day I was standing with a friend at a window in one of New York's tall office buildings looking down on Fifth Avenue at 42nd Street near the Public Library. The friend I was with, Amos Parrish, is one of the nation's great merchandising experts and a man with a picturesque, imaginative mind. I knew that an idea was agitating him because he was scratching his chin and had a reflective look. Suddenly, pointing down at the sidewalk in front of the library he said, "A lot of those people down there are shadow pushers."

"What do you mean, shadow pushers?" I asked.

"Why don't you see," he replied. "They are walking away from the sun and their shadows go ahead of them. They are shadow pushers. Those others," he continued, pointing again, "Are shadow leaders. They are walking toward the sun, so their shadows fall behind them."

The difference is very significant, for if you are leading the shadow, you are master of life; but if you are trying to push shadows, life can be hard indeed. You can't have any real fun in life if you always have your back to the sun pushing shadows.

Another important principle in leading a happy fun-loving life is to learn to love and esteem the best in people. My father taught me the great truth that how you think about people, how you treat them and react to them, is extremely important to your own happiness. "Treat each man as a child of God is the secret," he said. "Hold him in esteem and it will make both him and you happy."

On Christmas Eve, when I was very young, I was out with my father doing some late Christmas shopping in our home town of Cincinnati. My father had as big a heart of love as any man I ever knew. It made no difference who a person was, he loved and talked with them all. And he was an extremely happy man. He had respect and esteem for every person. He saw beneath their exteriors, not as they appeared to be, but rather as they really were. And he had sharp insight, too. He knew people.

On this occasion I was loaded down with packages and felt tired and irritable. I was thinking how good it would be to get home when a beggar, a bleary-eyed, unshaved, dirty old man came up to me, touched my hand with his and asked for money. I recoiled from his soiled hand and rather impatiently brushed him aside.

"You shouldn't treat a man that way, Norman," said my father as soon as we were out of earshot.

"But, Dad, he's nothing but a bum."

"Bum?" he said. "There is no such thing as a bum. He is a child of God, my boy. Maybe he hasn't made the most of himself but he is a child of God, nonetheless. We must always look upon a man with esteem. Now, I want you to go and give him this." My father pulled out his pocketbook and handed me a dollar. That was a lot for his means. "And do exactly the way I tell you. Go up to him, hand him this dollar and speak to him with respect. Tell him you are giving him this dollar in the name of Christ."

"Oh," I objected, "I don't want to say that."

My father insisted. "Go and do as I tell you."

So I ran after the old man, caught up with him and said, "Excuse me, sir. I give you this dollar in the name of Christ."

The old man looked at me in absolute surprise. Then a wonderful smile spread over his face. A smile that made me forget he was dirty and unshaven. I could see his real face through the streaks of grime. His essential nobility came out. Graciously, with a sort of bow, he said, "I thank you, young sir, in the name of Christ."

My irritation and annoyance faded like magic. And suddenly I was happy, deeply happy. The very street seemed beautiful. In fact, I believe that in the moment I held that man in full and complete esteem, I came very close to Christ Himself. And that, of course, is one of the most joyful experiences any person can ever have. Since then I have made every effort to see people as my father saw them. And that has brought me untold satisfaction. I have often returned to the exact spot where this incident took place, on Fourth Street, Cincinnati.

Giving is another joy producer. This may mean giving money or time or interest or advice; anything that takes something out of you and transfers it to other people, helpfully. Anything that gets you out of yourself, actually helps you find yourself. It's a strange principle but it's true, nevertheless, that those who give the most have the most of whatever they give.

I recall a young businessman who was ambitious. To get money and get ahead was his idea. And there is nothing wrong with that idea if you keep yourself in the center of a sharing process at the same time. He gave to his job all he had and then some. He was not naturally selfish, but he wanted to go places and so he concentrated upon himself rather exclusively.

He read everything that had to do with self-improvement. So it was that he bought *The Power of Positive Thinking*. It was "right down his alley" he said. He put positive thinking principles into action though he had a materialistic slant on it! But he went all out with it; and as a result, he "took off like a jet for the top echelon" to quote his picturesque, though not too modest, words.

But soon he began developing tension and anxiety symptoms, the former from overdrive, the latter because he feared he couldn't sustain the fast, competitive pace he had set for himself. Then developed a pathetic reaction often experienced by those who "get ahead." Such men have a lot of fun arriving, but when they arrive there isn't as much fun in it as they expected. The top can turn out to be a rat race and ulcers, if being at the top is all you're interested in.

"Why don't I get fun out of life any more?" this man asked me. "I've hit the top through positive thinking and look—I'm still not forty. What's the matter with me? Am I stale or something?"

We checked him over for the usual causes of unhappiness.

We started by looking into his participation, or lack of it, in things which wouldn't "get him something."

"Why, I can't believe it," I said. "You're not giving a thing to anyone except your family, to whom you give everything."

The church which he attended with fair regularity got exactly one big dollar a week from him—about a twentieth of what he should have been giving on his income. He gave the community chest just as little as he could get away with. It wasn't that he was tight. This dollar-pinching was rather a holdover from his old insecurity feelings when he was a poor boy starting out. As for giving of his time and thought to help others, this didn't check out at all on his personal evaluation test.

"No wonder there's no fun in life for you," I said. "You've got to get outside of yourself. You've stopped the creative process. You're run down because everything has been coming in and nothing going out. You're like the dead sea, inlets but no outlets, and that means mental and spiritual stagnation."

Now, he wasn't as bad as this sounds. The fact that he was worried about the way he felt and frankly was willing to discuss it, humbly asking for guidance, showed him to be a pretty real person. And a real person can always get answers to problems like this.

We therefore gave him a positive thinking program which he had missed by stressing the materialistic values in positive thinking. Sure you can use it to make money but if you use it only that way it will fold back on you as it did with this man. So, we stepped it up to a higher level, into a positive thinking he hadn't seen before. This was designed to release him and remake him and it did.

1. He was to increase his giving to the Lord's work to 10 per cent of his income. Some of this was to go to the church, some to individuals (for whom there would be no tax exemption claim) and some to other charitable institutions.

2. He was to look for someone who needed help outside his family and friends, someone who might never be able to help him in return. The help might be monetary or in the form of advice, or just friendly interest. Perhaps he might select a deserving boy and help him get an education or get started in business.

3. He was to stop rushing long enough to give himself to people—a few leisurely words with those who were part of his

daily life: the waiter, the policeman on the corner, the news vendor, the elevator operator, or even his wife and children.

4. He was to go to his pastor and offer to help in some of the church's business problems. More than that he was to offer to call on a few people to carry the helpful ministry of the church to them, people in the hospital for example.

"Gosh that sounds like a time-consuming layout to me," he complained.

"Sure," I said, "that's exactly right. You must learn to give, not only money and good will, but time for the benefit of other people. But the pay-off will be more than worth it. You'll get back your old sense of fun if you follow this plan. It's either-or, take it or leave it." I knew my man, I knew he wouldn't leave it. He went for the businesslike approach when he knew it was sound. And this was.

To sum up this case history, which strung out over many months, he did follow the program and he did recover the ability to get a lot of fun out of life. He became an active factor in his community life. Moreover, the tension and anxiety subsided. Maybe he staved off a heart attack, who knows?

Still another element in the total joy-in-life formula is to know for a fact that you are able to meet and overcome the hardships, sorrows and tough circumstances of this world. This kind of happiness is priceless. This is that deep fun we were talking about earlier.

One thing after another happening to you can literally "knock the life out of you." The expression is realistic, life is knocked out of you, for a fact. Blow after blow can leave you pretty limp and discouraged. Ultimately you may feel so beaten that you crawl through life instead of standing up courageously and masterfully, taking things as they come and handling them with sure skill and force. There is no fun in life for the crawler-through-life. The licked are always unhappy. But those who know in their hearts that they are equal to every challenge, minor or major, are the ones who get a huge amount of fun out of life.

A man on a plane said "I'm a positive thinking Exhibit A! I don't say that boastfully, but because it's done so much for me. I was the world's worst self-defeating person. I blamed everyone for my failures—even the government. But I knew who was my worst enemy. As someone put it, 'If I could kick the pants of the man causing all my troubles I couldn't sit down for a week!'"

"And believe me it wasn't funny." Then he described a series of defeats and disappointments sufficient to take the heart out of any man. "At first I shied off positive thinking because you tied God into it and I didn't go for that religious approach. I took the psychology in the book and let the religion alone. But while I mentally agreed with the psychology, it didn't take with me. Perhaps I was too negative. But I noticed that you were always urging your readers to read and apply the Bible to problems. Frankly, I hadn't opened a Bible in years. But finally I started reading. At first I couldn't get a thing out of it and wondered why you were so keen for it. So I limited myself to looking up your references. I really tried to follow the things you suggested.

"I was reading the 84th Psalm and the eleventh verse struck me . . . 'No good thing will he withhold from them that walk uprightly.' (Psalm 84:11) 'Walk uprightly'—what did that mean? But it wasn't hard to figure out that I was crawling like a worm. I should stand up like a man and quit griping and being sorry for myself. I was full of self-pity. *Uprightly*—that was the word! Stand up to things— that was what I should be doing! And I got the idea that if I did that, God wouldn't hold back any good thing. So I started walking as sprightly as I could, not cringing like I had been doing. I also saw that *uprightly* meant no double dealing. I decided I'd straighten some things out, with God's help.

"I now see why you tie religion and practical psychology together. Religion makes it work, puts the oomph into it."

That's really an idea to get hold of. Or better still let it get hold of you. "No good thing will he withhold from them that walk uprightly." It gave this man new fun in living. He really had it.

But what about sorrow and grief? An effective demonstrator of positive thinking who achieved out of sorrow a quiet joy in life is Mrs. Anne Scherer of Switzerland. I met Mr. and Mrs. Scherer several years ago at the Beau Rivage Palace Hotel in Lausanne where he was the manager. Some months later Mr. Scherer died suddenly. Mrs. Scherer worked on, under the new manager, as hostess of the hotel. Recently when I returned to Lausanne it was evident that in her modest way Mrs. Scherer had adjusted quite well to her sorrow problem. She had achieved a quietly serene spirit that obviously derived from a deep source of strength.

"I admire the way you have managed to pull through this sad time with such fine spirit," I said. "You did the right thing by going back to work and keeping yourself busy."

Then Mrs. Scherer answered with an extraordinary philosophy of sorrow. "Actually it wasn't going back to work that did it for, you see, work is not a medicine, it is a drug. It desensitizes, but does not heal. It is only faith that heals."

That insight is a classic. Work desensitizes, but it does not heal. It is faith that heals. When we are suffering from deep emotional wounds, of course, we cannot have real happiness; not until the wounds are healed. Some of us make the mistake of thinking we can cure them with work, or perhaps with play; with drink or attempted forgetfulness. As Mrs. Scherer pointed out, these efforts only desensitize the wound for a while. But they do not cure. It is when one learns to apply faith in depth that a true curative process is begun.

A man from out West used to come to New York every now and then on business, and he would call me on the telephone. He had a deep emotional wound and his mood was invariably dejected, his thinking gloomy and somewhat cynical. This negative reaction to sorrow, negative to the point of being abnormal, went on for several years and then, all of a sudden, he wrote me a ten-page letter. I left it lying on my desk for a while before undertaking to read it. But I got into it and I was amazed; it was full of joy and hope. Here was the buoyant testimony of a man who at last had found himself and was telling me how happy he was.

What had happened? Well, this man finally decided he was on the wrong track with his gloomy attitudes and resolved to study and "try to apply" positive thinking techniques to his sorrow problem. He said, "I evolved some techniques you didn't give in your book and they worked beautifully. Perhaps you would like to pass them along to others." And I am glad to do just that for these ideas are sound. I give them to you just as I received them.

This man's "five-fold program of faith" follows:

First, I pray twenty-five times a day. Yes, I mean that; but these are fragmentary prayers as I walk or drive or work at my desk. I guarantee that if anybody will pray twenty-five times a day he will change the character of his thoughts and change his life. Perhaps this is what the Bible means when it tells us to "pray without ceasing."

Second, I soak my mind with Bible passages. I must have committed a couple of hundred texts by now. I say them over and think of them as going down and down into my subconscious.

Third, I take a piece of paper and see how many good thoughts I can write down about people I know and about situations, too. This was the toughest thing in the whole process as I had a lot of gripes about lots of people. And as to situations, I was always negative and pessimistic. However, I've found that if you think mean thoughts about people it makes you unhappy. But pleasant thoughts about people make you happy all over. And if you make yourself think that things are going to be O.K. that makes you happier too; and thinking that way often makes them turn out that way.

Fourth, I see how many times every day I can tell the Lord how much I love Him. This love-for-God feeling really does something to you. There was a time I would have ridiculed such a thing, but no more. The more I express my love for God the happier I become.

Fifth, I try to keep all sin out of my life. This is a big order, but even making the effort gives me a clean and happy feeling.

As I said, I tried this man's program on quite a few people and where they really worked at it, it proved effective. It is my belief that this spiritual formula will, as he indicates, go far toward curing anybody of unhappiness.

Who wants to live with joy? Who wants to feel like whistling on Madison Avenue or any other street? Pray twenty-five times a day. Soak the mind with Bible passages. See how many good thoughts you can think about people. Tell the Lord you love Him. Get sin out of your life. It is not easy. It takes self-discipline. It requires your doing something about yourself. But really there is no need for you to be unhappy. Simply do a rehabilitation job on your thoughts. Try spiritual living, really try it. You will discover for yourself that there's lots of fun in life.

Chapter VI

THE WONDERFUL LAW OF ABUNDANCE

THERE IS a law of abundance operating in life. And this abundance is for you.

Abundance is a wonderful word. I like the sound of it; it's full and rich. The root of this word, I'm told, is the Latin *undare* which means "to rise up in waves." So actually, when you think and practice abundance you stimulate all manner of good things to rise up toward you in waves.

I received a letter from a young man in Washington, D. C. A year ago this man, Lloyd, was in all sorts of trouble. His marriage was on the rocks, he was drinking, he couldn't hold a job; he had been fired seven times from positions with the Hot Shoppes restaurant chain. Certainly Lloyd couldn't say that all manner of good things were rising up toward him in waves, or even in dribbles.

Then Lloyd began to hear about the amazing effect that positive thinking had on people's lives. He read and studied *The Power of Positive Thinking* and all the books and articles he could find on the subject, and he made up his mind to try these techniques for himself. First, he had to deal with the past. Who would hire him with his record? But that was negative thinking. Sure he had failed before, but that did not have to determine the future.

In *The Power of Positive Thinking* he had read those dynamic words from the Bible, "Forgetting those things which are behind, and reaching forth unto those things which are before, I press toward the mark . . ." (Philippians 3:13)

Lloyd went out once more and applied for a job . . . at the Hot Shoppes; right back where he had been fired seven times. With his chin held high, but scared and frightened, and saying over those words from Philippians, Lloyd walked into the office of the personnel director. His new faith enabled him to tell this man that he wanted to work again. And an amazing thing happened. The personnel director said that if he could find one manager who would take Lloyd on, he could work there again. This firm, as I have since learned, began and operates on positive spiritual principles.

"I'm thankful to say," writes Lloyd, "that I found a manager who remembered my good qualities as well as the bad, and gave me another chance." He was hired as a waiter at this drive-in restaurant. Then and there Lloyd set a new pattern for himself. His letter continues:

> I made two simple promises to God and to myself, something which I've never dared do before, for to me a promise to anyone is serious but to God it is more so.
>
> First, I promised to read my Bible and pray—really pray —every day. Second, I promised to tithe, to give a tenth of my income to God regardless of whether I had a good night as a waiter or a bad one. I decided to go for that promise in the Bible: "Bring ye all the tithes into the storehouse—and prove me now herewith, saith the Lord of hosts, if I will not open you the windows of heaven, and pour you out a blessing, that there shall not be room enough to receive it." (Malachi 3:10)
>
> Now, I'm no saint and have plenty of faults but for once in my life I've found a happy, peaceful, workable relationship with my God. Often on the curb (drive-in service) when someone has failed to tip and my blood pressure starts to rise, somewhere from the Bible, or some phrase from one of your books will come to mind and I try to give that much *better* service to the next car.
>
> This morning, after I came home from work, I was reflecting on the past year, and I suddenly realized that the problems I had a year ago no longer exist.

And then Lloyd made an amazing statement. I think of it as a most constructive result of positive thinking. Remember, this statement comes from a young man whose life has been remade.

> I never thought I could afford to tithe before. But now I can't afford not to!

What dynamic thinking! The exclamation point at the end of the sentence is Lloyd's own. He felt like exclaiming to the world the power of the new idea he had uncovered. When he began to tithe, to give in earnest of himself and his money, he unleashed one of the most potent spiritual principles in the universe. He discovered a basic fact of successful living: that to receive the good things of this life you must give.

This is the secret of the law of abundance.

Let me repeat it for you, because the idea contained in that sentence is literally life changing. It will make your life full and abundant and satisfying beyond anything you have ever imagined.

To receive the good things of this life, you must first give.

Firmly imbed that idea in your consciousness. Say it over and over. Let your mind dwell on it until it becomes a fundamental part of your thought pattern. To receive the good things of this life, you must first give. I cannot over-emphasize its importance. It can change anyone's situation.

This creative law of vital living is expressed in familiar words: "He that findeth his life shall lose it: and he that loseth his life for my sake shall find it." (Matthew 10:39) And the law is again stated in a sentence which I, personally, regard as one of the most important in the entire Bible: "I am come that they might have life, and that they might have it more abundantly." (John 10:10)

Poverty-stricken and defeated living has no place in the planning of a Creator who crammed this world to overflowing with riches and blessings beyond description. It is man who has messed up the supply of good to all. By his crude interference with the laws of Divine abundance, both socially and personally, he merely exists when all around him are values, not simply in sufficient supply, but in prolific abundance. Such a simple thing as the giving of self, of thought, of money, of time, of helpfulness starts it flowing.

Sometimes the results of putting this technique into practice seem almost miraculous. I choose the following illustration from among many because it is so down-to-earth and about plain everyday people like most of us. And it's one of those situations we call "desperate." But no situation need be thought of as desperate, really; not with the law of abundance to call upon.

A few years ago a woman living in Florida was really up against it. She had moved there from Illinois with enough, she thought, for a humble but secure future; she had a small private income from investments in popular common stocks.

Well, as happens to so many people, something came along to upset all her plans. "The best laid schemes of mice and men gang aft a-gley, and leave us nought but grief and pain for promised joy," wrote Robert Burns. And it's so true.

Certainly that was true for this lady because, when the

1929 crash came, she was completely wiped out. She lost all her money. Fortunately, her home was paid for, so she had a roof over her head but no income, and naturally she was worried.

"What can I do?" she wrote to an old and invalid aunt who lived in Pennsylvania. "Actually, things are so bad that I don't know where I'm going to find enough money to buy food. Right now, believe it or not, I have only a loaf of bread and some cheese in the kitchen, but by the time I get an answer back from you even that will be gone. I'm really up against it."

Well, when the invalid aunt got that letter she sat down and wrote a reply by return mail. She didn't have any money herself but she gave her niece something better, a dynamic motivation, the idea of abundance, the concept of supply. She gave her a formula for getting out of her predicament.

"The trouble with you," wrote the aunt, "is that you are thinking of starving when God will supply abundantly. You are thinking of getting instead of giving, so the secret of your situation is to give, give, give!"

You might say that's the kind of advice you can expect from an old aunt, living in a rocking chair; but as a matter of fact, the apparently unrealistic advice showed a sharp, keen insight into the deeper nature of things.

On the day the aunt's letter arrived in Florida, her niece was almost destitute. She had exactly two slices of bread left in the house. You may not remember, but I recall very well the unbelievable condition that developed during the depression back in the thirties. This type of situation was common then.

When the postman arrived, she tore open the letter hoping, perhaps, there would be something green inside. She didn't see anything green. She turned the letter over and opened the envelope wider and searched inside, but the aunt had sent no money at all. And then she read the note.

She was annoyed. Impatiently she tossed the letter aside. And just as she did there was a knock at the door. Still somewhat annoyed, she opened it and there stood a neighbor, an old man, a dignified elderly gentleman who lived down the road a way. He was embarrassed, terribly embarrassed to come to her door this way, he said, but would she by any chance happen to have something to eat. He was on his way home from a fruitless search for work. His wife wasn't well, and he just had to have something for her to eat. He couldn't believe, he said sadly, that he would ever be in such a condition.

The words from the aunt's letter came rushing back. "The secret of your situation is give, give, give." On impulse, this lady walked back to her kitchen and picked up a piece of bread. Half of all she had. She started back with it, and then she stopped. "The secret of your situation is to give, give, give!" She thought a moment and then returned to the kitchen and got the other piece of bread too, and she wrapped them both in a piece of paper and when she handed them to the old man she did so with an apology for not having more to offer. The grateful old man never knew that she had given him every bit of food there was in the house.

Now, the things that happened next are going to sound a bit on the extravagant side. They are going to appear exaggerated. All I can do is to assure you, further, that even more exciting things are happening to people every day. The door to this lady's house had hardly closed when there came another knocking. There stood a neighbor with a whole *loaf* of bread in her hand, fresh out of the oven. And the next day an unexpected dividend check arrived for $10, which this lady quickly shared. And then, a few days thereafter, a check for $50 arrived "as a belated birthday gift" from a brother. "It just occurred to me that you might be a bit low," he wrote. This, of course, was quickly shared too, because by this time our lady had come to the same conclusion that Lloyd was going to reach years later at the Hot Shoppes. She just couldn't afford not to share.

So this is the way the law of abundance works. It is there, ready to shower you with all manner of good things. All you need to do is stimulate the flow of abundance. And that is accomplished by developing certain stimulators; that is, certain attitudes and habits which will start and maintain the flow of abundance.

One is definitely and deliberately to work with abundance thoughts. Set yourself to eliminate all lack thoughts from your mind. Practice the abundance concept until it becomes habitual. See or picture your life as full of rich values. Conceive of yourself as being a stimulating part of the flow of good, not bad, of prosperity, not poverty. Help other people to think and act similarly, for there can be no permanent abundance for one unless it spreads to many. Prosperity, widely enjoyed, always lifts the level of abundance for everyone.

And there is another significant fact: those who apply the law of abundance, right thinking, right acting, outgoing service keep the flow of values in motion. Even when men, by wrong thinking, interrupt the smooth operation of another of God's great laws, the law of economics, those who keep in harmony are still able to draw upon the vast basic prosperity of God's abundant world.

Catherine Thrower tells of a study class composed of business people who were working with the principles in Charles Fillmore's book *Prosperity*. It was in a period of business recession. Each student was asked to "pour living words of truth into their situation," believing they would be prospered in their work regardless of recession. This was a city where the psychology of lack was very strong. Each class session began with such an affirmation as the following:

I am the rich child of a loving Father. All that the Father has is mine. Divine intelligence is now showing me how to claim my God-given blessings of wealth, health and happiness. All that is mine by Divine heritage now comes to me in abundance.

Each student was expected to pour positive thinking into the atmosphere of office, business establishment or home. He was to turn the energy of his thinking upon "plenty" ideas rather than upon "lack" ideas and thus to counter with thought-vitality the negativism expressed all around him.

These business people studied, learned and applied the simple principles of the law of abundance. They thought creatively, they helped each other, they shared with God and man, they worked creatively and thus they set the immense force of positive ideas against the dismal defeatism everyone was talking.

Results began to show. Two secretaries became so valuable to their firms that they received pay increases at a time when many salaries were being cut. A lawyer became so helpful to his clients that his receipts for professional services took a swift upturn. A steel man, whose business was supposed to be particularly affected by recession, unexpectedly received several good orders. One abundance student, a saleslady in a downtown department store, as a result of her application of abundance principles, did so much business in an organization riddled by negative thoughts that she was the only clerk to receive a commission for having sold more than her quota.

In such experiences as those mentioned, positive thinking stimulated fresh and creative ideas. Abundance begins in your thoughts, in the form of new slants, fresh insights concerning problems. These produce better results. Buried deeply in your mind are all the potential values you need for a complete life. The Bible tells us "the Kingdom of God is within you." What a promise! Think of it; all the riches of God's great Kingdom are potentially resident in your mind. It remains only to learn the method of releasing them into abundance. And by abundance, of course, is meant every good: health, well-being, sufficiency, usefulness—every creative value in life.

I have a friend in St. Joseph, Missouri, who showed me recently how right thinking can act as a stimulator of abundance. This friend's name is Jack Spratt. His first name isn't really "Jack," it's Elliott; but with a last name like Spratt it seems that no one can resist the temptation to call him Jack. And he is a living demonstration of the amazing results of positive thinking.

One day when I was visiting Mr. Spratt we got to talking about the law of abundant supply. "It's an amazing thing," Mr. Spratt said, "how a simple change in thinking can affect a man's whole career." And then he told me how, whenever he has a salesman who has begun to slow down on sales, maybe get a bit stale, he calls him into his office.

"Joe," he says, "I want you to give me your order book. I'm taking it away from you."

Well, that scares the salesman pretty badly; he thinks Mr. Spratt is discharging him. But Mr. Spratt is not; actually he is re-charging the salesman. He takes away the order book, but he gives the man an opportunity to find himself, to start abundance flowing again.

"Now Joe," says Mr. Spratt, "I want you to go out and make the rounds of your customers."

"But you've got my order book," Joe answers.

"That's because I don't want you to take a single order," says Mr. Spratt. "Don't even try to get an order. You're going out on a new angle of salesmanship. You are going to sell yourself on the law of abundance."

"What's the idea, I haven't been getting enough orders as it is, and now you want me to stop taking them entirely?"

And then Mr. Spratt says, "The trouble with you, Joe, is

that you've been hoarding yourself. You've got to give your-self away. Now here's what I want you to do. Make your rounds as usual; but this time, for one week, I want you to go to each of your customers and give yourself to him. I mean, do something good for at least one of them each day this week. Help them to have something they really need, something like courage, faith, hope. Give them just plain old friendship. Think about them as people, not as cus-tomers. Then, after you've given yourself away for a week, come back and see me."

Mr. Spratt told me that usually at the end of such a week, the salesman is quite a different person. A revitalized enthus-iasm shows in his voice and a kind of excitement has come into his relations with his customers. And then, in most cases, amazing things begin to happen to his sales record. Orders start to flow in. And they don't come out of grati-tude, either. A man substituting a go-out-to-give system for a go-out-to-get attitude breaks down barriers with people and releases creative qualities within himself.

"The key idea, of course," said Mr. Spratt, "is the tithing of yourself and your time as well as your money. When this is done miraculous things begin to occur in you, in your job, in your family life, in everything. I've seen it work a hundred times right here in St. Jo. The more you try to keep to yourself, the less you have to keep; and the more you give yourself away, the more you have to give away."

Tithe yourself, give yourself, share yourself. What a lot of power there is in that idea, and how it stimulates the flow of abundance whether your need is for abundant material things, or ideas, or happiness. Tithing yourself means giv-ing yourself to people and to God; doing something for your fellow man and for God's work in the world. As you do this humbly and sincerely, good things will flow back toward you. Try it for yourself. See for yourself.

At one time I received a letter from a young mother who complained that she was getting a raw deal.

Who is it that has to do all the cooking and all the iron-ing and scrubbing around here? Me.

Who is it who is scullery maid while the others play? Me! My lot is an unhappy one and I don't mind saying so. This house is not a place of love, Dr. Peale; it is a house where there is one overworked maid-of-all-work and that maid is me.

And what do I get out of it? Nothing! Absolutely nothing, but work and more work.

Well, I wrote back that I certainly was sorry she felt that way about her home. It is sad indeed when a woman does not like her job as wife-mother-homemaker. Obviously she had developed a self-centered thought pattern that was keeping her from receiving and enjoying the flow of love that her family would want to send out to her. She was blocking it off and in so doing was making herself tired and irritable.

I suggested to this young woman that she put into effect a new philosophy; just to see what would happen. Suppose, I suggested, that instead of waiting for love and appreciation to come from others, she stimulate the flow of these healthy emotions by giving them away first.

"When you cook," I said, "you use seasonings. You use salt and pepper and spices. Why not 'season' your home life? Try, for one month, adding a generous tablespoon of love to your recipe. As you stir in the other seasonings think these words, maybe even say them aloud: 'I am now adding love. This will make the meal more enjoyable for everyone.' Try the same thing with your cleaning. Sweep out your old, injured thoughts and bring in thoughts of love. Sprinkle thoughts of appreciation over your family's clothes as you prepare them for ironing. But the important thing is this: don't wait for someone else to begin. You start the love-flow yourself, and then write me again and let me know how things are."

Well, I didn't have to wait long to find out how the experiment worked. Three weeks later I got a letter from this woman. It went, in part, like this:

I must admit, Dr. Peale, that at first I thought your ideas were a little extreme. Imagine adding a tablespoon of love to a recipe, sweeping out negative thoughts, sprinkling clothes with affection! But frankly things were so bad around here and I was feeling so miserable that I decided to try your ideas anyway, as queer as they seemed. All I can say is, it's amazing how they did work!

The very first night, for instance, my husband paid me a compliment on my cooking; it was the first he had given me in a long time, and do you know what he said? "What's your secret ingredient, Baby? This is really good!"

Well, I was surprised to hear myself reply that it *was* a secret, but that I had lots more where it came from. And it's been the same way with other things around the house. Not always compliments; sometimes it's simply a look of appreciation, and sometimes it's even a helping hand. Anyway, I can see now that a whole new world lies before me.

These are but a few of the stimulators of the law of abundance. They all have one denominator in common; in each case the flow of abundance was started when a person dared to open himself up, ceased to be afraid, and believed that good things were going to flow toward him; and then underlined his belief by first giving away much of himself to others. It is a fact that negative thought will attract negative thought, and positive thought will attract positive thought. If you live on a basis of pinched, patched, poor, little thoughts, you will attract others of similar outlook. But if you make the first, bold move to get rid of your shabby thoughts, and replace them with fresh, healthy, abundance thoughts you will attract more such thoughts to yourself.

Abundance does not come by praying for things, money, possessions. Instead pray for insights and ideas. These you can turn into useful implements to enrich your life.

Actually, all values are in the mind. Creative achievement is in the mind. You have abundance within you. You can think your way to all manner of good if you will only *think: think* new thoughts.

Abundance is never likely to come to the "grooved-in thinker." That phrase was often used by the late great scientific genius Charles F. "Boss" Kettering, inventor of the automatic self-starter.

Some people, he pointed out, simply get into mental ruts and stay there. They have capacities, just as the people have who do things, but they won't ask questions and won't think, or if they do it's negative thinking. They can even defend their failures and sometimes actually call it the will of God, if they are piously disposed. In this abundant universe anyone, except the infirm and very aged perhaps, can think his way into abundance. And actually I could cite cases of people flat on their backs in bed who carry on worthwhile activities, even paying businesses.

Kettering shows how the negative or grooved-in thinker shuts off abundance and how the positive thinker stimulates it in full measure. He told the following story about his early experiences in the automobile industry.

In the early days of cars, we finished them off, like pianos, with varnish. For the cheaper cars, the job took seventeen days; more expensive ones took thirty-five. One day I called in all the paint experts and asked if we could shorten that part of automobile production. They thought maybe two days could be lopped off.

"Why can't you paint a car in one hour?" I asked.

"The paint won't dry," they said.

That was the best advice of the experts; so, with my question still in my mind I went looking. One day I saw lacquered pin trays in a jewelry store on Fifth Avenue in New York. I bought one for $11.50. The jeweler told me he bought the trays from a little laboratory over in New Jersey. So I went out there.

When I asked for a quart of his lacquer, the man was startled. He had never made a quart of it before. When I told him I wanted to use it on an auotmobile, he shook his head. "It won't work. Put it in your spray guns and it will dry before it hits the door."

"Can't you slow it down?"

"Nope, that's impossible!"

Of course it wasn't impossible. One question led to another, then another. Finally, by working closely with one of the paint manufacturers, we obtained a lacquer which could be sprayed on and a car completely finished in a few hours. Grooved-in thinking could have stopped us cold, back at the horse-and-carriage level.

And when we first put the self-starter in the automobile, the Detroit Edison people had a special meeting of the American Institute of Electrical Engineers. They wanted me to explain the self-starter, which I did; but about halfway through, a dignified gentleman interrupted.

"I move this meeting come to an end," he said. "This man doesn't know what he is talking about. He has profaned every fundamental law of electrical engineering!"

He was a victim of grooved-in thinking.

So, to stimulate abundance, *think*. Really think there is a way to better conditions. And, if you can think it in your mind, you can think it into actuality. Believe, pray, think, give—these are the four horsemen of abundance. Don't be a grooved-in thinker!

In Hong Kong I met a most remarkable man named Mr. Chou, a refugee from the Chinese communists. Mr. Chou, formerly a wealthy merchant in the old China, loved freedom so much that he and his family walked out of Red China with nothing; nothing, that is, except courage and faith and love; nothing, but positive thinking. He had known what it was to live abundantly in the material sense; but in Hong Kong he also knew what it was to live on a very, very meager scale. In fact, he was in plain, miserable poverty.

When he and his family first arrived without money or any source of money, they built a shack made of a couple of packing boxes insulated with burlap bags. They did their cooking on an open fire in front of their shanty home. After Mr. Chou had been in Hong Kong for several weeks, living on this subsistence level, he managed to get a humble job. It paid ten Hong Kong dollars a month ($1.60 U.S.)!

And yet the remarkable thing is that Mr. Chou was neither bitter nor resentful. He made every effort to improve his condition; but when his efforts failed he knew how to shift gears mentally and think abundantly regardless of setbacks. He tried to arrange for living quarters for his family in a Methodist housing project nearby called Wesley Village. Mr. Chou was a Methodist and Wesley Village was a nice cottage community especially built to house refugees. The two room cottages were situated on a sunny hillside and were neat, warm and attractive; but they cost 50¢ a day (8¢ U.S.). This was much more than Mr. Chou could afford so his dream was not realized.

But even so, on the day when his friends and neighbors who could afford to live there packed up their possessions and struggled up the hill to Wesley Village, Mr. Chou was on the spot to help them. He carried the heaviest boxes. He laughed and sang as he carried in the belongings of the fortunate ones. He was happy for them. He helped the aged grandmothers and the very young children. How much he wanted to move his own family there too; but since he couldn't, he rejoiced with those who could. Mr. Chou knew how to think abundantly. Wasn't he a true follower of Christ who promises: "I am come that they might have life, and that they might have it more abundantly." (John 10:10)

To me the wonderful point in this story is that Mr. Chou possessed abundant happiness, outgoing unselfishness, good will and cheerfulness even while his fortunes were at an extremely low ebb. But there is something about a personality such as his that attracts good will for others. You should see this man's radiant face—it warms your heart just to look at him.

Before long someone found a job for Mr. Chou that paid 35 Hong Kong dollars, more than tripling his previous wage.

The law of abundant supply was working. And shortly after that a vacancy occurred in the Wesley cottage community. Is it any wonder that Mr. Chou and family were asked to take it? This Chinese man will always remain in my memory as one of the truly great souls I have met in my lifetime.

His experience clearly demonstrates that the law of abundance operates even in most desolate and desperate circumstances. It stimulates forces which result in astonishing readjustment of conditions and, what is perhaps more important, constructive attitude toward conditions. Mr. Chou gave freely (at a time when many might have said he had nothing to give) and so he received abundantly. By this law of thinking and living one can do a creative job with the toughest possible conditions.

When you are in tune with the law of abundance the good things of life shall rise up toward you in waves. You will know emotional, physical (perhaps even material) wealth far beyond your present dreams. If today you are experiencing something less than abundant living, review this chapter and select one of the abundance stimulators that applies to your situation. Give it full cooperation. Live with it, believe in it, make it part of your unconscious thought pattern. You'll know this has happened when the new technique no longer requires effort. At the end of six months I am sure your life will be enriched beyond measure.

Chapter VII

WHAT TO DO ABOUT WHAT YOU'RE AFRAID OF

YOU CAN do something about your fear. You can overcome it. And to do that, simply develop faith as did this young naval officer.

He wrote me about his victory in the same factual manner he would report an engagement with an enemy.

> I am the commanding officer of this ship, a job which carries both pleasure and responsibility in large measure. It is as fine a task as could be assigned a young officer and I am grateful for the opportunity.
>
> My problems arise from the fear of failure, from the habit of worry, and from the lack of self-confidence. An imposing array of shortcomings, I know. Of all the methods tried to overcome or alleviate these weaknesses the only one proven successful has been Faith.
>
> From this realization stems my gratitude to you, for the simple, down-to-earth, and above all, believable manner in which you picture the power of reliance on God. I have been a skeptic in the past but you make further doubt so illogical as to be impossible. The strength I gather from you has enriched my life and made possible a hitherto unknown happiness.

How much time and energy do you spend on fear? None? When did you last knock on wood or walk around a ladder or throw a pinch of salt over your shoulder? When did you suddenly feel your heart pounding for no apparent reason? Was it when you awakened in the night, tense, mouth dry? Maybe you felt it as you went in to call on a prospective customer?

We are a curious generation when you come to think about it. We have developed the resources of the earth and advanced our scientific knowledge to a remarkable degree; we

are masters in so many areas. Yet we are not really masters
of our own anxieties. We still live in fear.

Actually, ours is a frightened generation. Albert Camus,
the French author, called this "the century of fear." There is
even a modern symphony called, "Age of Anxiety." That's
something when we make music based on fear.

Not only do we have all the normal, old-fashioned fears
but we now have a big new fear in the nuclear bombs
which can strike across oceans. And even if they never
strike, we can still worry about a sinister invisible killer
called "fallout" which may wreak its damage on us and
future generations. A scientist recently said, "We have a
free-floating anxiety induced by the atom bomb, by space
missiles and every destructive device."

"Free-floating anxiety!" What an apt way to describe the
fear of our time. This is not the fear which the caveman felt
when he heard the growl of the saber-toothed tiger. That fear
triggered the caveman to run, or (if he was inventive) to tie
a piece of rock to a stick and get himself that tiger's skin
for a coat. Of course, this is the basic and original purpose
of fear; to impel us to action in order to save our lives. And
this use of fear is as valid today as it ever was. When we
check our tires because we are afraid they are wearing thin,
that's healthy use of fear.

But this is not the type of fear on which most of us expend
our time and strength. Today we are afflicted more often
with a vague uneasy anxiety that's hard to name. We can't
fight back at this fear because we don't really know what
we're scared of. Or perhaps we are fearful of so many things
that attacking any of them seems futile. Fear, for us, isn't
always a specific pinpointed menace that we can act on and
do something concrete about, but a cloud that hovers over
us, just out of reach, and casts its black shadow on everything we do.

It's a hazy, pervasive apprehension. Some time ago I was
lecturing in Wichita, Kansas and had to fly to Cincinnati.
Mrs. Olive Ann Beech, of the Beech Aircraft Corporation
kindly loaned me a plane and pilot for that seven-hundred
mile flight. When we were flying over the Mississippi the
weather, which was sunny, became hazy.

"We'll have to go up above the haze level," said the pilot.
"Ground heat, dust and smoke often make a low-lying haze.
We'll go up another thousand feet and get above it."

We emerged into an altogether different world, one that

was clear and with far visibility. This is what we have to do in our thinking; lift our thoughts above the haze level of our own conflicted, fear-ridden thoughts. We need to rise above the cloud of fear, anxiety and worry into an upper level where we can think clearly and rationally.

It is most important to do something about fear. Fear is an enemy of your happiness. It affects your ability to think, thus hampering your efficiency, and poses danger to your health.

My own heart specialist and good friend Dr. Louis F. Bishop says: "It is not generally realized how many cardiovascular symptoms can be produced by tension and anxiety. Anxiety states are very common, and whereas it can be stated that a certain amount of anxiety is good for everybody, because it spurs you to get things done, at the same time it can be very crippling. It may produce symptoms affecting almost any organ of the body.

"The heart itself reacts in various ways to anxiety. The rate may be remarkably increased; the rhythm may be affected; a stressful or anxious situation may produce a serious irregularity of the heart. Anxiety may also produce, as is well known, particularly in the middle-aged, attacks of precordial pain, known as angina pectoris. Tension may play a role as a precipitating factor in the closure of one of the vessels supplying the heart with blood—the condition known as coronary thrombosis."

Dr. Leo Rangell, Clinical Professor of Psychiatry at U.C.L.A., says, according to the *Los Angeles Times*: "Bacteria and other micro-organisms find it easier to infect people who worry and fret."

But do not be alarmed. You have the power to overpower fear. It need not be allowed to harm you at all. The great fact is that you can, if you will, do something constructive about what you're afraid of. The ability to do this is one of the greatest results of positive thinking. Positive thinking presupposes a firm mind control. When you control your thoughts you will be able to control your emotions, including fear and worry.

I received a letter from a lady in Philadelphia whose little boy, named Carl, was troubled with fears. He was having nightmares; he was afraid of his playmates; he had grown thin and was constantly tired. She wanted to know if she could come to see me. Well, there is nothing sadder than a little boy full of fear and I wanted to help if possible, so we fixed an appointment.

When the time for the appointment arrived, it was a beautiful, springlike day, which was a bit unusual as it was the fifteenth of January. When this mother walked in (she came without Carl), I made some passing remark about what a fine day it was.

"Sickness weather," said this woman. "It's not healthy to have it warm this time of year. Watch out for influenza when you get a warm stretch in January."

That was just the start. This woman was afraid of everything. Within the first five minutes of our conversation, she mentioned that she had not brought her son with her from the hotel because she was afraid of the "dirty" air in the subways. She was afraid of all the "foreigners" she saw on the streets. She was afraid to go up on the Empire State Building for fear of the pressure on her ears. This was the tone of her talk. After we had visited in this way for a while, I brought the conversation around to Carl. I mentioned to her that his problem was by no means unique.

"So many children have fears," I said. "Where do you think they come from?"

This woman didn't know. She thought perhaps children were born with their fears.

"Not at all," I said. "Most fears are acquired from the people around them, especially, of course, from their parents."

"What you're trying to say is that Carl gets his fears from me?"

"I assure you this is nothing to be ashamed of," I said. "It is the way of human nature. You probably picked up your own fear thoughts from your parents and they from their parents and so on. The important thing is to break the chain."

"And how can I do that?"

"With positive thinking. Fear is a negative thought, and one helpful way to get rid of it is to think of your mind as a scale, a balance. On one side of the scale are all of your negative thoughts. On the other side are all of your positive thoughts. Right now, your scale is pretty badly out of balance; your negative thoughts far outweigh your positive thoughts . . . and, of course, these are being reflected in your son. The solution is to outweigh your fears.

"Try this method. The next time you have a negative thought, put a positive thought in the other scale. Take, for instance, the weather. It's a beautiful day outside. When you leave here, say to yourself, 'What a health-giving day! In fact it's so unusually clear that this would be a good day to take Carl up the Empire State Building to see the view.' "

The woman laughed—but doubtfully, "Do you think it would really work?" I replied, "It will work. Stick with it until that emotional scale is completely balanced; and then stick with it some more, until your positive thoughts outweigh your negative thoughts. When you have done this for, let us say, three months, let me know how Carl's fears are coming."

It was more than three months before I heard from this woman, nearer six, actually. But she really did make the experiment. When she finally wrote me, her letter reflected a state of healthy, happy excitement. She said:

> You've no idea what an amazing effect on our lives this simple plan of outweighing your fears has had. We have had to do a lot of struggling with them, but I do believe they are under much better control. Carl is much more relaxed and has fun with his playmates. He no longer seems so afraid or tense. I like to feel that I have, at last, broken that chain of inherited fears. One of these days I hope I can report that they are conquered altogether.

The basic idea employed here is an indirect approach to the problem of handling fears. Instead of tackling the anxiety and fear directly, by which process they often refuse to budge, we tried the indirect method of floating the fears out.

This is one of the best strategies for ridding yourself of fears; much better than trying to force them out by mustering your will power, which may be weak anyway. Rather let the rising tide of faith do the job for you. Fill your mind with such a large quantity of faith that your fears will actually be floated away. By this method God's power will do for you what you cannot do for yourself. Your part is simply to believe, trust and surrender yourself to His power. Let His tremendous strength lift you above fear.

Those who have used this principle of positive thinking in dealing with fear have had amazing results. But how do you fill your mind with faith to this degree? One of the methods is what we call the practice of the presence of God.

For example, I received a letter from Mrs. Grace Lichtenstein of Oakland, California, telling how one lady used this

same positive technique to handle a situation that usually
arouses panic and fear.

A woman was caught in an elevator which had stopped between floors. The manager of the building called to her and
asked if she were alone. She replied, "No, not alone." He
assured her the elevator would soon be repaired and urged her
not to worry.

When finally the elevator was repaired, and the door opened,
the lady was quite alone. The man looked at her in surprise,
"Lady, you said you were not alone."

"No," she replied calmly, "I wasn't alone. God was with me."

How many people, who constantly live with fear thoughts,
could have answered as calmly as she did? There is a profound comfort and security in believing, for a fact, that
God is with you. Perhaps the greatest comfort in this world
is, "I am not alone." When you know this for yourself, your
fears will lose their hold upon you.

Next time you are afraid, next time your heart pounds or
anxiety clutches at your mind, repeat the following eight
confidence-building words from Isaiah 41:10: "Fear thou
not; for I am with thee." Say them over and over to yourself,
listen intently to them as if God were actually with you
speaking to you. He is, of course, so try to sense His presence. When you are able to do this with a sense of conviction, then you will experience release from your fears.

In the great crises of life, when men really need to have a
sense of the Lord's presence in order to endure, they can get
it. In Belgium I visited what was once a notorious Nazi prison, located midway between Antwerp and Brussels and
known as the Breendonk. It is now maintained by the Belgium government as a sacred place of memory, and the flag
flies over it proudly.

To the Breendonk during the Occupation, the Nazis took
loyal, patriotic Belgium citizens who had the audacity to op-
pose their tyranny, kept them like animals in miserable cells
and strove by indescribable maltreatment and torture to
crush their spirits; but the prisoners stood up against all this.
Passing through the dark, dank, dismal passageways that have
been left just as they were in those days, one gets an awful
sense of the degradation of man and at the same time an
uplifting sense of the greatness of man.

I said to our guide, "How could people stand up against
anything so terrible?"

"I'll show you the answer," he said, and he took us back into one of the darkest of the cells. There in the corner, carved crudely in the stone, was an outline of the face of the Saviour, Jesus Christ. The guide said, "When the going got hard these men, one by one, would come in here and put their hands on His face. It was their way of remembering that they were not alone.

"One night the Nazis came to our house and took my father. We never saw him again. We heard, after the war, that he probably died here; but we cannot be sure. We were told that he was one of those who came to this very cell to feel the face of Christ. I know he would do that for he was a devout Christian. I am comforted by the thought that our Lord was with my father to make him unafraid of whatever he had to suffer."

What an answer to fear. *We are not alone!* Practice this tremendous truth until it becomes a positive conviction. I AM NOT ALONE. Make it personal. No fear on earth is greater than this thought.

This truth suggests that one big factor in doing something about fear is to keep your head and not panic. As long as you can think calmly, you can think rationally. When you can do this you will get along all right. The only way God can guide you is through your thoughts and even He cannot get through panicky thoughts to direct you. But God will help you maintain calmness as you practice positive thinking. In a radio talk describing certain aspects of positive thinking, I said: "There is a passage in the Bible, in Luke, ninth chapter, first verse, where we are told that Jesus called unto His disciples and 'gave them power and authority over all devils.' "

Nor, did you ever have any idea you might have a devil in you? By devils I mean the devil of hate, the devil of sensuality, the devil of dishonesty or the devil of fear? When the Bible says men may be possessed by devils, it is of course a truth. And modern psychological medicine confirms it. I have known people who have had devils in them. In fact I have felt devils within myself: meanness, hate, fear, resentment, jealousy. These things are well named, for devils they are, considering all the misery they cause. But an enormous fact to depend upon is that Jesus gave his disciples power and authority over devils so that they may rise up in a vast strength and cast them out in His name.

A businessman in Tennessee wrote me of his experience with this truth.

Dear Dr. Peale:

About three years ago I found myself engulfed with doubts and fears. They crept in and peace crept out. For months I was swamped with a tormenting depression. I felt as if I were almost lost and there was no God. I prayed and I did everything I could think of.

One day I found myself impatient, if not angry, that He would let me go on this way. I told Him I was angry and asked Him to forgive me.

I found informaton in the writing of Reverend J. A. MacMillan of the Christian and Missionary Alliance faith about the authority of the believer. I saw I was a victim of doubts and fears which are really evil demons. I acknowledged it. I cried out to God and I asked Him for this authority.

Then, as if I were in the presence of a person, I spoke to these doubts and fears and commanded them to leave me in the name of Jesus. A miracle happened. As if a light were turned on, the doubts and fears fled and my soul leaped for joy in a peace that is hard to describe.

For five months now I have been getting up around five o'clock to read the Bible and to meditate and pray. Peace has so flooded my soul that it is like liquid joy.

This man learned that Christianity is not some little, nice thing, a mere intellectual system of thought. It is rather a very strong power given to those who truly accept it. It is the power of God unto salvation to all who will believe. And if you really want freedom, Jesus Christ will give you power and authority to say to these devils of fear, or hate or sensuality or whatever: I command you to leave me.

That is man-sized Christianity and its blessings are yours if you want them badly enough. But you will have to develop some very real and strong faith. Say to the Lord, "I am tired of fooling with this fear; I want peace and relief." Don't go cringing and crawling in front of life. We are supposed to be men, strong men of faith, filled with power. Take the Gospel of Jesus Christ, really take it in depth; and transplant it into your mind, and you can have power and authority over your fear. Stand up to your fear and in the name of God and His son Jesus Christ command it to leave you. Then believe it is gone. Repeat this process until you feel a deep sense of victory.

One thing we must watch is that a fear thought has a way of popping into your mind when you least expect it and when it can do the most damage. At such times it is particularly important, as we have said before, not to try a frontal attack against the fear, but to use the displacement and substitutionary method of eliminating it. If you constantly fill your mind with faith thoughts, the fear thoughts will be firmly and surely displaced in due course of time. Of course, no change of personality of this character may be accomplished without effort. But that it can be accomplished there is no doubt at all.

A woman wrote me in French from Switzerland to report on the remarkable effects of such thought changing and displacement.

Dear Friend:

Allow me to start my letter so. You do not know me. I know you well after reading your book.

I am the daughter of a French Presbyterian minister. I have been brought up by real Christian parents, but having lived through two wars, I lived in terrible fear of the future. What would I ever do if I lost my husband? How would I ever bring up my three boys with very little money? And so on.

Then I became dreadfully ill with eczema, which was real torture. It lasted, on and off, for seven years. The doctors could not find the origin of this eczema. But I found it in reading your book. Fear had actually poisoned my blood. As I was itching on the inside, so also I itched on the outside, and I assure you it was agony.

So after reading your book I followed your advice. I started reading the Psalms. I copied all the verses which were helpful. I followed the way you said, of letting these verses soak into my mind. At last I fell upon the last verse of the Fourth Psalm: "I will both lay me down in peace, and sleep: for thou, Lord, only makest me dwell in safety." (Psalm 4:8) Security, that is what I needed. I can find it in God. I have found it in God.

And as for money, I found these verses in Job which set me free from money worries: "Then shalt thou lay up gold as dust . . . Yea, the Almighty shall be thy defense. . ." (Job 22:24-25)

So now at last I have understood, now that I am over fifty, that the spiritual reserves within me are unlimited, and I can call upon Him and be well and joyful.

This woman literally crowded out fear by crowding faith

in, faith in the form of great spiritual truths which were received deeply into her mind.

Harold Medina, you recall, was the famous judge who presided over the long trial of eleven top U. S. communists who had been charged with conspiracy to overthrow the United States government by violence. This trial was an extremely difficult experience. Emotions were high; tempers were short. And a great deal of the emotion and temper was directed at the judge in person.

He soon became aware of the fact that this was not entirely an accident. Something unusual was happening. It seemed that the defendants were more interested in breaking up the trial than they were in obtaining an acquittal. They were after a mistrial. They could achieve this goal in one of two ways: either by creating a tremendous confusion, or else by putting Judge Medina himself under such a strain that he would break.

The defense worked both plans at once. Throughout the trial, there was great difficulty in keeping order. Witnesses were insolent; attorneys were devious. But the attack that came closest to breaking up the entire trial was directed against Judge Medina himself. Somehow or other the master planners for the defense found out that the judge was afraid of high places. He had what is known as acrophobia, a fear of heights.

When Harold Medina was a small boy his father took him to Niagara Falls. Harold saw the crowd of people pressing up against the railing, looking down at the falls, but he could not go near that rail. He was afraid he would jump over. Time and time again throughout his childhood and young manhood, Medina faced this fear and handled it simply by avoiding it.

But now, suddenly, he could no longer avoid it. Judge Medina's chambers were on the twenty-second floor of the skyscraper federal courthouse in New York City overlooking Foley Square. One day the judge became aware of crowds down below shouting about him. "Medina will *fall,* like Forrestal." It was just a few days after Defense Secretary James Forrestal had fallen to his death from a hospital window. Was it just his imagination, Judge Medina wondered, or were these people stressing the word "fall." Quickly he stepped back from the window.

Bit by bit, Medina became aware of the deliberateness of the campaign. The word "fall" began to be stressed all around him. He found it underlined in letters, circled in newspaper clippings; he heard it stressed in conversations. He managed to carry on, but the strain was beginning to tell. One evening as he was preparing to go to bed, his wife opened the window of their apartment to let in some air. It was a stifling night, but Judge Medina said:

"Close that window, please, Ethel."

His wife looked at him, puzzled. He had never mentioned to her the fear of falling that he had had as a child. "I'm not fooling," he said, and then he told her about the signs, the chants, the whispers and the underlinings. Mrs. Medina was convinced. After that, they slept with the window open only a crack, from the bottom.

"Now the problem was," said Judge Medina talking about the experience later, "what do you do when you cannot avoid your fears? When I was a child the solution was simple; I just shunned the things that would make me afraid. Now I couldn't do that. What could I do? How does a man face a fear he cannot avoid? I'll tell you the answer . . . prayer.

"I don't mean a prayer directed only toward my fear of falling. I didn't suddenly say, 'Now, Lord, You have got to take away my acrophobia.' I mean a whole prayer pattern that asked for strength and guidance in *all* that I was doing. It was prayer that I had been building since I was a boy, when my mother knelt with me at bedtime to read from her Episcopal Book of Common Prayer. I inherited not just a Sunday kind of prayer, but a daily, often hourly kind of prayer. I prayed constantly, on and off throughout the day, any time when I was thankful, or under stress, or when I was in any kind of trouble.

"It was prayer alone that kept me going during the sixth and seventh months of the trial. There was no visitation, no sudden apparition, but there was the slow renewal of strength. With it came the firm realization that I would be able to meet whatever lay ahead of me . . . free of my old fear."

Do you see what Judge Medina was doing? He did not try to fight this one fear; he did not struggle and strain trying to rid himself of his acrophobia. He floated his fear away with a total prayer program that acted in the same way the tide did in raising that old tanker out of the Jersey mud flat. He so completely filled his mind with faith thoughts, that there simply was no room for fear thoughts, and they were firmly and finally floated away.

Judge Medina told this story in our monthly, inspirational magazine, *Guideposts*. It illustrates how a man can use prayer to eliminate his fears, even old deep ones. But this is not the only way that prayer can be used to conquer anxiety. There is also intercessory prayer when many people pray for a given objective.

One of the editors of *Guideposts* is a man named John Sherrill. In September, 1957, John had an experience which convinced him of the power of other people's prayers to dispel fear. Right up until the morning September 20, of that year, John was leading a fairly normal life. He was married, he and his wife (and the bank) owned a house in the suburbs of New York; they had three children and a four-year-old Ford automobile. Theirs was a happy, creative life.

Then, on this morning, John got a telephone call from his doctor. The doctor wanted to see him right away. A few days earlier, John had had a small mole removed from his left ear. Now he was told the shocking fact that it was highly malignant. Without an operation, the doctor said, his chances of being alive at the end of a year were one in nine. With an operation, he had one chance in three. Further examination by specialists at Memorial Center and Presbyterian Hospital confirmed the diagnosis. Immediate surgery was recommended by every doctor.

A few days after that operation, I received a letter from John which I would like to share, in part, with you. This is what he had to say about the fear that took hold of him when he learned about the cancer:

> . . . Fear is such a devastating emotion, Dr. Peale . . . it harried us day and night. I woke up in the night and knew that I was afraid. I answered the children's questions automatically; my mind was elsewhere. I spent hours with Tibby [his wife] going over insurance, wills, finances. When I tried to force my mind to more healthy matters, I could not: I was afraid.
>
> And then, Dr. Peale, something remarkable happened. As our friends began to hear the news of the cancer, they needed to feel they were helping and their immediate response was to pray. The first prayer that we learned about, I think, was the one that you said for us from your pulpit that Sunday. After that, prayer rose about us like a flood.
>
> There was prayer at *Guideposts,* both in the New York and

Carmel office. Did you know, Dr. Peale, that your friend, Tessie Durlac, asked her synagogue to pray for us, and that she called long distance to the Prayer Tower at Unity? Our assistant art director, Sal Lazzarotti, told me he almost drove off the road saying the rosary on his way home Friday after he heard the news. "I haven't been saying the rosary too regularly, God," he said, "but starting tonight it's going to be different."

Prayer was in the air we breathed. We were surrounded by it, submerged in it. Early the following week I was admitted to the hospital. To my amazement the atmosphere there was one of prayer, too. No sooner had I settled down in my bed in Room 609 when I heard a weird and haunting note, almost a cry, permeate the corridor. In the room next to mine an Orthodox Jewish patient was celebrating Rosh Hashana, the Jewish New Year. The nurse told me I had heard the cry of the ram's horn, which for centuries has been used to summon men to prayer.

During these days in the hospital, I was praying too. But there was something strange about my own prayers; they were not for myself, they were for others. I must emphasize, Dr. Peale, that I am trying simply to report facts. I prayed for others, not from any deliberate sense of selflessness, but because I genuinely did not feel the need to pray for myself. This struck me as odd until I realized the reason. *Suddenly, on the night before the operation, I was aware that I was free of fear!*

Was this the tangible result of all the prayers? I think it was. On the night before the operation I felt such a surge of health that it was hard to realize I was in a hospital. At six o'clock the next morning a nurse roused me and gave me a needle.

"This will make you sleepy," she said.

I laughed. "You wake me up to give me something to make me sleepy?"

They came and wheeled me into the operating room. It was as if I, and the white-masked nurses, and the doctors were in the center of a force that dispelled fear. The closest I can come to describing it is to say that I felt as if I were deeply and personally loved.

And that, of course, must be a perfect condition for healing.

The operation was over. There was a week of tortuous waiting. Then the doctor brought me his report. He did not tell me the results of the operation right away. He shined a light into my eyes, probed and thumped, and then, in a matter-of-fact voice, he said: "Your report is the best one I could possibly have for you. There is no evidence of residual melanoma."

Does this mean that there has been a cure? I am not a doctor, and I do not pretend to understand the vagaries of cancer. Has it all been removed? Will it come back? No one really knows. But I do know about another kind of cure, one that may be more important.

With as much honesty as I can possibly muster, I must say that I personally have experienced the power of prayer to heal the most devastating disease of all—the power of prayer to heal fear.

So John Sherrill's fear was healed. And of course this experience means that yours can be healed also—no matter what it is—if you will let prayer open for you the tremendous world of faith. We have God's own promise that our fears can be overcome: "For I the Lord thy God will hold thy right hand, saying unto thee, Fear not; I will help thee." (Isaiah 41:13)

And He will, too. Place your fears in God's hands and leave them there.

And now let's sum up what to do about what you're afraid of:

1. Know what it is you are afraid of. Pinpoint it. Isolate it. Set it off and see it for what it is. Know exactly what you have to deal with.

2. Study the origins and reasons for being afraid of this or that. If you are not absolutely sure that you know the reason or reasons, then you had better get some expert counseling.

3. Get the fear out into the open. Divest it of all the mystery. Get it out where you can really attack it. Often you will be surprised what a puny thing has been frightening you all this time.

4. Cram your mind full of faith thoughts, for fear cannot occupy the mind when it is full of faith. Remember always that faith is stronger than fear. So, the more faith you have the less fear you'll have. It's that simple, though this process requires some hard discipline.

5. Just do your very level best. You can do no more. Then practice until you strongly develop it, the ability to leave results calmly to the good Lord.

6. Stand up to your fear and challenge it to do its worst. Usually there will be no worse, for actually most fear is an unreal bluffing of the imagination.

7. For the real fears that have substance in fact, you have what it takes to meet them. God will help you release the necessary mental and spiritual strength. Pray.

8. Affirm always that by the grace of God you are more than equal to any fearsome situation.

9. Keep uppermost the most powerful thought and fact of all—"*I am not alone.* God is my friend, my *support*. He is always with me."

10. Finally, if you would like further help, I shall be glad to send you free upon request, my pocket-sized twenty-four page booklet entitled, *Quit Worrying.* Write to: Foundation for Christian Living, Pawling, New York, if you would like a copy.

Chapter VIII

How to Feel Real Security

A SENSE of security is one of the most priceless assets you can have. With it, you can be efficient and contented. Without it, you may not be able to function effectively at all.

I received a letter recently, a really remarkable letter, from a woman who had lost all the security props that one usually depends upon. She was fifty-four years old and had been married thirty-one years when her husband suddenly asked for a divorce. So, she lost her husband. She simultaneously lost her "home" since, for her, home meant the place where she and her family lived. She lost her son when he was killed in an automobile accident. And then her daughter married, and in a very real sense this was a loss too—as any mother knows who has ever cried at a wedding.

So where did she turn? Here is an excerpt from her letter:

> It wasn't easy to lose my son or give up my daughter in marriage, or my husband, or my home, or my friends; but I found that security is within one's self, and not in persons, places or things and we really don't possess anything except in our consciousness.

That is a philosophical classic, that sentence. She tried finding security in the three traditional ways: persons, places and things; and she came to the conclusion that she couldn't possess anything except in her own consciousness. What she meant by this is that security is a spiritual matter and not a physical one. The fact is, *only* in spirit will we ever be able to find security. In order to feel confident and secure we must have a secure spiritual life; that is, we must get close to God.

This precept has very good foundation in psychology. Victor Frankl, world-famous psychiatrist and professor at the University of Vienna, practices what he calls *Logo*

Therapy, or God Therapy. It has been his observation that much of the mental trouble we experience today stems from the fact that "we have broken with the sense of the reality of God." Along with this goes a loss in the sense of life's meaning. We feel a decline in well-being; we feel hopelessness and insecurity. But when a person does establish a closeness to God, a great sense of security follows, says Dr. Frankl.

How practical a sense of God's presence can be is shown in this letter from the vice-president of an important company in the midwest:

> You have gotten me to going around talking to the Lord just like I talk to the president of this company. I do not call that praying, or what the average prayer sounds like. But in reading and following your advice these past years I have come to actually feel that the Lord is with me in my office, or when I am traveling, or walking, or in a conference. In fact, I know He is near me and I have frequent conversations with Him just as naturally as with any friend. You have taught me that the Lord is a constant companion.
>
> I can tell you that in the last six years since I have been practicing this, it does not make any difference what the problem is in this business, the Lord is with me and helping me. I do not talk to Him, perhaps, in the same way in which you do. You are working on the sacred front and I am working on the secular front, but it all comes out at the same place. You and I know that God is with us.

So runs this letter from a businessman. This man's life has been revitalized and renewed, his whole outlook changed, his grip on himself strengthened, his record of achievement enhanced. He has found security in God.

So we are on very realistic grounds when we talk about getting close to God and finding security. But the big question is, how does one get close to God? Since many people ask me this question, I have worked out a formula that I have tested often and found very helpful.

> Why did I have to be sixty years of age before I discovered the wonderful, practical value of religion in my daily life! Everything has been different since I discovered the amazing truth that God can be my constant companion.

1. Feel a deep need of God.
2. Have a deep desire for God.

3. Pray in depth to God.
4. Live in partnership with God.

The most difficult part of this formula, I think, is to learn how to pray in depth. When this happens, lives are really altered. It is as if you are able to focus all the strength-giving, life-changing powers of God on your soul at once. God's power is around us all the time. Occasionally we are able to focus it on our problems with definite effect. And sometimes we are able to focus it with a mighty power that shakes us to the depths of our very beings.

It is as though God's power were sunlight. The sunlight is around us daily, affecting our lives. As children we learned how to bring the rays of the sun together with a piece of glass and generate enough energy to set fire to paper. Recently, the Army engineers developed a series of lenses and mirrors which concentrate and re-concentrate the simple rays of the sun to such a degree that they could develop the thermal power of an atomic bomb! This force is so great that it can cut through a four-inch beam of steel as easily as if the beam were composed of ice. And this astonishing force is simply the concentrated rays of the sun. Similarly, the power of God through concentrated positive faith can cut through our problems with tremendous results.

This is what it is like to pray in depth.

Have you ever had that experience? You can have it, when you reach for it and pray with all your heart and soul and mind. When you really pray with powerful intensity of belief and earnestness, you can burn out your insecurity and gain new confidence in yourself and in life.

I had such an experience twenty-five years ago, which is as vivid to me now as when it occurred. Mrs. Peale and I were in England staying in the little town of Keswick, in the English Lake District. And it was there I had one of my most profound experiences of prayer. This was the situation.

I was filled with insecurity and lack of confidence. I had just become pastor of the Marble Collegiate Church, a famous and distinguished church on Fifth Avenue in New York City. I was young, had come to the big city from up-state New York; and some people said I couldn't handle the job. I became convinced they were right. I floundered and was frightened and just knew I was going to fail. That was the mental condition I was in when my wife and I took this trip to England and found ourselves in Keswick.

We were sitting on a bench in the lovely, formal garden of the Keswick Hotel. We had been married for only two years and my wife was young, but she was a forceful young girl, and a spiritual one. She said to me very plainly, "Norman, I don't know what to make of you. I listen to you preach sermons and know you are sincere; but I also know that you are thinking of yourself too much. You have ability but it will never be realized until you surrender your self-consciousness and all your insecurities to God."

She put her hand upon mine. A soft hand, but a determined one. She said, "Let us sit right here and pray this thing through. We are not going to leave this garden or this bench until you really let God take over your life." I looked into her eyes, and I know that what she was saying to me was the truth.

So we sat there together for a long, long time. Then I started praying. And by some self-releasing I really prayed; and it was an agonizing prayer, trying to get free from myself. Finally, in the depths of that prayer, I felt a Presence giving me release. It was an amazing sense of release and from that moment my feelings of insecurity and lack of confidence had less strength. Ultimately, with God's help, I was able to break their power over me. Years later when Ralph Edwards on his "This Is Your Life" program suddenly asked me what my greatest spiritual experience had been, I unhesitatingly told him, and the millions watching, that it was this one at Keswick.

Anyone can find an answer to insecurity if he will pray with everything he has, and pray until he actually senses God's presence. This isn't easy or superficial: it is like drilling for deep water. The shaft has to sink far below the usual water levels, but once these deep-down sources of supply are tapped they will not dry up with every passing drought.

The Power of Positive Thinking has brought me many good friends. One is Elmer Cary and he has developed a very workable technique for living close to God and overcoming insecurity.

Now, Elmer has an unusual job. He sells cemetery lots. As a matter of fact, he is the world's greatest salesman of cemetery lots, having set a record during an international contest. You might think he would be a long-faced, lugu-

brious character, but this is not so. He has brought a
warmth, a genuine naturalness and a spirit of dedicated
service to his work. Elmer is really a great persuader; so
much so that, although he sells lots in Houston and I live
in New York City, I find it all I can do to keep from buy-
ing one of his properties whenever he unleashes his salesmanship on me.

One time we were traveling across the ocean on the *S.S.
Constitution*. It was the first time Elmer had ever been
overseas, but even so, he was a better sailor than I. The
weather, actually, was rough and after a couple of days of
being tossed about, I became slightly green around the gills.
In fact, I went to bed.

Well, I'd not been in bed long when Elmer knocked on
the door and came bouncing in looking unpleasantly healthy.
There's nothing worse, when you're seasick, than seeing one
of your shipmates feeling good.

"Well, what's the matter with you!" he asked. He seemed
genuinely surprised to see me flat on my back.

"I just thought I'd lie down a while," I said wanly, trying not to show how I really felt.

"You're not sick?"

"Well, you might say I've felt better in my life. As a
matter of fact, I do feel kind of woozy."

"Now look," he said, "where's your positive thinking?
Let me give you a lesson in right thinking. The trouble
with you is you're not in harmony with God and His wondrous works. The sea is His—He made it. God made this
ship through men's hands. And here it is in its natural
element, moving like a thing alive on the waves. It rides the
sea with graceful and beautiful symmetry. You ought to come
up on deck and feel the spume flying off the waves, and
watch the great billowing clouds in the sky, and hear the
whistling of the wind. It's really great! And up there you
will know one of the best fellowships with God, in the
wonder and glory of the elements."

"My, that's wonderful talking," I said admiringly. "Where
did you get it?"

"From one of your talks," grinned Elmer.

So I got dressed and went up on deck with Elmer and
we stood there facing the flying spray and spume that he
had spoken of so rhetorically. After the first few wobbly moments I began to get the feel of it. We stood swaying to
the ship's motion and identifying ourselves with God's ocean

and His waves. And I, too, began to sense the rhythm and wonder of a ship mastering a sea. Never again on that trip did I feel the slightest edge of seasickness.

Elmer says that the secret of his confidence and security is living with God. He used to feel quite insecure. One thing, he is short of stature; and this shortness bothered him a lot, especially since he was quite slender as well. And for another thing, Elmer once told me that he never liked his name. "I didn't like 'Elmer,' " he said. "Why any mother and father ever named me 'Elmer' is something I will never know! But I discovered a long time ago that confidence doesn't come from the way you look, or from what people call you. Confidence comes from living close to God. You can't live close to God and feel insecure."

"No," I answered, "and the size of a man is not determined by the length of his legs but by what's in his head."

I think that one phrase Elmer used is worth memorizing. "You can't live close to God and feel insecure." Elmer Cary spends a lot of time at the task of living close to God. He told me once that every morning he spends more than thirty minutes, figuratively putting on the whole armor of God.

"I protect myself with 'the helmet of salvation' . . ." he says with a twinkle in his eyes. "That keeps my mind and my thoughts safe. Then I put on 'the shield of faith' to protect my heart and keep it strong. But I still have fears to live with, so I put on 'the sword of the Spirit' and with it I go out to do battle with the things that otherwise would frighten me." (Ephesians 6:13-17)

Is it any wonder that Elmer Cary is full of self-confidence? "You can't live close to God and feel insecure," he says. That, my friends, is it! The Bible puts it another way: "In the fear of the Lord is strong confidence." (Proverbs 14:26) What does "fear of the Lord" mean? I never did like that phrase too well because I feel certain the word "fear" conveys the wrong concept. Either "awe" or "respect," I think, would be closer to the intended meaning. In respect of the Lord there is strong confidence. When an individual is close to God, in harmony with God, then his weaknesses, his self-doubts, his shyness, his bashfulness disintegrate.

I know another man who spends a particular time every day getting close to God, and in this way achieves a strong confidence. He is the well-known writer, Roy L. Smith. Not long ago he suggested that instead of having the usual "coffee break" we should have a "Bible break." "Why, wouldn't that be a good idea?" he suggested. "Well, as a matter of fact, we could have a Bible break right along with the coffee break."

This idea impressed me as unique and sound and I advocated it in my own writings and speeches. One reader became particularly interested in the idea and decided to try it. So, five days a week he read the Bible while having coffee in his office. He began with the New Testament. He read it through and then went back and read it through again, for it had gripped him. Then things began to occur that had life-changing potentialities. "I found things were beginning to happen to me. For one thing, surprisingly, I wasn't as nervous. I didn't feel so negative about things. Then I discovered that people were more friendly. There were some curious situations which could only be ascribed to God's guidance. All in all, the Bible breaks gave me a new insight into the nature of security and confidence."

This is a wonderful confidence-producing technique. I am absolutely convinced that if a man were to carry out such a program faithfully, five days a week, for one year, he would be an altogether different person. Nothing would floor him. The reason I am so sure of this is that I have seen it work; not only with a Bible break explicitly, but with a little booklet called *Thought Conditioners* that we wrote and published back in 1951. In a small footnote at the bottom of page 109 in *The Power of Positive Thinking*, I offered a free copy of *Thought Conditioners* to anyone who would like to have one. As a result we have given away well over one million copies of this forty-page booklet.*

The ideas we worked out in *Thought Conditioners* seem to have caught on. Time after time people have told me that these powerful nuggets of scriptural thought have altered their lives. Since this volume you are reading is a book about the amazing results of positive thinking, I would like to mention two ideas from this booklet.

Thought Conditioners is a pocket-sized booklet containing forty creative and dynamic Scripture passages. The idea is this: As you can air-condition a room, so you can thought-

---

* Readers may still obtain a copy of *Thought Conditioners*, free of charge, by writing to Foundation for Christian Living, Pawling, New York.

condition your mind. First of all, you must be willing to go into the program with the idea that you are about to perform a major operation on your thoughts. You are definitely going to get rid of all those old insecure thoughts. In their place you are going to substitute real faith and security thoughts. It will be an operation by displacement. One way in which this is done is by a simple memorization of each and every one of the texts suggested in *Thought Conditioners*. Take one example:

> What things soever ye desire, when ye pray, believe that ye receive them, and ye shall have them. (Mark 11:24)

Next you meditate briefly on the technique for using this Thought Conditioner. For this one the explanation reads:

> To pray successfully you must employ affirmation and visualization. From a picture in your mind, not of lack or denial or frustration or illness, but of prosperity, abundance, attainment, health. Always remember you will receive, as a result of prayer, exactly what you think, not what you say. If you pray for achievement but think defeat, your words are idle because your heart has already accepted defeat.
>
> Therefore practice believing that even as you pray you are receiving God's boundless blessings and they will come to you.

Throughout the day refer to the Scripture passage and repeat it until it is thoroughly memorized. Then, on the second day, select another Thought Conditioner, and *add it to the first*. This is the way thought-conditioning works. As you repeat one right after the other, the second will "hammer and drive" the first deeply into your mind. The next day a third is added, then another and another on successive days. This will strongly displace any negative thoughts that are now resident there. Keep this process up steadily for forty days, each day saying all the verses you have learned before until finally you have committed to memory all forty and know them so well you can repeat them in your sleep. The effect upon you will astonish you. Thousands of people bear testimony to the powerful results of this method.

I will defy anybody to remain insecure, or to lack confidence, if he will deeply saturate his mind, and keep it saturated, with these creative thoughts. How well thought-conditioning works was illustrated by a man I met at a luncheon meeting of a state association of businessmen. A diamond-in-the-rough type of man walked up to the head table where I was sitting and said, "Doctor, I just wanted you to know that I am in the state legislature today because I read *The Power of Positive Thinking* and sent for that *Thought Conditioners* booklet of yours. They mean so much to me that I couldn't carry on without them. They turned me from a person full of insecurity into a man of real confidence. Through following the plan of using those Scripture texts, I was able to overcome my fears and inferiority so much that I went into politics which, as you know, means liking and working with people. By thought-conditioning my mind I emptied out my insecurity. No, I didn't do it," he corrected himself, "God did it for me. Now I am trying to do something for God and my country." The man seated beside me at the table overhearing this conversation said, "I've seldom seen such a change in anyone as in Jack. So it was thought-conditioning that did it!" He asked for the booklet to work the plan on himself.

A few months later I stopped at a motel out West. The manager came up and handed me an old, dirty, battered copy of *Thought Conditioners*. "I just wanted you to know, Dr. Peale, that this little book is the reason I'm successful in this business today. I used it to pull myself out of a very bad debt situation, and now I'm doing right well."

I suggested to him that he get a fresh copy. His copy looked pretty dog-eared. "Let me send you one when I get back to New York," I said.

"No, sir," he said. "This is the one that did it. I've got sentiment for this particular copy and I wouldn't exchange it for anything." Then he went on to say, "At first I thought the idea of merely committing Bible verses to memory was too simple, and that your idea of reconditioning your thoughts was sort of on the queer side. I'd never heard anything like that before. But then, from somewhere I found the will actually to do the memorizing. It was so helpful that I kept on doing it and all I can say is that this simple practice has changed my life. It burned out all the old negative, defeatist thoughts and substituted more confidence than I've had in years."

A man from Connecticut who experienced some pretty bad times tells in the following letter how he found security and a new business career. His is another demonstration of the amazing power of positive thinking:

While going through a very trying period of losing my business about five years ago, a friend suggested *The Power of Positive Thinking* and I became a disciple of your teachings from the first chapter. I also sent for a copy of *Thought Conditioners* and followed instructions to the letter, working, studying and praying for a way out of my difficulty. I know that you won't be surprised to hear that the way out appeared before I had committed all the verses in *Thought Conditioners* to memory. I was led to close the business and talked to each of my creditors in person and was surprised at the way my fear of them was suddenly taken away. I found them all very agreeable to give me a chance to see what I could work out without having to resort to bankruptcy. I was led to talk with my banker and was able to arrange a mortgage loan of $3500 on my home and was able to pay all my debts in full. I just can't put into words the relief I experienced in clearing this mountain of despair up in such a short time, truly proving "The things which are impossible with men are possible with God," and your words in *Thought Conditioners*: "Keep relaxed. Don't worry. Avoid getting panicky . . ."

The very next day after this demonstration of the power of prayer I landed a job with an aircraft company as an aircraft mechanic, after having been away from that field for over ten years, and have rapidly risen to my present position where I am trusted with the most difficult repair jobs on the aircraft in the factory. Another proof of God's POWER.

A few months later I formed my own band with a group of dedicated musicians. This was the first time I had fronted a band in fifteen years and we were a success from the first date we played, and new fields are opening for us all the time.

So to develop more confidence within yourself, try using *Thought Conditioners*. Saturate your mind with them. Let these dynamic principles work for you, and I am sure you will have a deeper feeling of security than you have ever enjoyed. Actually, you do not need the booklet, though I will be glad to send you a copy. You can go through the Bible taking out your own texts which speak of faith, and peace and strength. But insert at least one every day deeply into your mind until it really takes hold of you.

There is one last thing which is quite important in living confidently. And that is the values which the church affords you. A church is a wonderful source of security because this is where people, for generations, have congregated in an effort to bring the health-producing, life-changing laws of God together in a single concentrated experience. Church worship is much more than a formal duty to perform. It is your exposure to the greatest of all power. In fact, a vital church is the greatest power relay station in existence. Through it flows the vibrant life-changing energy of Almighty God Himself.

The church has probably produced more real, sensible and effective positive thinkers than any institution in the world. And that is because it reaches the power of faith. It provides peace of mind and heart, and these qualities are very essential to efficient mental processes. The church puts hope and love and confidence into men's minds. True, you will find some gloomy, depressive, negative, even mean people in churches. There are two things that may be said about this phenomenon: First, the exposure just hasn't taken; and second, it's good that such people are in the church, for it means there is still hope of doing something with them. Of course the basic reason the church produces positive thinkers is due to the life-changing force in Christianity, the basic genius of which is that, when taken into one's life, it can dramatically eliminate weaknesses and add strength. Christianity can literally make a new man of anyone who wills it so.

In *The Power of Positive Thinking* the reader was constantly urged to practice the teachings of Jesus Christ, or if not of the Christian faith to practice the laws of God as he has been taught. Church worship was advocated as an invaluable aid in solving personal problems, of contributing to human welfare and helping one to know God.

One of my readers, a man who had no church contact whatsoever, resisted that particular emphasis in the book. He said, "I took the common sense of the book but skipped the religion. As a matter of fact, I thought you just brought that in because you happen to be a minister." However, he became convinced by my insistence, and one Sunday he attended a neighborhood church. Unfortunately, the minister devoted his sermon to a denunciation of businessmen, strangely seeming to regard them all as evil influences. The church was only partially filled and the spirit was without lift or enthusiasm. This man did not sense or note the spiritual power I had promised he would find.

My reader was so incensed that he sat down and wrote me a rather sharp letter and ended by saying that this finished him with the church. However, he did admit that he felt a real sense of need and would continue to work with the book—but no church, that was "out, period!" for him.

I wrote back suggesting that it was hardly fair to judge a minister by one sermon or to dismiss such a great and vast institution as the church because of one unfortunate contact. I gave him the name of a church not too far from his home where I knew the minister to be a pastor of radiant spirit and infectious faith.

My friend, a bit mollified, went to this church. He found it filled with a great congregation of eager people.

They all struck me as happy and everyone was so friendly. The minister was obviously a man of conviction. He was so sincere and kindly and down-to-earth that he got to me. I kept on going.

The minister called on me and invited me to join a group of fellows who met for lunch once a week. To my astonishment they actually had a good time together talking about religion and how they were applying it to personal and business problems. I was amazed by all this and continued attending these luncheons. I soon realized that you were right in your book; Christianity is actually a way of life. At least it was for these guys. One day one fellow told how insecure he had been, how he had suffered all his life from feelings of inadequacy and inferiority.

Well, that was me all over, and I listened carefully as he told how, through this fellowship of spiritually-minded men, he had found peace and a new strength to solve his own problems. So I decided that this was for me if I could only get it.

On Sunday in church we have a quiet period and the big congregation silently prays. Some real power is developed—there's no doubt about that. Suddenly, one Sunday, I felt a wonderful sense of peace. It wasn't like me, or at least like I thought I was, but tears came to my eyes. I actually felt God's presence. It had to be that, for all that old insecurity seemed gone. It was simply wonderful, the greatest thing that ever happened to me.

So ends the letter of a man who found security through spiritual fellowship.

Finally, to sum up, I recommend the use of the following formula for gaining a sense of security and confidence:

1. Study yourself to discover where *your* real security lies. Check over the things upon which you are now depending for security. Persons? Places? Things? Are they really satisfactory? Or do you need to look for a more basic security in the spiritual realm by getting close to God?

2. For getting close to God, practice the following:

> First, feel a deep need of God.
> Second, have a deep desire for God.
> Third, pray in depth to God.
> And fourth, live in partnership with God.

3. Take God as your actual working partner. Let God guide your thoughts and actions.

4. Practice systematic thought displacement to dislodge your insecure thoughts and replace them by confidence thoughts.

5. Associate with people of a confident and secure frame of mind. These feelings are contagious.

6. Read and implement positive ideas about everything in your life.

7. Find a positive, dynamic church where victorious living is taught and practiced. Become a vital part of such a creative spiritual community. Give to it. Draw from it. Believe, share and practice a power-packed faith.

Do the above and a strong confidence will displace your insecurity.

Chapter IX

How to Handle Your Difficulty

A DIFFICULTY can break you, or it can make you. It all depends on how you take hold of it, and what you do with it. "Mishaps are like knives, that either serve us or cut us, as we grasp them by the blade or the handle," said James Russell Lowell.

Grasp a difficulty by the "blade" and it cuts; grasp it by the "handle" and you can use it constructively. It may be hard to get hold of that handle but it can be done—that's for sure. And there are some practical techniques for so doing that have been tried and tested.

But before we get to them let me say that actually you ought to be glad you have some difficulties; life would not be worth living without them. While this element in life may have its unpleasant aspects, difficulty is still essential to growth and direction.

Recently on a flight from New York to Los Angeles on a Boeing Jet 707 airplane, I noticed a line of small blades midway down the wing surface and also on the tail. These blades I was told are called vortex generators. Their function is to cause the air flow to swirl as it passes over the rear wing area. Engineers tell me that the rear assembly of these big planes does not steer truly if the air situation is too smooth, so vortexes must be generated. The element of roughness must be inserted to attain precise directional accuracy. God's wisdom is demonstrated by the fact that He installed vortex generators in our human experience.

Many people write to me complaining about the problems they have. "Why must there be so many problems?" they ask.

Actually, problems are a sign of life! In fact the more problems, the more you are a part of life. The only place I've ever been where people have no problems is a cemetery and there they are all dead. Be glad that God trusts you with some problems. Thank Him for the compliment. He believes you have what it takes to handle them.

In this chapter we shall outline a technique for handling difficulty and this can be very important to you for, as Confucius says, "Settle one difficulty and you keep a hundred away."

In handling difficulty, first of all, get yourself as quiet, calm and composed as you can. You can never competently handle a difficulty unless you are quiet mentally. It is so very important to think calmly. When a difficulty arises, the first tendency is to become upset, even panicky. Nervously we assume that the problem has to be solved right away, quick; that something must be done immediately.

When you are mentally hectic, rational answers to difficulties tend to elude you; but when you become quiet your mind gets down to its real busisess, which is rational thinking.

So I must stress the importance of learning the use of silence in meeting life's difficult problems. "Silence is the element in which great things fashion themselves," said Carlyle. Silence conditions the mind to those sharper illuminations which surely come from God working in your thoughts. Divine guidance is always spoken in a still, small voice. You can scarcely hear it in confusion—certainly not in excited panic, nor when your mind is filled with anxiety. You cannot perceive God's will or receive His guidance in the midst of noise, especially noise within. So, the technique is to let yourself down into the relaxed and deep quietness of faith and confidence in which clear thinking is possible. Then a sense of direction will be opened to you for dealing with your difficulties.

The Japanese seem to practice quietness to a high degree of efficiency. It is one of their characteristics that I admire most—their ability to be quiet, composed and unruffled in the face of difficulty. Recently when I was in Japan, I spent some time studying quietness techniques. The practice of quietness is actually an important ritual in Japan; sometimes it is called *Ryōmi*. In English perhaps the nearest meaning of the word is "the taste of coolness" or "a refreshing." What a wonderful idea! When you have a problem, get "the taste of coolness." We put it another way, "keep cool." But to keep cool you must first get cool. In Japan this is done in an unusual but effective manner.

Let us say it is a pleasant summer evening. The first thing

is to sit in a hot Japanese bath and reflectively soak yourself. A bath is frequently more like a pool—a hot thermal pool. Everybody goes into the same bath together. Most Westerners balk at this beyond the family group. You relax, become quiet, and after awhile you feel like philosophizing.

Then you come out of the bath and put on a *yukata,* the name for a cotton kimono. You proceed into a cool room which is without furniture and sit on the floor on a soft straw matting called *tatami*. You sit quietly, listening to the wind bells tinkling in the gentle breeze and watching the *gifu* latterns swaying overhead.

Then you are brought a little bowl of amber tea. You don't gulp the tea down hurriedly in American style; rather you savor it thoughtfully, even commune with it. The Japanese linger long over a cup of tea, making of it an act of serenity. The idea is to induce quiet reflection; to relax and grow still, thus entering into the essence of peacefulness. You talk very little but rather meditate in an effort to cultivate the creative values of silence. In this way your mind brings the scattered ends of life together, the heat goes out of your thinking, and you get the taste of coolness. The effect of this practice on problem solving is amazing. Problems seem the more readily to dissolve. And they are resolved. This is a most effective method for perceiving difficulties clearly in their deeper implications. It is extraordinarily helpful in arriving at sound solutions.

Since you and I don't live in Japan, we have to develop our own kind of *Ryōmi*. Actually, one already exists in our own religious tradition. Christianity and Judaism are basically Oriental faiths and the value of quietness and meditation is emphasized in the Bible. "Come ye yourselves apart into a desert place and rest a while." (Mark 6:31)

Indeed, one of the best places to find creative quietness in our country is in a church. If you have a problem that you have difficulty in solving and wish to find a quiet place for meditation, I suggest that you go into an empty church when no service is in progress. Sit quietly in a pew and think of your mind, and then of your muscles, as letting go their tension. Let down and down, until you are relaxed.

Then practice consciously sensing God's presence. Say the following affirmative prayer, repeating it several times slowly: "You are here, Lord . . . You are now touching me with Your healing peace . . . My mind is becoming quiet.

You are now giving me the answer . . . Your answer . . . The right answer to my problem." Then empty out any wrong thinking which you may be holding. Forgive everyone. Quietly say, "I forgive—————(mention name)." Enumerate a few things for which you are thankful and others for which you ought to be thankful. Don't hurry, but rest quietly in the Lord. Try this experiment in creative quietness. It's really a wonderful method for handling difficulty.

Another method is to associate yourself with spiritually-minded people who have developed some skill in the use of creative quietness. I once had a very perplexing personal difficulty and had not been able to get an answer. While I was struggling with it I attended a Quaker Meeting. In a Quaker Meeting the practice of silence is a well-developed spiritual skill. It is a practical demonstration of the principle suggested in two Scripture passages: "Be still, and know that I am God." (Psalm 46:10) and "In quietness and in confidence shall be your strength." (Isaiah 30:15) Even to the unpracticed, the deep and vital silence-power of a Quaker Meeting has a way of getting through to you.

Before the silence period began, a man said something which was most enlightening: "If anyone here has a problem, drop it now into the deep pool of spiritual quietness."

It was an apt description, for the silence that followed was indeed like a deep pool. I took that problem, which had been baffling me, and said, "All right. We'll see what happens." And I let it drop into that pool of spiritual quietness. We continued to sit and wait and pray and listen to the silence and to the Reality within the silence. I don't know how long we sat there, for the passing of time was not important; but suddenly as clear as crystal, came the answer to my problem. And it proved to be so right an answer. I saw that I had been thinking and searching in wrong directions. But intuitively I now recognized this solution for what it was: God's answer.

It is always very important to find God's answer, and then to follow it. Mencius (second only to Confucius among the sages of China) says: "To follow the will of God is to prosper; to rebel against the will of God is to be destroyed."

One of the greatest people I ever knew for handling problems through mind-power plus Divine guidance was a wonderful old man, Harlow B. Andrews, who lived in Syracuse, New York. "Brother" Andrews we all called him. Brother

Andrews is said to have operated the first supermarket in the United States. Years ago he brought in perishable goods from California by fast express trains and sold them in his big Andrews Brothers store. He is credited with developing the first dishwasher. He was a highly effective businessman.

Brother Andrews had only three years of schooling, but his was a great mind and he used it to the maximum. His method of thinking through a problem was an amazing combination of common sense, scientific analysis, intuition and prayer. I had a chance, once, to see his mind at work on a tough problem of my own about which I had asked Brother Andrews' help. As I outlined my problem I paced nervously up and down in front of his desk.

"Wait a minute, hold your horses, don't pace around so much," said Brother Andrews. "Sit down and get relaxed. Let's get that mind of yours untensed. How do you expect to think when your mind is so tied up."

After he had me sitting relaxed and laughing a bit with him, he said, "Now let's examine this difficulty." He began talking the problem through, step by step, detail by detail, with consummate exactitude. He really took it apart and studied every aspect. He gave me the impression of walking around the difficulty, poking at it here and there with his gnarled old finger saying: "Let's see if we can find a soft spot." Or, "Let's chip a little off here, a little there and get it down to size where you can handle it, son."

He walked around it mentally, and I walked around with him. "Every problem has a soft spot," he declared. "But we don't know enough. What are our little minds compared to the great mind of God. Let's take it up with God." So saying, he prayed, outlining the problem in detail. The prayer itself was a process of thinking it through, of analyzing it. He knew God so well that he talked to God as though He was right there with us. (I believe He was, too.) And as Brother Andrews talked to the Lord about my problem it began to clarify in my thinking. It was remarkable how my nervousness passed off and suddenly I just knew the solution would come.

Brother Andrews' advice came to mind recently when I had a phone call from a well-known figure in baseball. He told me about a difficult decision he had to face. "I'd like you to pray with me about this matter. Will you?"

I told him I would, and advised him, "Don't worry. You'll get the right answer. Don't push it."

He answered, "I'm not worrying, nor am I tense. It's only that I have to have the answer by tomorrow, that's all. But I know I'll get the answer that God wants me to have." Then he used a phrase which I liked very much. He said, "I'm walking around this problem with prayerful thought." That really is an interesting idea: "I'm walking around the problem with prayerful thought."

Later I learned that my friend had made the choice that had seemed to him the more difficult of two alternatives which he described at the time he talked with me. In explaining his decision he said, "I took the job I thought the Lord wanted me to take." That had been the outcome of walking around the problem with prayerful thought. Incidentally, it turned out very well indeed.

Use the power of your human mind fortified with Divine guidance to organize the attack against a difficulty. No matter what your situation or however difficult the nature of your problem, or how hopeless it seems, this organized, analytical-spiritual attack will get results, and right results, too.

Another very good technique for handling a problem is just to stay with it; in other words, don't give up. It's amazing what simple *persistence* will do where you use it intelligently on your difficulties.

When everything goes wrong and you seem particularly inadequate, what shall you do? Just keep on pitching. And tenaciously hold a positive picture of the outcome. Put your faith in God . . . all your faith. You will get through if you persevere.

That's the way the great men of history handled their problems. It is a good idea to read about those men and get acquainted with the inspiring persons of all time who didn't know how to quit.

There is another element in winning victory, and that is the element of belief. "Believe you can, and you can." Belief is one of the most powerful of all problem dissolvers. When you believe that a difficulty can be overcome, you are more than halfway to victory over it already. One of the greatest of all principles is that men can do what they think they can do.

For example, it was generally accepted for a great many years that it was impossible to run a mile in four minutes. But then along came a lanky, frail-looking English physician named Roger Bannister who didn't look like he had the strength to run a mile at all. But one fine day, back in 1954, Roger Bannister ran the mile in four minutes flat.

Why had no one ever run the mile so fast before? Bannister feels it was because people didn't think it could be done, and that seems to be a very reasonable conclusion. Back in 1886, a man named Walker ran the mile in 4:12 3/4, a world record. And thirty-seven years later Paavo Nurmi ran it in 4:10¾ shaving two seconds off the earlier record. That was a wonderful achievement. I remember reading about it in the papers at Boston where I was living at the time. The fastest man on earth—Nurmi! Nobody, they said, will be able to beat his record!

But thirty-one years later Roger Bannister broke it. For the first time in history a man ran a mile in four minutes flat.

And now, what has happened? Since Bannister's feat no less than twenty-three other runners have run the mile in *less* than four minutes. When asked whether this is due to scientific improvements in the style of running, Bannister says that it cannot be explained that way. He believes it is due to a change in psychology. Once the mile had been run in four minutes, the mental conception was accepted that it could be run in less, and this belief in the runner's mind was responsible for its being done.

This, of course, is positive thinking in its purest form. And the use of positive thinking in overcoming difficulties is becoming more and more widespread. I can tell this from my mail. Letters come in by the hundreds, even by the thousands, telling how faith thoughts and positive thinking attitudes have helped in surmounting difficulties.

For instance, one man says that he keeps a card index of every passage in the Bible dealing with faith. He commits these to memory. One text among hundreds which he has collected is this one: "I can do all things through Christ which strengtheneth me." (Philippians 4:13) Another text is: "If God be for us, who can be against us?" (Romans 8:31) He substitutes the pronoun "me" for "us" in the latter text.

Read the Bible regularly and when you come to a passage that states positive thinking in a fresh new way that appeals to you, put it in your collection of faith ideas. As you fill your mind with these great thoughts your own attitudes will become more positive and more vitally strong.

So keep positive thoughts from the Bible at your fingertips or more properly your "mindtips" throughout the day—

thoughts that will be ready to help you meet any new difficulty that may arise. This method is a practical one and we recommend it.

In this connection I am reminded of my friend Arthur D. Rodenbeck of Dayton, Ohio. When I spoke to the National Home Builders great convention in Chicago, I had a very unique and dramatic introduction. The stage was set, special lighting arranged and dialogue prepared and rehearsed. The "star" of the cast was Art Rodenbeck, a successful home builder who told how positive thinking had pulled him through some difficult experiences.

To that big hushed audience Art Rodenbeck gave the healing potency of God's Word in practical human problems. He said:

I had plenty of problems, not financial, but with people. You know, people in the office, salesmen, foremen, mechanics —a big turnover—and nothing seemed to go right. Well, I was getting nervous and irritable and it began to affect my health. I was in pretty bad shape and actually on the verge of a crack-up. I read *The Power of Positive Thinking* by Dr. Peale and it helped. But then I went further. I got one of his pamphlets called *Spirit Lifters*, and I memorized thirty-two verses from the Bible. Everytime things were going bad, I'd mentally recite one of those verses. It did the trick; saved my mind and maybe my life.

Later I went to New York and I found out about his Foundation, The American Foundation of Religion and Psychiatry, where people are helped by a permanent staff of specially trained pastors, psychologists and some top psychiatrists.

Well, just a year ago I was having the same trouble and the *Spirit Lifters* saved me again. I was in deep trouble, financially this time, and I couldn't see my way out. But I drew all the strength I needed from those Bible verses just as you'd draw money from the bank, and it worked again. Right now, I'm sold out in Dayton and in Florida and my lumber company is doing fine. And I know that nothing can ever get me down again.

And here is a letter from a family in Massachusetts who describe another type of satisfying experience with positive thinking:

None of the letters that you receive can be more inspired by a deeper gratitude than that which is in our hearts. My husband (an engineer) and I sincerely feel that our seventeen-year-old boy would have lost the opportunity of a lifetime if it had not been for our daily letters based on your book, *The Power of Positive Thinking for Young People.*   ..

After high school graduation this spring, our son received a full scholarship to a famous school in New York. This is a specialized, completely endowed college, necessarily very small. Candidates are carefully screened and admitted by their standing on the Board Exams. Only twenty are taken each year from all over the United States. The course is extremely tough, and a test of character as well as brains.

The first six weeks were a severe strain on our son who concluded from the evidence available that he was flunking. It would have been the first failure of his life; he was so upset we feared for a complete nervous breakdown.

I wrote him every day, and his father wrote as often as possible—the gist of our letters being to think positively. He began to do this, and also to pray seriously, from his heart, for the first time in his life.

As a result, he kept plugging instead of just giving up! And he has passed his mid-terms this month with an average of 84 per cent, standing seventh in his class. Only seventeen of the boys are left now, as three freshmen did flunk out! After questioning our son, we have concluded that their failure was due more to attitude than to lack of ability or intelligence. I just felt that I should let you know this story.

A chief reason that people are beaten down by difficulties is simply that they allow themselves to think they can be beaten. And one of the greatest techniques for overcoming difficulty, as we have said, is to learn to believe that they can be overcome; and that you can do the overcoming with God's help. In order to accomplish this you may have to do considerable growing, both mentally and spiritually; but that can be done also. It is possible to grow tall in the mind, taller than any problem. This is another way of saying that you are bigger than any difficulty.

I had lunch recently with a friend, John Powers, president of Prentice-Hall, Inc., my publishers. He makes interesting use of diagrams to illustrate his ideas. He draws them all over the paper at hand, and then perhaps over the tablecloth as well. On this particular day he drew a picture of a huge mountain, and next to it a small man. "This mountain symbolizes a difficulty," said John. "Now how is this little man going to get on the other side?"

"That's easy," I said. "He will go around the end."

"Too wide, he can't do that."

"Well then, he will skirt the other end," I said.

But John shook his head, "That's just as wide."

"He will crawl over the top."

But John replied, "That won't work either for it's too high."

I thought and then said, "He will burrow under it."

"Too deep," he replied.

"O.K. then," I declared, "he will just haul off and plow right through it."

"That's out too," said John. "It's much too thick and he would only break himself."

"Well," I said, "it looks like an impasse; though I'm sure there is a way."

"There is indeed," said John Powers. "The answer is in your power of positive thinking. Rise over the difficulty by the enlargement of your thoughts. The man will grow tall in his thoughts until he is taller than the difficulty."

Of course that is the secret. There is apparently an unlimited extension facility in the human mind. Physically a man's height is limited. I once saw a man 7′6″ tall; but I presume the average height for man is from 5′8″ to 5′10″. But man has the unique mental ability to extend far beyond those limits. In his mind he developed the ladder which made him, let us say, about twenty feet high. His brain produced the elevator which made him, perhaps, two hundred to three hundred feet high; and the jet airplane which raised his height to thirty thousand feet. You have a tremendous extension power within yourself.

"You teach that fact in positive thinking," John declared.

So here is our little man apparently blocked and baffled by the big mountainous difficulty confronting him. This is how he meets this seeming impasse. He starts thinking pure, unadulterated, positive thoughts. He explores the matter from every angle. He affirms that with God's help and his own creative powers he will get the answer. Then he prays and this prayer takes the form of affirmation, the expression of the belief that he can rise above even this huge difficulty. In his prayer he receives guidance about how to do it. Through prayer, also, comes the inspiration and motivating force which supplies lifting power. As a result he begins to grow in mind and spirit until he is taller than the problem and looks down upon it.

You are indeed greater than any difficulty—always remember that. Grow until you're bigger than your difficulty. That's really a power-packed idea, and the way to achieve this growth is through understanding of yourself, and through prayer and spiritual development. You can grow bigger than any difficulty you may face.

One of the great things that positive thinking does for people is that it teaches them to stop working against themselves. So many people actually practice self-defeat. By their thoughts they actually convince themselves that they can not handle their difficulties. They are defeated in their minds. And since you are intended to be master of your thoughts, if you have used your thinking negatively you are responsible for your own inability to deal successfully with your difficult problems.

One of the greatest blessings of my life is the association I have had through the years with laymen in the church. As a pastor I was supposed to be their guide and teacher but it's a two-way street; and I can never pay the debt I owe to them for their guidance and inspiration to me.

In my first church in Berkeley, Rhode Island, I formed a lifetime friendship with Rob Rowbottom. When I recently went back to Berkeley to speak at the dedication of the remodeled church, I had an interview with reporters from Pawtucket, Providence and Woonsocket newspapers. I was asked if I had learned the idea of positive thinking from Mr. Rowbottom.

I replied that many had contributed to my thinking but to Rob I owe the conviction that sound thinking and prayer to God will take you successfully through any difficulty. In my young and acutely impressionable years I watched him meet up with some very difficult problems. Nothing ever floored him. He would say, "Well, now let's see, let's pray and think and we'll come through this all right." Then he would chuckle and keep on hacking away at the difficulty, always with good spirit and always believing. It was marvelous the way things worked out. This quiet but determined man was actually an indomitable personality.

We discussed the principle of positive thinking after the reporter had raised the question. "Tell me your secret, Rob," I said.

His reply was priceless, one of the wisest statements I have ever heard. "When a problem arises, I think it through patiently and carefully. I analyze it and analyze it some more. Sometimes, in doing so, I go off alone where I can talk to myself. I can understand better by talking out loud." Then he added, and this I hope you will never forget, *"I never build a case against myself."*

That is so very important. Stop working against yourself down in that mind of yours. God, your creator, is not a poor workman. He made you and He never intended that life should defeat you. He made life hard, to be sure, but He wants you to know that He will help you. "Hope thou in God: for I shall yet praise Him . . ." (Psalm 42:11) is one of the great words from His book. And another is, "God is our refuge and strength, a very present help in trouble." (Psalm 46:1)

So, with faith in that help, print those words of my friend Rob Rowbottom indelibly upon your mind: *I never build a case against myself.*

What thrilling victories people have who practice these principles of positive thinking. I have before me a letter from a man who was faced by one of the toughest kinds of problems. This is what he has to say about his difficulty:

> For twenty-five years I had been progressing from a heavy drinker to a hopeless alcoholic. I had lost position after position; had been locked up for common drunkenness; had been confined to alcoholic wards; spent many weeks in mental wards where alcoholics were confined while being given treatment. I spent a year and a half a hopeless drunk on skid row in Philadelphia.
>
> For years I was completely out of touch with my family. My marriage, never a happy one, dissolved. I am a photographer. At one time I had two portrait studios. These I lost. About 1950 I heard about Alcoholics Anonymous and attended some meetings. I tried to work the program but had too many reservations. Then, in a Jacksonville, Florida AA I met a fine woman and a year later we were married. However, not long afterward we both began drinking again and things went from bad to worse. Hospital after hospital.
>
> One day I took to my bed with a bottle—my usual routine when a difficult problem arose—and passed out. My wife, to pass the time, went downtown to the library. Somehow she stumbled across a book of yours, *The Power of Positive Thinking*. She glanced through it and as she later told me, rushed home and put it on my night table. When I came to in my drinking bouts I usually liked to read something, as it seemed to calm me down.
>
> So I reached out and picked up this book and began reading it. At first, of course, none of it made much sense. I remember closing it and placing it on the table. But a phrase

I read made its way through my muddled thoughts. "If God be for us, who can be against us?" I tried visualizing Him there beside me and immediately felt assured and stronger. I then picked up the book again and commenced reading it from the beginning, feeling better as I went along. During the next days, reading a little each day, I could feel a resolve within me becoming stronger and stronger to regain and keep my sobriety.

My wife and I celebrated our fourth anniversary the other day. Four years without a drink. We don't have too much in the way of worldly goods, but we are very happy. I manage a portrait studio in a small town in Massachusetts. We have nice clothes, our own car, attend the Episcopal church, and hope to build our own home next year.

Here is a man who grew. He grew over his difficulties through the power of that one phrase, "If God be for us, who can be against us?" Completely defeated, he got hold of this tremendous force, the power of the Almighty, and with this he began to grow. And he built a case not against, but for himself!

There is a corollary to this idea. If it is true that by growing you can overcome your difficulties, it is also true that your difficulties can help you grow. Difficulties are growth stimulators. The Russians have a proverb which I find interesting in this connection: "The hammer shatters glass but forges steel." If you are like steel, if you have good, malleable stuff in you the difficulties of life will forge you in strength and power.

It is interesting how many of our outstanding leaders have had this philosophy. President Eisenhower told me one day about an early memory he had of his mother as one of the wisest persons he had ever known. And her wisdom came from her religion. She created a wonderful spirit in the home, and she herself was the center of it.

He recalled one evening playing some kind of game with cards and complaining about the bad hands he was getting. Suddenly, his mother stopped the game and told him that when you play a game you have to take the cards as they come, and play them! She reminded him that life is like that. God deals the cards in life, and you've just got to play your best with what you have.

The President said he had never forgotten that advice and follows it to this day.

Thomas A. Edison took life in this same man-sized manner. He too was a tough, positive thinker. Former Governor of New Jersey, Charles Edison, his son, told me this fascinating story about his father. On the night of December 9, 1914, the great Edison industries of West Orange were practically destroyed by fire. Mr. Edison lost two million dollars that night and much of his life's work went up in flames. He was insured for only ten cents on the dollar because the buildings had been made of concrete, at that time supposed to be fireproof.

Young Edison was twenty-four, his father was sixty-seven. The young man ran about frantically, trying to find his father. Finally he came upon him, standing near the fire, his face ruddy in the glow, his white hair blown by the winter winds. "My heart ached for him," Charles Edison told me. "He was no longer young and everything was going up in flames. He spotted me. 'Charles,' he shouted, 'where's your mother?' "

" 'I don't know, Dad,' I answered."

" 'Find her!' he bade me. 'Bring her here. She will never see anything like this again as long as she lives.' "

The next morning, walking about the charred embers of all his hopes and dreams, Thomas A. Edison said, "There is great value in disaster. All our mistakes are burned up! Thank God we can start anew." And three weeks later, just twenty-one days after that disastrous fire, his firm delivered the first phonograph.

To sum up, I recommend the following:

1. Thank God you have difficulties. It's a sign you are alive.
2. Learn to stand back from your troubles and take a calm survey of them. The best way to do this is through the practice of quietness. In quietness and peace, take a level look at your problems.
3. Use your full mind power to analyze your difficulty. Then systematically chip away at it, bit by bit.
4. Think positively about your difficulty. Believe that you can overcome it. Do this and you are already well on the way to victory.
5. Learn the spiritual-practical method for handling a difficulty.
6. Let persistence work for you. Keep everlastingly at it, and you eventually will be victorious.
7. Grow to the high point where you can look down on your problem, and then use your problem to help you grow.

8. Calmly take life as it comes. Deal with your difficulties with controlled emotion and steadily keep on working for victory.
9. Never build a case against yourself.
10. Make use of the available power of the Almighty. Troubles will defeat you without God, but with His help you can handle any difficulty.

Chapter X

Don't Let Pressure Pressure You

IT IS a generally recognized fact that we live in a world that is full of tension. Tension surrounds us. It is in the rhythm of our cities and of our machines. It is in our talk and on our faces and in our bearing. It is built into our society. Certainly it shows in our work. Believe it or not, in New York City you can get the correct time by dialing N-E-R-V-O-U-S!

Fortunate indeed are those who do not let tension push them around; who do not let pressure pressure them. One evening, not long ago, when I was out on the West Coast, I had a very interesting talk on the subject of tension with Desi Arnaz. Desi and Lucy had just finished a hectic week at the studio, where they were filming scenes for a new show. But when I saw them in the living room of their country home, they were both as calm and cool as if they had just finished a refreshing week on vacation rather than on location.

"I've read that book of yours about positive thinking," Desi said suddenly. He has a way of fixing you with those wide-open, deep brown eyes of his when he talks. "You know," he said, "there're some pretty good parts in it."

Lucy laughed. "Just pretty good?" she asked.

"Especially that part, there, where you talk about tensions," he went on. "I really liked that part because we're in the business of tension, Lucy and me."

"You know what I did after I finished your book?" Desi said. And then he came up with a unique result of positive thinking. He leaned forward and pulled back his sleeve to show a bare wrist. "I threw away my watch."

I was a little startled. This wasn't exactly the kind of effect I had expected when I wrote *The Power of Positive Thinking*. But I felt better when I got the whole picture, because it turned out that although Desi does throw his watch away, he does it for just a few hours.

During the week, Desi's time is very tightly scheduled.

145

At 8:05 in the morning he must do this; at 11:40 he must do that. Commercials must fit smoothly into the program, timed down to the exact second. And, of course, there are always delays and last minute changes to gum up plans and create tensions that mount higher and higher.

But always, after a while there comes a breather. Maybe it's a break in the production schedule. Or just a weekend, or a holiday. On these occasions, if it's winter, Desi and Lucy drive out to their house at Palm Springs, or if summer, to one they own on the ocean. Both are beautiful places. The desert home is rimmed around by glorious mountains. The seashore home sits right on the edge of the Pacific. Out there in the desert and mountains, or next to the surf, they are far away from deadlines and appointment pads. But this is not enough. Just to make sure they won't be hounded by time, Desi throws away his watch.

He literally takes his watch off as soon as he walks into the house, tosses it into the dresser drawer and closes the drawer with a bang.

"After that," he said—and then he came up with a wonderful phrase—"I take a vacation from tension."

Isn't that a great idea! Take a vacation from tension. Desi does it by ignoring time. "I go down to the beach," he said. "And I lie down and let my mind and body relax. Then if someone calls me and says that it's time to eat, I tell them it isn't time to eat because I'm not hungry. If they come and say it's time for bed, I tell them the stars are out and the moon has just come up. It'll be time for bed when I get sleepy."

Later, of course, after the little vacation-from-tension is over, Desi has to go back to the dresser drawer and put the watch back on again. But he does it with a new sense of vitality; he is refreshed and ready to get back to work.

It isn't the Desi Arnazes of this world who need to learn how to handle tensions. Almost everyone these days faces the same problem. Thousands of children no longer stroll out the door and walk leisurely off to school, thumping picket fences and breaking the ice that has formed on puddles along the way; they must hurry to catch the bus at the corner—it leaves precisely at 8:12 A.M.

Even the routine business of getting to work has become a tightly scheduled affair. I know one pathetic fellow who has to meet three deadlines before he can sit down at his desk in the morning. He must get up in time to catch the

7:28 bus that takes him to the railroad station. He must be at the station in time to catch the 7:43 train to New York. He must arrive in the city in time to catch a car pool that takes him fifty blocks uptown. The schedule is so tight that at every stoplight he wonders if he's going to be at his desk by the time the 9 o'clock "starting bell" rings.

I once asked this man what time he had to set the alarm in order to make that series of deadlines. His answer was a classic. I think about it whenever I think about twentieth century man and the way he is pushed around by time.

"Oh," he said casually, "I usually set it for approximately 6:32."

Approximately 6:32!

This is symbolic of a problem that thousands upon thousands of men and women face daily. How to handle unwanted tension.

Notice that word "unwanted." A certain amount of tension is a good thing. Normal tension keys you up, it stimulates you and keeps your creative processes operating at top efficiency. But perhaps it would be a good thing if we learned how to turn tension off and on as we turn off the energy that flows through an electric wire. We would then be able to use tension when it served our purposes, and stop it when it begins to overpressure us. When it came time to relax, all the pressures could be drained off with little vacations from tensions.

Actually, that turning off of pressurized tension can be done. Here's one way to do it. First, consciously tense up your whole body. Start with your eyebrows. Draw them together into a frown. Now move on down to your jaw muscles and your lip muscles and your throat muscles. Tense them without relaxing. Hold the tension in all these muscles and move on down to your shoulders; tighten the muscles there and clench your fists. Contract the muscles in your stomach and press your knees together. Finally, push your feet down against the floor.

If you have done this as outlined, just about every muscle in your body is now tight. Hold that for a minute. Note the amount of energy that it takes to keep yourself tense!

I suggest this experiment to demonstrate what we are doing to ourselves, for many of us go through life pretty much tightened up like this twenty-four hours a day. Not every muscle at once, perhaps. Maybe it's just the throat muscles, or the shoulder muscles. For a great many people it's the stomach muscles. But the point is that because of such tension much energy is being wasted. It is being dissipated through effort that shows no results except fatigue and irritability.

Now, go on with the experiment; let the tension relax. Reverse the process described above. This time consciously relax every muscle. Carry this relaxing through your eyebrows, your jaw muscles, lip muscles, throat muscles. Now your shoulders and your fists. Your stomach. Your legs. Think of yourself as letting go. Relax all muscles and sink back in your chair until you feel limp all over. Imagine that the chair is carrying every ounce of your weight. There is nothing for your muscles to do—you are relaxed, completely relaxed.

I have a friend who works in a health club in a large city. George gets his clients to try this experiment of tensing all the body muscles and then relaxing them. He may sometimes use an additional relaxing method. With the muscle tensions eased, George tells them to bring the thought of God to mind.

"You are now perfectly relaxed," George says. "The tensions are leaving your body. In place of the tension, healing thoughts are coming into your mind and into your body. Now, let's go deeper. Say to yourself, 'God is in me. God is in my whole being. Just a moment ago I was rushed and anxious. I was tense, but now I am released from tension. My energies are now operating in a normal and creative way.' "

And then George asks, "Do you notice anything different about yourself?"

And one does indeed. I have tried the exercise myself many times, and know that something very different is present. I feel refreshed, invigorated, a new sense of control, as if I had the power to tackle the most difficult problem.

"That's relaxed power," says George. "You can now take that power back with you to the office, or back into your home. You can take relaxed power into the most tensed-up situation and the pressures won't bother you at all."

This is an excellent technique for handling the physical tensions that have a way of seizing us and not letting go. But I am of the opinion that most physical tension is really mental tension that has been translated into a new dimension. Our minds get to racing with a problem; pretty soon our bodies get to racing too. Even when seated in a chair our bodies can race. The muscles tense up as if they were in motion, and before we know it, we find ourselves knotted up. You must find ways and means to keep pressure under control, to keep the great quality of relaxed quietness.

Some years ago my wife and I bought a farm about seventy-five miles north of New York City. While the chief purpose in getting the place was to give our children the benefit of country life, I also wanted that farm to try an experiment on myself. I had a theory that everyone should have a private retreat where he can retire from the hurrying, scurrying, tension-filled world, and renew his spirit. My theory was based on the words: "In quietness and in confidence shall be your strength." (Isaiah 30:15)

I was born a country boy and they say you may take the boy out of the country, but you can never take the country out of the boy. At any rate, I wanted an actual place away from the city where I could retire at times and give God a chance to re-create in me a quiet mind. I wanted to see if this return to the country had a noticeable effect on the mental and muscular tensions that I was feeling.

Out back of the old farmhouse, on the place we finally bought, there is an orchard. To reach it you walk past the barn and follow a little path over a small stream, then through a corn patch and along an old stone wall. Finally you come to a little hill hard by a woods. You are completely alone up there. If you strain your ears, you can hear the wind in the trees, or the far-off whistle of a New York Central train working its way up the valley. Occasionally, you might hear the lonesome barking of a dog.

Nothing happens to you right away, up there on that windswept hilltop. You have to give God a chance to reach into your soul with His healing power. It requires a sort of settling down. But after a while you become aware that there is a certain rhythm in nature, a rhythm you had not been conscious of before. You look around you. It is autumn, say. The world is slowly going to sleep. A squirrel chatters to himself as he gathers nuts for the winter. A leaf falls; its very fall is lazy and relaxed. Down in the valley the corn is standing in shocks; the harvest is in, the fields are asleep, not to awaken for months. The entire world, as you see it from up there on the hilltop, has a rhythm of its own.

And it is a slow, relaxed rhythm. It is not the hurried pace that you brought with you from the city. You came racing up the hill with your mind running to keep pace with your body. But up there on that elevation, if you sit back and let the rhythm of the universe seep into your bones, or more importantly, into your thought processes, you find that your mind has slowed down; you simply are not in the same rush you were before. You find yourself repeating, with a new sense of meaning, the words: "In quietness and in confidence shall be your strength." God has heard your prayer. You feel less tension, more peace, and greater strength.

Once recently, when I was telling this story to a tired and harassed business executive who had come to me for help, I had it pointed out that not everyone has a convenient, lonely hill to which he can retire. "No," I said, "but anyone can find a quiet place if he really wants one."

On a recent trip to the Orient I noticed that the Japanese have beautiful, small gardens scattered throughout their cities. Maybe it's a garden of stones or of sand or of moss; it doesn't matter. They can retire to their gardens for a few minutes of contemplation. And it is a most effective practice, as I myself discovered.

During the weeks I was in Japan I made good use of the quieting and relaxing qualities of those unique Japanese gardens. Two in particular were so unforgettable that I often find myself returning to them in memory to experience anew their healing touch.

A moss garden in Kyoto was the scene of frequent relaxing meditations. There, where the sun falls gently through lacy-leafed trees onto a soft floor of moss and gleams on little lily pads in miniature ponds, the confusing world retreats and peace abounds. One is supposed to sit as immobile as possible, letting the eyes rest upon this beauty and permitting the mind to open wider and even wider to receive peaceful impressions. The effect, when you have learned to yield to it, is amazing in its ability to heal tension.

The stone garden of Kyoto will ever remain a significant spot in my long study of the techniques for reducing tension. Located within the confines of a Buddhist temple, the garden is an area perhaps 75 x 40 feet. It consists only of sand in which are set fifteen stones of varying size and shape: Sand and stones, that is all. The stones, according to one theory, are supposed to represent the fifteen basic problems of human existence. They are so placed that only part of them are in your line of vision, on the theory that it is too much for the mind to consider all human problems at one time.

One is supposed to become physically and mentally still

and, without being conscious of time, to contemplate life's deepest meaning.

On my last visit, the Japanese taxi-driver volunteered, "Do not hurry from Stone Garden. I will wait. No charge. If you worry about time you will miss what Garden has to say." I was the only Westerner in the Stone Garden at the time. Two venerable men in kimonos, a woman of uncertain age in Japanese dress, and a young couple in western clothes, holding hands but not speaking: these were my companions in meditation.

We all sat quietly, each thinking his own thoughts. Deep stillness prevailed, but I recall thinking that it was an alert stillness, full of dynamic force but no tension. Suddenly a phrase came to my mind: "Motion in stillness." I realized again that out of quietness comes vitality and force. Tension swirls one apart, but motion in stillness puts one together again. Quietness does not curtail, but stimulates drive; however, it is a drive that is organized and controlled.

The experience gave me an extraordinarily acute awareness of God. "In him we live, and move, and have our being," (Acts 17:28) was a Scripture passage I found myself repeating.

Later I addressed the Kyoto Rotary Club on "How to Live and Work Without Worry and Tension." In replying to my talk the club president said it was, "very appropriate since Japanese businessmen are Far Eastern Yankees, full of stress." I suggested that they visit their own shrines of healing quietness, just as I advise Americans to seek "the peace of God, which passeth all understanding." (Philippians 4:7) So, find your place of quietness for the practice of meditation, contemplation and prayer. It is one effective answer to tension.

A good friend of mine, Jesse L. Lasky, one of the founders of Hollywood as a motion-picture center, did this most impressively. In his house Mr. Lasky had a special room set aside which he called his Silence Room. It was simply furnished with a table, one stiff-backed chair, and a picture of the Matterhorn on the wall. On the table was a Bible.

Whenever Jesse became tense or found that pressure was mounting in him he would go into his Silence Room, shut the door and just sit for a while gazing at the picture of the majestic Matterhorn. "I will lift up mine eyes unto the hills," (Psalm 121:1) he would say to himself. Then he would open his Bible at random and read.

Jesse Lasky told me that he never failed to come out of his Silence Room refreshed and renewed in spirit. Anyone can find a quiet place of his own, if he really wants to. It is significant that a good many people nowadays are arranging, if not a room, at least a little spiritual meditation nook in the home. Islands of spiritual quietness, you might call them, in a time of tension.

Actually, a quiet place doesn't have to be a physical place; it can be in the thoughts. Years ago I developed a technique of my own for storing up peaceful experiences in my mind. I have used this technique literally hundreds of times, and can personally guarantee its effectiveness. It has done much in helping me master tension.

Here is what you do. Let's imagine that you are standing alone on a beach. The rest of the world has gone to sleep, but you were restless, so you got up, dressed, and took this walk on the beach. All of a sudden you find your eyes rising to the heavens. For the briefest moment you throw your soul out into the universe. You consciously expand yourself into an identification with the great God and His vast creation. You stand there and become at one with the pounding surf and the infinity of the skies.

Then you memorize the experience. It is like memorizing a poem. First you start with the things you can hear: the ocean and the wind and the sound of the beach grass rustling. Then you memorize the things you can feel; the spray in your face, the bite of the cool night air. And taste? There is salt in the air; if you run your tongue over your lips you can actually taste the ocean. Down your five senses you go, memorizing each one so that as you stand there you can bring it back at will.

And then the next time you find yourself tense, close your eyes and bring the scene back by conscious memory re-creation. Run down each of the senses and re-create the peaceful experience. In just a few moments you will bring back into your mind the feeling of harmony and of relaxation that you knew that night on that vast and empty beach.

One night at Pensacola a high-ranking naval officer told a group of us a wonderful story illustrating the importance of calm, emotional control in doing a vital job.

The aircraft carrier *Essex* was entering Pearl Harbor, the first of her class, loaded with planes and gear from San Francisco, including five thousand Marines. All officers and men in

Pearl were eager to see the first of the replacement ships, and her arrival was a significant event in the war.

As she entered the channel a fire broke out on the hangar deck. Simultaneously a merchant ship was sighted coming out. The channel at Pearl was not wide enough for two ships under normal conditions and the situation was critical. Word of the fire was passed to the bridge and the officer of the deck called to the captain, "Fire on the hangar deck!"

Every captain is seriously concerned about a fire on the hangar deck because of the many gasoline filled aircraft always present there, and because of the proximity of fuel and ammunition stowage.

The captain was closely watching the approaching ship and did not appear to have heard, so the officer of the deck repeated his report more loudly. Without turning his head the Captain, who was noted for his imperturbability, said quietly, "Put it out."

The two ships passed safely, and the fire was put out with little damage.

But some people are always telling me that the times are so filled with tension! Tension, they complain, is all around, so how can you keep from being tense. I repeat—tension exists in the mind, in your attitude toward confusion, noise and problems.

How do successful positive thinkers keep their lives poised and relaxed? There seems to be a definite pattern that they follow. For one thing, they do what Bernard Haldane suggests. They "study their successes." Some people keep poking around among their failures for know-how. There's not much wisdom in a failure, otherwise it wouldn't have been a failure. It's really only good as a reminder how not to do something.

But when you have succeeded, study how you did it, and see if you can apply the technique to the next job. You will then know that you know, and that you can, and your tension and nervousness will give way to the calmness of the man who knows that he can, and does it.

The successful person has had to learn how to organize, so that he is free from those swamped feelings that cause pressure to rise.

A great many of the successful positive thinkers with whom I have talked, or who have written me, are men who were thoughtful enough to realize they couldn't handle everything on their own. They were part of a team in which many others were important. They learned to train and encourage others, and trust them to do their part.

And, finally, men of this caliber know the real source of strength and peace. Having big minds, they are able to comprehend the importance of spiritual values in life. The bigger they are, the humbler they are.

And now, what about the times when it is *necessary* to live with tension. I guess one of the most confusion-ridden, ten-square-feet of real estate in the whole world must be the area under the information sign on the upper level of Grand Central Station, New York. I went there one day to ask a question. Out of the surging crowds there was constantly a little knot of people clustered up against the booth, each with a burning question that had to be answered right *now!*

I watched the man behind the desk handle people. And he showed no signs of tension. It was fascinating. Here was a small, bespectacled man, subjected to heavy pressures, trying to answer the questions of impatient and confused travelers. And yet he was one of the calmest people I have ever seen.

The next passenger to get his attention was a short, plump woman, a shawl tied over her head. I remember that she had little whiskers growing from her chin.

The information man leaned forward so he could single out her voice from all the noise around him. "Yes, madam?"

The information man looked up slowly and focused his eyes on this woman through the bottom lenses of his bifocals. "Let's see . . . where was it you were going?"

A smartly dressed man with a briefcase in one hand and an expensive hat in the other tried to break in with a question. The information man just kept on talking to the woman in front of him. "Where was it you were going?"

"Springfield."

"And that was Springfield, Ohio?"

"Massachusetts."

Without looking at his timetable he gave her the answer. "That train leaves on Track 25 in just ten minutes. You don't need to run; you have plenty of time."

"Did you say Track 25?"

"Yes, ma'am."

"Twenty-five?"

"Twenty-five."

The woman turned to leave and the information man focused his attention on the man with the expensive hat. But once again the woman asked him the track number. "Did you say it was Track 25?" she asked. This time, however, the man behind the desk was giving his attention to his new passenger, and he would no longer listen to the little woman with the shawl tied over her head.

Finally, there was a momentary lull, and I took the opportunity to ask the information man a question. "I've been admiring the way you handle the public," I said. "Tell me, how can you do it and keep so calm?"

And then this man raised his head and looked at me through his bifocals. "I don't deal with the public," he said. "I deal with one passenger. And then with another passenger. It's just one person at a time right on through the day. Now where was it you were going?"

I've never forgotten that phrase: one person at a time right on through the day. And I don't intend that I ever shall, for it is too important in the proper regulation of factors that make for tension. It's been a great help to me when many multiplying problems compete for my attention at once. When things start coming at me from every direction I remind myself: "One thing at a time." That's it. That policy can undercut tension and keep your emotions under good control.

"This one thing I do," said St. Paul. (Philippians 3:13) There is magic in that phrase. If life is crowding you, if pressures are mounting inside you and tensions are leaving you high-strung and irritable, memorize that phrase. "This one thing I do." Refer to it before you start to work, and then determine to live by it. Develop the habit of saying, "Just a minute please" to interruptions, whether they come in the form of people, ideas or noise. As you perfect the technique of doing only one thing at a time you will find that much of the tension has been eased away, and in its place has come a smooth power-flow.

If you learn to think in terms of peacefulness then, no matter how hectic your circumstances, you can live with calmness and peace of mind.

I saw this demonstrated in the case of a man I met one winter morning. To begin with, I make it a practice in my morning prayers to ask the Lord to guide me to anyone He wishes me to help during the day. I recommend this practice. It will lead you to many exciting adventures.

Well, on this particular day the telephone rang and a tense voice reminded me of a meeting I was supposed to attend in midtown Manhattan. I got the impression from the tense person who was calling that if I failed to show up or was late, civilization would fall. I dashed out of my apartment building urging Mike, our genial doorman, to get me a taxi-cab. But it was the morning rush hour and none was readily available. I live on upper Fifth Avenue and, failing to note a cab in sight, started walking rather rapidly toward Madison Avenue, a block away, where I felt the chances for getting a cab might be better.

Then I decided to practice the tension-free control which I advocate for others. I slowed down to a relaxed pace and humbly suggested to the Lord that if He wanted me at that meeting He would just have to make a cab available. And that is exactly what happened, for there at the corner was an empty taxi. And, as I soon discovered, my earlier prayer was answered, for this driver was certainly a man who needed help.

He was extraordinarily tense, gripping the wheel so tightly his knuckles showed white. He talked ceaselessly in a nerv-ous manner, complaining about all the other drivers throng-ing the avenue. Pushing through the maelstrom of traffic, listening to him, I got the naïve idea that he alone, of all the drivers on Madison Avenue, knew how to drive. He leaned out of the window and instructed the others vociferously. In fact, he communicated with them in theological termi-nology.

He created a very tense atmosphere despite the fact that a sign in the cab urged his passengers to "Sit back, enjoy the ride." I really felt very sorry for this high-strung, nerv-ous man and employed a spiritual technique I have often used of sending out quieting prayers toward him. I tried to surround him with God's peace as we pushed on down the jampacked thoroughfare.

Then I noticed something that explained much. It was a printed sign, not hand-lettered, but apparently done by a printer. It was appended with Scotch tape to the instrument panel at eye level where one could easily see it. I became quite amused by this sign which read: "If you can keep your head amidst all this confusion—you don't understand the situation."

I asked the taxi-driver what it meant and he said he didn't know but it comforted him. Well, of course, we are not likely to escape from the confusion of this world. We have to live in it and we must understand the situation. And that is just

the point; we *can* understand and adjust to outward tension,
living in it successfully, because we have the secret of peace
of mind.

When we reached our destination I said to the driver that
I was sorry he was so nervous, that unless he conquered it
he might become ill. He assumed from my remarks that I
might be a physician and anxiously asked me how a nervous,
tense condition might be cured.

I told him that I was not a medical doctor, but could recommend a Doctor who could heal him. In fact, I knew that
Doctor's methods, and could give him a prescription. It
would not be a liquid in a bottle or a pill, but a healing
thought which, lodged in his mind, could fill him with peace
and strength. Whereupon, I took a sheet of paper and let-
tered the following words; "The peace of God, which passeth
all understanding." (Phillippians 4:7)

"Put that up alongside your other sign," I said. "Keep looking at it until those eight words are printed upon your mind
so deeply that they sink into your consciousness. They have
healing power. They can draw off your tension."

The man looked long and intently at what I had written.
That the words impressed him was evident. "Guess that's
what I need," he said. "I'll try taking your prescription."

I could have given him other tension-healing words, but
this seemed sufficient for the time.

But for you who may work with the teaching of this book,
I shall add others. The procedure is to cancel out your tension thoughts by the systematic and deliberate use of more
powerful thoughts of peace. Inject into the mass of tension
thinking which fills your mind with some really potent and
healing thoughts that have the power to change the condition. Physicians tell us that certain thoughts can make you
sick, actually physically sick. Such thoughts are hate, fear
and tension, to mention only three. Alexis Carrel says: "Envy,
hate, fear, when these sentiments are habitual, are capable
of starting organic changes and genuine diseases." And other
thoughts can make you well; such long-held thoughts as love,
faith and peace.

But they must be directed and systematic thoughts, taken
regularly into the thought stream. In due time they will
change its essential character. Then the tension which has
agitated you, which has perhaps even affected your blood
pressure, your heart and certainly your disposition, will sub-

side and you will return to a normal and satisfying condition of mental, emotional and physical well-being.

For one week "take" the following thoughts daily. Read each one thoughtfully several times to perceive its deeper meaning and to get the feel of the words. Then commit each to memory. Keep saying it until it is firmly lodged in your conscious mind. Then conceive of it as sinking steadily and deeply into your subconscious, there to do its healing work.

Proceed similarly each day with each one. After these seven have been fully integrated into the thought stream, go through the Bible on your own, culling out the many texts that are especially designed for tension curing. Saturate your mind with them, "soak" them deeply into the inner consciousness.

This may seem a strange and curious method, but it will work miracles, so what else matters? Hundreds, maybe thousands of people tell me the great things this procedure has done for them; how finally it has freed them from tension. It is truly one of the most amazing results of positive thinking thoughts:

Monday	"Peace I leave with you, my peace I give unto you . . . Let not your heart be troubled, neither let it be afraid." (John 14:27) (Where it says you or your, use your own name.)
Tuesday	"Thou wilt keep him in perfect peace, whose mind is stayed on thee; because he trusteth in thee." (Isaiah 26:3)
Wednesday	"My presence shall go with thee, and I will give thee rest." (Exodus 33:14)
Thursday	"Rest in the Lord, and wait patiently for him; fret not thyself." (Psalm 37:7)
Friday	"Come unto me, all ye that labour and are heavy laden, and I will give you rest." (Matthew 11:28)
Saturday	"Let the peace of God rule in your hearts." (Colossians 3:15)
Sunday	"He maketh me to lie down in green pastures: he leadeth me beside the still waters. He restoreth my soul." (Psalm 23:2,3)

Another point at which to attack tension is in your conversation or talk. Actually, you can easily talk yourself into being tense. A verbal statement is simply an articulated thought. So, when you talk tension you are thinking tension; and as you think tension you develop a tense state which results in high-tempo talk. Manifestly then, if you stop making tense and nervous remarks you will in time starve the thought that produces tense talking. The process can be encouraged by speaking calmly and by reducing the tempo of speech, using quiet, composed tones and words.

Take it slow and easy when you speak. Watch the elevation of the voice, keep a curb on its intensity. If someone breaks in before you are finished, just realize that maybe they are tense, so let them break in. If you want to resume your line of thought later, very well. But maybe you'll just let it slide. It's a kind of nervous habit nowadays just to jabber, whether anything is said or not.

Easy does it in speech as in all human activity.

There is one final technique that I would like to tell you about. It is a technique that is always used by the men and women who have learned to live successfully with pressure. Sometimes it is used instinctively; sometimes, as in the case of the business executive I am about to tell you of, it is used with planned deliberation.

I met this man on a railroad train and he taught me a good technique for reducing tension. A distinguished looking gentleman, he was headed for a business convention in the South. He settled down in his roomette across from me, pulled out a small briefcase and proceeded to surround himself with various stacks of paper. He had brought his office with him, and he was getting ready to go to work right there on the train.

But before starting, he did a strange thing. From his briefcase he pulled a black enamel plaque about the size of a postcard. Written on the plaque in large white letters were two words: PLAN BACKWARD. The man propped these words on the table before him and went to work.

Curiosity finally got the better of me, and I leaned across the aisle and said, "Pardon me, I hope you don't mind if I ask you a question?"

The gentleman took off his glasses and looked at me and said that he didn't mind at all: what could he do for me?

"Well," I continued, "I've seen a lot of these signs that say PLAN AHEAD. But I've never seen one that says PLAN BACKWARD."

He laughed. "All it is," he said, "is a reminder to myself that I've got to organize my time."

"But why the backward? Why not ahead?"

"Because," he said, "planning backward contains the idea of a specific goal. You choose a goal, picture yourself accomplishing it, then plan backward until you know exactly where and when you must start."

What a clever idea that is, really. Plan backward! I have tried it and it works. The big thing it helps you do is to organize yourself so that you start a project in time. I am a firm believer in the idea that every program has an ideal, intrinsic time-value of its own. To allow less time produces tension; to allow more time produces waste.

Try to discover this intrinsic time-value for the tasks that make up your day. How long does it really take you to handle your correspondence thoughtfully? How long does it really take you to prepare breakfast, walk to the bus stop, get the children off to school? Plan backward from these goals, and you will know when you have to *start* in order to reach them effortlessly, efficiently and without rush. This really cuts down tension. Simply start in time.

Of course, as previously suggested, the basic cure of tension and pressure is through God's peace. "Peace I give unto you: not as the world giveth, give I unto you. Let not your heart be troubled . . ." (John 14:27)

Knowing that modern people need the peace of God, I introduced a period of creative spiritual quietness into the services of worship in Marble Collegiate Church. Everyone is urged to let the body relax and to think only of God and Jesus Christ. A deep, a very deep silence settles over the large congregation. The only sounds are those on Fifth Avenue, but they are muffled by the thick marble walls of the ancient church.

When all is still I suggest quietly that everyone "drop" his problems, fears, tensions into the "deep pool of quietness" which has been created. The effect is deeply moving. The peace of God does indeed move over the people, taking life's fitful fever from minds and hearts.

And, as an illustration of how we all need the peace of God, I want to close this chapter with a touching letter from a young woman:

> First of all, I'll tell you that I'm twenty years old and a Roman Catholic. I've been brought up to practice my religion faithfully, and I have always done so. But lately, I had begun noticing that my faith in God, and His powers, was leaving my thinking more and more. I knew my faith was slipping away, and so I prayed that my faith and belief in God be renewed and strengthened. God, through your book, has done just that for me.

I cannot tell you how much happier I am . . . how much peace of mind I now have, and how much more I love life. As I read your book, I practiced every suggestion you gave with all my heart, and so I will continue practicing those suggestions until they become so much a part of me that I will do them naturally.

The other day, I had a rather upsetting experience. I have, for about a year, lived with an acute guilt complex about something I did. This feeling kept me from being happy, and in fact, kept me constantly nervous and miserable. I have confessed this sin to God many months ago, and have received absolution. Yet, in my mind, this wasn't enough. I let it eat at me, and imagined all sorts of terrible things that could result from it. Just the other day, reminders of this sin, and memories were brought back to me, and my guilt feeling kept telling me that I might some day do these things again, thus falling back into sin. The whole day I was a case of nerves, and even though I kept trying to apply your suggestions of relaxation, etc., to myself, I was still very upset. That night, in bed, I couldn't sleep, but suddenly I thought that by my talking it over with God, He would give me peace and relief. I told Him I knew He had forgiven me, and that He knew how sincere I now was to better myself. I asked Him to let the guilt feelings leave me. Instantly they did, and I fell into a peaceful sleep. These feelings have never again haunted me, and I know that they never will.

In your book, I felt, as I read it, that you were sincerely trying to help me personally. And so you have.

Take a vacation from tension when you can. Throw away your watch temporarily; build little islands of peace into your day; learn the art of storing up relaxed power. But for those times when you must live with tension, learn the art of saying, "Just a minute, please . . ." Cram the mind full of peace producing thoughts. Keep the speech tempo down. And avoid getting tense in reaching objectives. Plan backward; allow yourself enough time for the jobs you have to do. And, finally, and most important of all, practice the peace of God every day.

Follow these simple rules regularly, and there is no reason why your life cannot become one of peace, tranquility and poise. You don't need to allow pressures to pressure you.

Special suggestion. I have written a forty page, pocket-sized pamphlet called *You Can Relax* which contains other practical suggestions for dealing with tension. I will gladly send you a free copy if you will write to me care of the Foundation for Christian Living, Pawling, New York.

Chapter XI

BETTER HEALTH THROUGH POSITIVE THINKING

IN MY OFFICE at Marble Collegiate Church is a small, toy coal bucket containing miniature lumps of real coal. I think I shall always keep that bucket, because it symbolizes an effective secret of health through positive thinking.

It happened in this way. A well known political personality asked me to call upon his wife's aunt who was in the hospital. This woman proved to be an amazingly interesting and able person. "I'm already getting better," she said. "It's my coal bucket that's doing it."

"Your coal bucket," I repeated. "I never knew coal buckets had healing properties. Besides, who has coal buckets in this era of better heating."

Then I saw it. There she was, propped up in her hospital bed, surrounded by the usual bottles and buzzers and vases of flowers; and on her bedside table, right in the middle of it all, was a miniature coal bucket, an exact replica of the black, old-fashioned kind our grandparents used.

"Well," I said, "this is certainly the most unusual piece of hospital equipment I've ever seen. Does it have something to do with how well you're looking?" And she did look very well, sitting straight up in bed, her eyes sparkling.

"It does indeed," she said. "It is my symbol of victory. Let me tell you about it. Here I was in the hospital, sick in body and despondent in mind. One dark trouble after another went through my thoughts. Then someone gave me a copy of your book about positive thinking. I was particularly struck with the idea that negative thoughts can do damage to our bodies. So I decided I would get all the old, black thoughts out of my mind and put bright, hopeful thoughts in their place.

"I started praying and reading the Bible as you suggested,

but the black thoughts continued. Then one day I got to thinking that a black thought was something like an ugly black lump of coal. Strange the ideas we get, but I believe God gave me this one. So I sent out and got this little bucket of coal. Now, when a black thought comes, I pick up a lump of coal and say, "With the help of God I now cast this thought out of my mind and I toss the coal into that receptacle over there. I'm sure my nurse thought I was going daft; but then she saw how much my spirits were improving. This simple technique has helped me no end, and I thank God for the bright thoughts that have come to take the place of the dark old thoughts which had so much to do with making me ill. You have no idea, Dr. Peale, how much this silly, little coal bucket has had to do with my recovery."

When she left the hospital she sent the miniature coal bucket to me and there it stands atop a bookshelf to remind me of an important truth about well being—get rid of black thoughts.

I have been impressed many times by the effect of positive thinking on health and how dark negative thoughts tend to induce illness. Holding negative thoughts is very dangerous. Job said, "The thing I greatly feared is come upon me." (Job 3:35) And Job was not the last to find that you can bring catastrophe upon yourself by unhealthy thinking.

Occasionally one comes across some dramatically clear-cut example of this fact. In England I read a story in the *London Daily Mail* describing the curious death of Gem Gilbert, a British tennis star. She had died as a dentist was about to extract a tooth.

Years before, when Gem Gilbert was a small girl, she had gone to the dentist where her mother was to have a tooth pulled. And a most unusual and tragic thing happened. The little girl, terrified, watched her mother die in the dentist's chair. So what happened? Her mind painted an indelible picture of herself dying in the same way. The picture became a mental reality. Gem Gilbert carried it in her mind for thirty years. This fear was so real that she would never go to a dentist, no matter how badly she needed treatment.

But finally there came a time when she was suffering such acute pain that she agreed to have a dentist come to her house at a seacoast place in Sussex to extract a tooth. She had her medical doctor and her pastor with her. She sat in the chair. The dentist put a bib around her. He took out his instruments and at the sight of them—she died.

The writer in the *Daily Mail* remarked that Gem Gilbert had been killed by "thirty years of thought." It is an extreme case, of course, but everywhere there are people who are doing great damage to themselves just as surely, if more slowly, by sickness-producing attitudes compounded of defeat, hate, fear, guilt. Obviously, then a most important technique of good health is ridding the mind of all unhealthy thoughts. It is important to have regular mind cleansings. We must get rid of mental infection in order to have healthy bodies.

It is astounding how often the pattern of resentment causing illness is repeated. Bernard Baruch says, "Two things are bad for the heart: running up stairs and running down people." It's true not only of the heart but of the entire physical being. And forgiveness has an amazingly therapeutic effect. I received a letter from a woman who had suffered an accident, while hunting with her husband, which bears this out:

> I had an accident in 1946, when a gun I was firing gave a hard recoil and injured my right shoulder. Great pain ensued, and some time later I went to an orthopedic specialist. X-rays revealed a bony spur, with a great amount of calcium, and a nerve spasm was also present over the site of injury.
>
> I was given an injection of procane into the nerve spasm and put on cortisone. But the pain came back again and I was unable to lift the arm beyond a certain degree in motion. I had made an appointment with my orthopedic surgeon to begin X-ray treatments when he returned from a trip.
>
> Then I started reading *The Power of Positive Thinking.* After reading about resentments and their effect on physical conditions, I put the book down and did some thinking. I had had some trouble over family affairs with my only sister, and we were not on good terms, though we observed the amenities when meeting. We had not visited nor made personal calls for over four months, and had not been truly friendly for a number of years.
>
> After a great deal of thinking I called her on the phone, had a pleasant talk with her, which was a great surprise, and I found myself offering to help her, if I could, in any way. When I laid down the phone I was weeping silently.
>
> Then, much to my astonishment, I had a burning sensation on the inside of my forearm. It's hard to explain the sensation only to say it felt as if the glands were secreting backwards, with a warm burning sensation. So intense was this sensation that I just looked at the spot on my forearm expecting to see it break out in some rash. It lasted for a few seconds only, and the pain went.

I then, gingerly at first, began putting my arm through motions and found I could move it freely, in flexion, extension, supination. Since then I have had complete free motion of the arm without soreness or pain.

Resentment! What is this powerful emotion that wreaks so much havoc with our bodies? Apparently what happens is that we make ourselves feel painful experiences over and over again. "Resent" is an interesting word: it comes from the Latin words meaning "to feel again." It operates in the following manner. We have an experience that is full of hurt to the personality. We resent it and so make ourselves miserable and sick by constantly re-feeling it. But finally the conscious mind may refuse to relive the actual painful memory. However, instead of forgiving and forgetting, it forces the memory down into the subconscious and then the smothered, emotional reaction may break out in the form of physical pain or sickness.

A physician told me about a woman of fifty who kept coming to him with various kinds of sores on her body. He would cure the sores with local applications, but sooner or later they would reappear and so would she. Finally, the doctor began to suspect that his patient's trouble was more spiritual than physical, and he decided to make an experiment.

"Do you know," he told her the next time she came for treatment, "I believe you are terribly afraid of something or else you are holding some deep resentment. I don't know what it is, and unless I do know I'm not going to be of much help to you."

There followed a prolonged counseling session in which it became obvious that the doctor's suspicion was well founded. This patient, as a child, had suffered a shocking traumatic experience. She had a beautiful sister, while she herself was always considered a homely child. When they were both still very young, the pretty sister died. Alongside the casket, the mother stood weeping. Suddenly she whirled around on the homely daughter and cried, "Why wasn't it you!"

This was such an extremely painful experience for the girl that her mind tried to avoid accepting it. How incredible that her own mother did not love her! But she did not want to remember that. So she managed to bury it in the unconscious, but still it remained very active in total consciousness. She developed a hatred for her mother and this, too, was an emotion that she could not accept and would not admit. She also buried that in the subconscious. So these unhealthy emotions were driven deep underground and there they festered, sending off ill health.

Things would go all right until for some reason (perhaps it was a telephone call from her mother, or maybe she saw someone on the street who reminded her vividly of her mother) the old resentments were stimulated again. She resisted the painful, remembered emotions, but they came out anyhow, in the form of another *kind* of pain. But once she recognized the real source of her physical troubles, she was able to empty out her resentments to her doctor. When she utilized the therapy of forgiveness she finally was rid of hate. The spiritual health she achieved led to mental and physical health. Thereafter she was also rid of the constantly recurring sores.

This patient had buried her feelings of ill will for many years before they erupted into ill health, but sometimes the effects of such feelings are much more immediate. Just the normal frictions of day-to-day life can result in headaches, back troubles, aching joints, and that "gray sickness." A case of this kind came to my attention recently in a rather amusing way. An old friend blurted out that he was "feeling lousy" and that he "hated his mother-in-law." He, himself, saw the connection between the unwell feeling and the cause.

"Let me tell you about her, Norman," he said. "If you want to hear about witches, listen to this one. I have to get up early each morning, earlier than my wife; and while I'm getting breakfast in comes the mother-in-law. She's a hag. Underneath a frayed kimono she wears a sloppy old nightgown that's dragging along the floor, and she shuffles along in dirty carpet slippers that keep kicking off and on. Her hair is never combed and it falls down in front of her eyes. But the thing that I hate worst of all is the way she grinds her toast. She puts it between her false teeth and grinds it back and forth like a horse. I set there every morning, just waiting for her to start grinding the toast."

Well, it's no wonder my friend was having stomach troubles, starting his day off with such emotions. I suggested a simple solution. "You're not distinguishing between your mother-in-law as a mother-in-law and as a woman," I said.

"She's no woman," my friend said firmly. "That's all she is, a mother-in-law."

"Well now, that just isn't so. She was a woman before she

was a mother-in-law; and if you want to find a solution to your problem, I suggest you start treating her like a woman. Some morning soon, when she comes to breakfast, why not invite her out to lunch. That will surprise her. She won't know what to do with that one, and she'll at least be so surprised she'll stop grinding her toast for a couple of minutes.

"Invite her to lunch in a nice place. Say to her, 'I'm going to take you to a swank spot that I know, so you'll want to dress your best.' And when she meets you at the restaurant, usher her in like you were proud of her. Buy her a corsage, and pin it on her. Compliment her on her hair-do, and on her dress. And then, say this: 'I never realized how pretty you were, just seeing you at breakfast and all. My, but you are really a pretty woman.' Then drop it. Have a good meal, be full of fun, give her a good time and see what happens."

It worked like a charm. The morning after that luncheon the mother-in-law came down with her hair combed and as soon as she had the opportunity she purchased some new slippers and a bright, pretty housecoat to replace the shabby old kimono. In time the two became as thick as thieves, and all the old symptoms of tension and stomach distress disappeared.

But you may say, "Dr. Peale, your ideas are all very well for the person who has an emotionally induced illness. But not all illness is caused by the emotions."

This is very true. But in one important way, it makes no difference whether the disability is functional or organic. In either case, the patient's spirit can be healed. And that is a large element in healing, even if the physical disability remains.

In fact I believe that, whatever your problem—it can be solved. I make that statement with complete awareness of all the terrible, heartrending problems to which human nature is subject.

I preach no easy philosophy because we do not live in an easy world. But neither do we live in an impossible world. Never forget that fact. We have available the help of Almighty God in the problems of this life. And underscore that word *Almighty*. The help we get from God is tremendous help. We all know of the astonishing victories which are achieved in the lives of human beings through that vast Power. For example, take this letter from a woman in Wisconsin:

My husband was a strong, healthy man until, in his early forties, he was stricken with arthritis. Many days of suffering extreme pain followed, but after the first bout was over he continued to travel his sixteen states as a salesman.

Finally he had to use a cane. The joints on his feet and fingers became horrible knobs. I was with him on one of his trips. It was so pathetic to see this once strong man hobbling along the streets, complaining about his inability to take a step without pain.

Suddenly a young man in his thirties passed us, whistling merrily. As he went by, to my dismay, I noticed that he had only hooks for hands. I called this to my husband's attention. It suddenly presented a picture of a young man with a lifetime ahead of him, having hooks for hands. And yet he was happy.

So my husband braced himself and said, "I'll never complain again." He never has. He has had phlebitis, gangrene, and lost the sight of one eye. Three weeks ago he had an operation for a ruptured gall bladder, has an eneurysm of the lower aorta, and the liver growing around the gall bladder. His fingers are so bent he cannot button his shirt.

But he is happy, victorious. He never complains. He is grateful for all small or large favors. When the ambulance man deposited him in his chair, he turned to me and said, "I've come through this just great. God has been so good to me."

This man's problem was not removed from him, but he solved it. There are many situations like this, where problems are not eliminated, no matter what one does. But the person who has faith in God, even though his problem remains unchanged, shall indeed gain victory over it. This arthritic man emptied himself of his negative and self-pity thoughts, and while his arthritis was not cured, his spirit was healed. He is not an unhappy man today. He is not victimized by his condition. And as a result, he has the blessings of mental and spiritual health despite his physical handicaps. So it is possible for us to improve our spirits even though, occasionally, we may not be able to improve our physical condition. Many times our physical condition is beyond control. We inherit our health from our parents and from our grandparents. Frequently, fortunately, it is good health we inherit. Sometime ago I had a letter from President Harry S. Truman in which he pointed out this fact:

I have always been of the opinion that to live a long, healthy and happy life, you must be careful to pick the right grand-parents on both sides of the house. Apparently, that is what I did. Of course, I have obeyed the rules the best I could about the forms of exercise best suited to my age and about eating habits. I eat what I want when I want it, but not as much as I would like.

Mr. Truman, however, does go on to say that living by spiritual principles has effected his health:

> One of the principal contributions to good health is a moral code that considers the welfare of the people around you as well as your own. I have found the 20th Chapter of Exodus and the 5th, 6th and 7th Chapters of the Gospel according to St. Matthew to be nearly perfect guides by which to live. The 10th Chapter of St. Luke also has a wonderful effect upon people who are trying to find the true definition of a good neighbor.

Dr. George W. Crane says, "In modern medicine we are beginning to realize that positive thinking seems to exert a beneficial tonic to many of the internal organs. On the other hand, negative thinking can throw a monkey wrench into the smooth functioning of those inner organs and glands. Drugs and chemicals can influence glands, but the mind can do so too."

Ronald J. Smith discovered that fact. The *S.S. Homeric* was moving slowly up the St. Lawrence River and Ronald Smith, who had long been plagued with a nervous disorder that affected his stomach bringing the chances of an ulcer within distance, was standing in his cabin looking at a large jar of stomach tablets in one hand and a copy of *The Power of Positive Thinking* in the other.

Ronald Smith's cabin companion ventured: "You have been reading that book for five days now. Are you going to ignore what you have learned from it? Go ahead and throw the tablets out the porthole." After a brief hesitation, Smith gave one throw and the jar of stomach tablets splashed out of sight.

Smith has never again had need to revert to the habit of taking tablets. He learned the amazing power of positive thinking to heal. Let me repeat. The technique is to believe that you are going to be better, believe that positive thinking is going to work for you, and remedial forces actually will tend to be set in motion.

The newspapers carried a story about a man who was hit by a truck while crossing a street and was killed. An autopsy established that he had lesions from tuberculosis, ulcers, bad kidneys and heart trouble. Yet he had lived a vigorous life to the age of 84. The doctor performing the autopsy said, "This man should have been dead thirty years ago." The widow, when she was asked how he had lived so long, answered, "My husband always *believed* he would feel better tomorrow."

One definite step that some have found helpful in applying positive attitudes to physical well-being is that of affirmation or the use of definite positive statements. Words are dynamite. If you constantly use negative words concerning your health, you may stimulate negative forces that can adversely affect you. Words, habitually used, are reflections of strongly held thought, and thoughts can affect internal organs negatively or positively. But this fact also works to your advantage in that forces favorable to well-being may be stimulated by the constant use of positive words of affirmations. And it is a fact that positive thinking is stronger than negative thinking as faith is stronger than fear.

Alfred J. Cantor, M.D., former President of the Academy of Psychosomatic Medicine, in speaking of the effect of affirmations on health cautions against even such qualified statements as, "I am not going to be ill today." That is a half-positive assertion. Use instead, "I am going to be better today," which is a wholly positive statement and therefore much healthier. "Affirmations," says Dr. Cantor, "are based upon proved, scientific facts—the facts of biology, chemistry and medicine. Properly employed, such affirmations will improve your health, lengthen your life, rejuvenate your body, increase your happiness, give you success and guarantee for you the most important gift of all—peace of mind."

Here are some examples of health affirmations which have been used successfully by many persons. Try them for yourself, but be sure to use them daily, thus training the mind to think in positive concepts.

I see myself as whole—every organ of my body operating perfectly in harmony with God's perfect laws.

My whole being is fulfilled with health, I think health, feel health, practice health.

The healing grace of the great physician Jesus Christ is flooding my life. In Him was life. His life is in me.

I am a child of God. In Him I live and move and have my being. I am strong, vital, joyous. The kingdom of God is within me and I am grateful to God.

Here is a prominent medical doctor who recognizes the role of affirmed belief in health and who recommends affirmation as a road to well-being.

Actually, making affirmative statements and holding affirmative thoughts is a major first step toward causing the affirmed belief to be actualized. A second step is to put the affirmations into action. And to do that, act as if the thing affirmed is already true. As you think, affirm and act; just so will you strongly tend to feel. Act vigorously and energetically and you will be amazed at the new energy and vigor you will enjoy.

Recently I sat beside James A. Farley at a luncheon. I marveled at his obvious good health and vigor. He seemed to be in the very best of condition and didn't appear any older than he had twenty years ago when I first knew him.

"Jim, don't you ever intend to get old?" I asked admiringly.

"No, sir!" he answered, smiling at me broadly, "not on your life."

"Well, I can believe it," I said. "But what's your secret?"

"I never think any old thoughts," he declared.

Jim Farley by thinking and living on that positive basis is actually demonstrating the power of positive affirmations.

Sessue Hayakawa, the Japanese actor who played the role of the prison camp commander in the film "Bridge on the River Kwai," is often mistaken for a man in his forties, although he is seventy. How does he accomplish this? By acting quietly and sincerely as though he were in his forties. "I stopped counting the years when I became 45," he said recently. "Aging is often a matter of the spirit. It exists in the imagination before it exists in the body. It is in the mind. It does not matter how long I sleep or what I eat. When a person gets little sleep one night, he usually says to himself, 'I didn't get enough sleep last night, I must be tired.' And so he is tired. His body did not need the sleep. Only his imagination did."

What sound insight! Our bodies do not need to become tired, sick, exhausted and old. Change your "image" of yourself; see yourself well, of course observing and practicing all the rules of health, and you will tend to be that which you visualize and practice.

This has long been a personal theory of mine, one that I have applied to myself through actual personal demonstration. I am humbly grateful to God that through the practice of His mental, physical and spiritual laws I have, in sixty years, been inside a hospital, as a patient, exactly twice. Once was when I was still a youngster and had a slight ear operation. The second time was when I was twenty and had my tonsils and adenoids out.

I am not a strapping athlete but have been fortunate in having good health. In twenty-eight years at the Marble Collegiate Church I have missed just one Sunday due to illness, and that was because of a cold that settled in my vocal cords and I couldn't speak. Since then I have discovered principles of relaxation and right thinking that would have overcome such a voice difficulty. What are the principles I use? Simply those I have advocated in previous books which many have applied effectively.

They are all sound principles, adapted from a lifetime of observation and experiment, not merely by myself, but in the "laboratory" demonstration of thousands of people who have shared their practice with me. They will work. I know that they will work because they have worked for me, and for the many others with whom I have shared them. They are part of the amazing results of positive thinking.

1. Affirm that you are healthy. Say to yourself, "I feel well today. God created my body, mind and soul; so today, I feel as God intended, healthy and vigorous."

2. Hold constantly before your mind a clear picture of yourself as a well person.

3. Thank God frequently, every day, for the wonderful feeling of vitality. I asked Dr. John Riley who, at 91, was the oldest practicing physician in the state of New York the secret of his good health to ninety plus. He said, "Every day I thank God for the amazing organs of my body. I name them over and say, 'Thank you God, for my excellent stomach; thank you God, for my wonderful heart; thank you God for my marvelous blood stream.'"

That this rather unique procedure added to his life of health and longevity Dr. Riley had no doubt. In daily thanksgiving he was firmly establishing the image of good health in consciousness and it demonstrated itself in fact.

4. Make every effort to keep your mind free of unhealthy thoughts. Flush out negative thoughts such as antagonisms, regrets, mean or vindictive images, disappointments. Replace

them with healthy, kindly, positive thoughts. Did you ever hear the Balinese proverb, "If you get angry you will quickly get old"? I am told that in Bali there is less heart trouble than anywhere in the world.

5. Take nothing into the system that debilitates.

6. Keep your weight down. Find out what the doctors think your weight should be and keep it there. The solution of the weight problem requires a kind of strength that is essentially spiritual in nature. Control of extreme appetite whether for drink, for power, or for food is a problem of character. And character, of course, is spiritually conditioned.

A few years ago I became increasingly concerned about my own weight. It was far beyond the point at which I should have tipped the scales. Still, I kept on eating. I wasn't cutting down and realized that fact all too well. I began to wonder if I really could. It became an issue with me, actually a moral problem; was I defeated by a food appetite?

So I went on a diet that took off thirty-five pounds. Several years later, having re-added some fifteen of the lost poundage, I repeated the process—thirty pounds this time—to reduce to a level that has seemingly become a permanent weight. To accomplish this desired weight reduction, I employed certain spiritual and mental procedures which are described in *Live Longer and Better* which I wrote jointly with my brother, Dr. Robert Clifford Peale, a practicing physician.*

7. Regular daily exercise is essential to good health. I prefer push-ups, calisthenics and swimming, sometimes a little golf, and hiking. It is important to choose a form of exercise that you enjoy enough to keep up regularly without its becoming a bore.

Personally I walk at least a mile every day, usually just before retiring. And when I am at my farm, I follow Dr. Paul Dudley White's advice to ride a bicycle.

Dr. White says, "A long brisk walk in the evening may help more to induce sleep than any medication. Nervous stress and strain can be counteracted and even prevented by regular, vigorous exercise. It is the best antidote I know."

* A copy of this 40-page, pocket-sized booklet, *Live Longer and Better*, may be had by writing to the Foundation for Christian Living, Pawling, New York. No specific charge is made: publication and distribution costs are defrayed by voluntary contributions.

Dr. White further points out that "good muscle tone in the arms and particularly in the legs resulting from regular exercise maintains an improved circulation in the veins. Since the veins have valves which, when in good condition prevent the blood from going the wrong way, the compression of the veins by the skeletal muscles helps to pump the blood back to the heart. Soft unused muscles do not accomplish the job as well and also make clotting in the veins more likely. And," adds Dr. White, "deep breathing exercises several times a day are of definite value." I have added this latter to my own exercise program with excellent results.

8. Have regular examinations by a doctor. Prompt attention to any imbalance helps restore the proper health conditions.

9. The greatest point of all, in my opinion, and this is based on personal experience, is to open one's life to the inflow of God's renewing power. The words "meditate" and "medicate" are almost identical in root meaning. Right thinking is medicinal. God creates good health, and He re-creates it as well. The word health comes from the Anglo-Saxon word "wholth," which is also the root of the word "wholeness," and of the word "holy." Thus health is directly related to the idea of wholeness, and to the idea of holiness. In fact, holiness means to be a whole person, not a disorganized one; more than it means to be pious.

This brings to mind Plato's famous statement, "So neither ought you to attempt to cure the body without the soul." Indeed the whole man must be well, body and soul, if health is to be sound. So I keep in mind always that to be a healthy person it is important to be spiritually vital. When one becomes filled with positive thoughts and God thoughts there is no room for negative, unhealthy thoughts that are so often at the root of ill health.

Chapter XII

How to Be Married and Enjoy It

Do you want a successful and happy marriage? Of course, everyone does. And many couples have learned through positive thinking how to be married and enjoy it.

Take, for example, that cynical young man who sneered, "Me marry—nothing doing. I'm too smart for that." He began attending the Young Adult activities at our church shortly after the last war. He went out on dates, but made it clear that he wasn't going to marry. That was that!

Eventually we discovered the reason for his cynicism about marriage. In the first place he had come from a broken home. Then, he had seen too many unhappy marriages among the couples he knew. When he was overseas with the Navy as a pharmacist's mate on a small ship, he got the idea that "not one of the married men aboard was faithful to his wife." As soon as the ship pulled into port, the married men, it seemed, were the first ashore, "running to cavort" with whatever women they could find.

The result of such negative experiences was that this young man firmly decided that marriage was not for him. He had kept his eyes open. He knew the score and he was going to steer clear of it. That was for sure.

Well, it happens that in our church there is a wonderful couple, the Merle Wicks. The Wicks are happily married. It was arranged for the young man to visit the Wicks in their home. He spent several days with them. He watched them laugh and play and pray, and even argue, disagree and make up. He saw them in a variety of moods and situations, handling a variety of problems; and what he observed proved to be a revelation.

"Do you know," he said later, his face animated with a new discovery, "these people actually know how to be married and enjoy it!"

I've always liked that phrase: "How to be married and enjoy it!" This is a vitally important factor in successful living. When people know how to "enjoy" such a close relationship it means that they have a healthy, creative marriage in which both partners are encouraged, helped, built up. Each bolsters the other. It is a relationship in which the children know genuine warmth and affection. It produces a home that radiates happiness and emanates well-being.

The National Education Association held a meeting at which the presidents of practically every important university in the country were present. The purpose of the meeting was to discuss what education could do about the country's most pressing need. And what was the most pressing need? More scientific education to compete with the Russians? More space education? Better training in economics? Not at all; these educators felt that the most pressing need of today is happy and substantial home and family life. The happy, healthy home is the cornerstone of a healthy society. Create health in the home and that health will radiate outward, touching business, industry, education, government, all phases of society.

So, how to have a successful marriage is a vital matter, a top concern of our time.

In collecting material for this book, I have separated my correspondence according to categories, and one of the thickest folders is marked "Marriage Problems." Week after week the letters pour in:

> I have been married fourteen years and not at all happily, though I do have three wonderful healthy daughters for whom I thank the good Lord. My husband, age forty-nine, treats me shabbily. Sometimes he strikes me so hard with his fists. I think the real trouble is that he needs rest and relaxation. He doesn't take his vacation. He'd rather have double pay, though we don't need it. He makes good money. He owns his home. And we have never been in debt. Well, I wonder what should be done tactfully about him. Can you give me any suggestions?

> We have a daughter who is married to a man who does not work steadily and is otherwise very irresponsible. They have three young children. She has made regular trips for a long time to a guidance center, as the pressures were affecting her nerves and mind. Her condition is better, but she has been advised that her only hope of complete recovery is divorce.

> There is always a lot of talk and advice about the "little

woman" keeping herself attractive, not to let herself show the effects of child bearing, housework and worry; keep herself as pretty as the office secretary. How about the husband; a paunchy, bald male is no longer a jaunty Romeo. How about a bit of advice to him?

I have a problem in my marriage, and I don't know what to do. I left my husband nine months ago, one month before our wonderful little son was born to us. I haven't been happy since I left him. The reason for leaving my husband was that he started running around with single men and drank an awful lot. Also, he would never let me have any money in my purse. Just enough to pay the rent and get groceries with. You see my real problem is that I live with my parents and they want me to get a divorce and they are planning on it very much. I'm afraid of losing their love if I go back to him, and I still love him very much. He has told me of the mistake he has done and wishes me to come back to him. What should I do?

It seems the thing that disturbs me most of the time is my relationship with my wife. I never know how to take her. We have been married eighteen years and I love her very much, but she, being the type she is, quiet, self-sufficient, and satisfied to be by herself. I find it difficult to feel that she needs me for anything. Sometimes she volunteers some affection, but seldom cares for me to go any further. When I try to tell her how I feel she simply won't listen. Can you help me?

And so it goes, on and on, week after week the letters pouring in, giving intimate glimpses into problems people face in their married life.

One of the outstanding results of positive thinking has been its effectiveness in difficult marital situations. When people who are having trouble with their marriages begin to apply positive attitudes to their situation, the marriage almost always strengthens. New appreciation, esteem and regard come into the relationship. When two people begin to think constructively about marriage they get constructive results.

Not long ago I was making a speech on the West Coast. When the talk was over a man came up to me and said he wanted to tell me how positive thinking had affected his life.

He said that he had been married for nine years. Two weeks after his wedding he began to realize that he had not chosen his mate wisely.

"That marriage was a mistake," he said. "Right away both of us knew it. It had been a case of physical attraction, but my wife turned out to be just plain dumb. She was selfish, too. I had to face the fact that I wasn't ever going to get along with her, and I had to make up my mind whether or not to stick it out."

This man chose to stay with his wife. He told me that he decided to make the best of a bad situation and endure the marriage. He said that as soon as he made this decision he stopped griping and tried to get along as well as he could with a woman he did not love.

Things went along this unhappy course for five years and then this man read *The Power of Positive Thinking*. He began to use the principles outlined in this book in his business life. They worked very well. One day it occurred to him that if the principles of positive thinking worked in business, perhaps they would also work in his personal life.

"What would happen," he asked himself, "if I applied *The Power of Positive Thinking*, chapter by chapter, idea by idea, to my own home situation."

He began to do this. He began to analyze his wife, asking himself why she was selfish and why she appeared to be stupid. The thought came that perhaps his marriage had been a form of guidance. He started to picture his wife as an entirely different sort of person: as a stimulating, attractive life partner. He began to pray for her and eventually even out loud with her. Simultaneously he examined his own personality objectively and honestly for the flaws which were making his wife unhappy. This was important to the process for he, too, had not a little selfishness and self-centeredness, as he readily admitted.

This process lasted for four years, but "the results were very good," he declared. And it was evident how sincerely he meant that. From a marriage which was simply endured, the relationship between these two people became a warm partnership in which each tried to give more than he received.

"Positive thinking," this man told me, "was directly responsible for the remaking of our marriage."

Now the fact of the matter is that the married relationship is one of the most touchy and difficult of all human relationships requiring, as it does, the adjustment of two different personalities in intimate association. Making a marriage succeed cannot be left up to chance, or even to hope. A definite, practical program needs to be established so that each party to the marriage may grow and mature; so that the children may have full, rounded, happy, creative lives. These are the purposes of marriage and should always be held firmly in mind. A happy marriage, let me repeat, is one in which all parties concerned—husband, wife and children—are fulfilled to the maximum.

Let us examine a few of the problems that arise in marriage and see how they have been met successfully.

One of the most common complaints about marriage is that couples do not have common interests. Admittedly, it is sometimes difficult for a husband and wife to develop common interests. The husband leaves on the 8:10 train every morning and returns on the 6:57. His day has been filled with active business interests, but these he never explains to his wife because he has learned that she is not interested, or else he is too tired to talk. On the other hand, the wife has perhaps filled her day with Town Hall or club lectures, and when she tries to regale him with the details of the lectures he is bored to distraction. The result is that these two people never really communicate. Their interests become more and more divergent.

Some years ago I had a rather amusing example of conflicting interests when a member of our church told me that he and his wife had begun to argue over who was going to watch television. This was back in the days when TV was new and most people could afford only one set. So there they were sitting in the living room each night, the husband wanting to watch fights, sports programs and westerns, and the wife wanting to see programs on the cultural side. They began to argue over the television. They said cutting, mean things to each other, and while the marriage never came close to divorce, things definitely were not smooth.

This problem may seem too petty to bring to a pastor, but what seems petty can be a symptom of a deeper problem, or it can work up into a major cleavage. The husband could not understand his wife's dumb interests, and the wife could not understand her husband's stupid interests. Well, this went on for quite a while until both husband and wife decided they would have to do something about the situation, so they came to see me. After talking with them I decided upon a little strategy. Privately I made an arrangement with the husband, then later with the wife, on the basis of the principle of ". . . in honor preferring one another." (Romans 12:10)

"Now what this means," I said, "is that you should prefer each other: by that I mean that you insist that the *other* party shall have the preferred treatment. I want you to apply this Bible principle to your problem with the television. When you get back home tonight," I said to the husband, "you insist that you both see her cultural program, and really get something out of it." A little later the same day, I said to the wife, "When you go home, you insist that you and your husband watch the ball game. See if you can't enjoy it yourself."

At first this had a rather unhappy turn. That night the wife turned on the TV—to the ball game.

"Oh no you don't!" said the husband. "I *insist* that you listen to the Philharmonic tonight."

"Not at all," said the wife. "We are going to watch the ball game, whether you like it or not."

So that first night, believe it, they got into a terrific argument trying to follow the Biblical injunction, ". . . in honor preferring one another."

Later, when they came back to my office to complain, they saw the humor of the situation, and after that we got down to the more serious question involved. Actually, their problem was only a lack of common interest. Their lives were too narrow. They were living by themselves, for themselves. They needed to find outside activities which would take them together, away from their television set into the great world outside.

Since then this couple has become so active in community and church activities that they seldom watch television. Together they have achieved the goal of finding mutual interest. They are one of the happiest married couples of my acquaintance.

The matter of common interest raises the question of marriage with a member of another faith. I have received hundreds of questions dealing with the problem of whether a Protestant should marry a Catholic, or a Christian marry a Jew. Few questions so agitate families as this one.

If people truly practice positive thinking they can work out an interfaith marriage successfully. But it involves complete mutual respect for each other's faith, and an equal balance of every factor relating to the marriage. However, on the basis of considerable experience, I strongly urge young people to marry within their own religious group: Protestants with Protestants, Catholics with Catholics, Jews with Jews. Many hazards are eliminated by selecting a life partner from your own background. Marriage has many problems of adjustment as it is, and it's wiser not to add a difference of religion.

But a mixed marriage, as indeed any marriage, can rise to high levels of happiness if the home is packed full of love and faith and esteem for personality. Fill any household full of a love of God and of each other that transcends theological differences, and men and women and children can dwell together in peace and joy.

Another pesky problem that keeps coming up is the holdover of the ancient concept of the husband's role in marriage; that he is lord and master of the home. He handles the money, doling out an allowance, while the wife supposedly has the business sense of a babe in the woods.

Paralleling this is another anachronism: that many women, consciously or unconsciously, regard themselves as objects of art, to be taken care of by a father substitute in the form of a husband. This immature, infantile, ungrownup state of mind assumes as the wifely right that the woman is to be made happy. In her thought, apparently, the whole purpose of marriage is to provide happiness for her; meaning, of course, that she shall receive all she wants from this kind "Papa" husband whom she has taken as a spouse.

But it often happens that the "Papa" husband becomes disinclined to act out the father figure. He indicates that he expects a real contribution from the supposedly mature woman whom he has taken as his life partner. Then she is likely to react emotionally according to the immaturity on which her concepts are based; and the marriage starts to disintegrate.

So one of the really major steps that a couple needs to take in developing a successful marriage is to become mature individuals. Perhaps this is the most difficult assignment that life gives us. Dr. Smiley Blanton, the psychiatrist who heads The American Foundation of Religion and Psychiatry, with the assistance of Dr. Irwin Smalheiser, psychologist, has worked out a Maturity Score. This simple test will give some clues as to whether or not you need to work on the question of maturity in your own married life or in your life generally, for that matter.

Maturity Score

Yes   No

1. Do you lose your temper, stamp your feet, throw or kick things?
2. Do you always give the other person equal consideration with yourself?
3. Do you criticize your wife or husband in the presence of other people?
4. Are you insistent upon always having your own way, and sulk if you don't get it?
5. Are you a chronic worrier?
6. Do you put your trust in God and then just do your best?
7. Do you accept the ups and downs, and things that are inevitable, with serenity of spirit?
8. Do you have a positive conviction that you can meet and solve your problems?

Yes to questions one, three, four and five indicates immaturity.

Yes to questions two, six, seven and eight is a sign of a mature personality.

With the results of this test as a guide you will be able to know whether you need development of your emotional maturity. Certainly a major difficulty is that many people have an immature concept of love. A great deal of damage has been done to marriage by our Hollywoodish ideas of love. We seem to feel that "love" has got to be one prolonged moonlight and roses thrill.

Just the other day a young wife came to my office complaining that there was no thrill left in her marriage. She had been married nine months and now her husband's touch ceased to start her heart pounding. She had, however, found another boy who did give her this Hollywoodish sense of excitement. She wanted my advice about divorcing her husband to find married happiness with the second boy. She "simply must recapture the thrill of romance," she said.

"Well, young lady," I said, "suppose this new excitement lasts, as did the first, for only nine months; then what? In fact, the next might last only five months, for thrills tend to diminish with repetition. By the time you are forty you could be nothing but an old hag desperately looking for this so-called glamour that forever eludes you. You need to realize that this thrill you seek is something special that belongs to a certain stage in your development, but to expect it to last at high intensity is pure Hollywood hokum. It won't do that and it should not. It is against all the facts of human psychology that it should."

This young lady had never been apprised of the fact that sexual excitement is only one facet of a successful and enjoyable marriage. My father, who was first a physician and later a minister, and always a wise man, used to say that thrill-love was nothing but a biological trick on the part of nature for the simple purpose of perpetuating the race.

Far too many young couples think that as soon as sexual excitement begins to wear thin, they are falling out of love. They haven't adjusted to each other on any other basis than sex, and in their immaturity they do not want to work at marriage in all of its many aspects. The physical, while it is important, is certainly not the whole by any means.

In a newspaper I saw the results of a survey in which some four hundred happily married couples were interviewed. This survey indicated that the *average* time needed for two people to adjust to each other was six years! Note the fact that this is the average length of time; for many people it must have taken considerably longer. So when a young couple tries marriage for a few months, or even for a few years, and finds that the sense of excitement has abated somewhat, they should not become discouraged. Learning to be happily married takes time and patience. It is a mistake, indeed it is preposterous to think that as soon as the first flush of romance passes, it is time to seek another partner.

Now I do not want to indicate that sexual enjoyment should be confined to the first, few, pink-cloud months. Sexual adjustment is vital to a mature marriage. And in the overwhelming majority of successful marriages, sexual interest and capacity lasts into old age. Certainly sexual maladjustment can cause deep problems as many letters indicate:

You have said many wise things about sex, so I turn to you with a serious problem.

I have a perfectly good relationship with my wife in everything but the sexual area. She is about one-third as needful as I am. What should I do with my psycho-sexual difference? I don't want to express myself with another woman, yet my wife, whom I love, does not fulfill me.

My wife is a dream girl, very attractive. She has the personality that attracts friends, especially children, who love her. It is her dream to have a child. I love her very much, and she is everything in the world to me. My problem is that we have been married two years and I have not been able to have sexual intercourse with my wife.

I have been to one doctor after another, and all they tell me is that there is nothing wrong with me physically. Finally, one doctor told me that it was a combination of emotions, nerves and subsconscious mind that was blocking off any successful attempts.

Do you think I have the right to ask her to spend the rest of her life with me when I cannot fulfill the part of the husband and man to make a happy home and marriage? Is there anything you could suggest that might help me?

My husband and I have been married a year and one month. I haven't enjoyed our sexual relations at all, don't get any pleasure in love making, and dread even kissing him for fear it will lead to intercourse. I have never actually wanted intercourse and my life would be perfectly happy without it. I've explained this to my husband. It disgusts him, which I suppose, is normal. Should I divorce my husband and let him have another chance at happiness, or should we go through life like this?

My daughter was married last July. I tried to prepare her adequately for the physical side of marriage. I felt that she was quite mature and ready. She seems to be having trouble adjusting—wonders if, after all, she is "frigid." I wonder sometimes if we read too much and become completely confused. Would you have a word of some sort that might help her?

I have been married eighteen years and have a wonderful husband and four children. But, Dr. Peale, I still have an indifferent attitude toward sex relations. Possibly it is because I was led as a child to look at it as a vulgar act. Does the Lord look at it that way? Is it to be entered into only for conception's sake and the bringing of babies into the world?

So very often this question of vulgarity comes up. Apparently our Puritan backgrounds have left an indelible mark on our attitudes toward sex. I think it is important to state firmly that a full, natural enjoyment of sex is normal and right, else God would never have created people as He did. Love is both physical and spiritual. Therefore, a complete enjoyment of the physical senses within a spiritual marriage is never an expression of vulgarity.

The sexual act is a sacred expression of love between two

people who have spiritually become one through marriage. "The twain shall be one flesh," the Bible says. While sexual union itself is physical in nature, it is also a fundamental expression of the highest and purest emotions in love. To regard it as vulgar indicates a warped concept, probably originating in childhood when, to make you moral, a dirty connotation was put upon God's principle.

Notice, however, that while we have been talking about the physical aspects of love, we have consistently brought the spiritual side of married life into focus. The spiritual element is where its real strength lies, and this is one of the areas where positive thinking becomes most important. Positive thinking says that through the proper mental and spiritual attitudes we are able to overcome our difficulties, whether they are marital or otherwise.

One of the most effective aspects of positive thinking is positive prayer. I am a firm believer in a statement originally made, I believe, by Father Patrick J. Peyton, "The family that prays together stays together."

A young couple told me they happened to be walking on Fifth Avenue in New York City at the moment the boy asked the girl if she would marry him. She said, "Yes." These two youngsters were both religiously inclined. Their first impulse was to drop into church and dedicate their engagement to God.

The nearest church happened to be St. Patrick's Cathedral, and although they were both Protestants, they entered the church, knelt, and prayed together. They felt that their forthcoming marriage was thus spiritually consecrated to God long before it was officially sanctified at the altar. It isn't surprising that their marriage turned out to be highly successful. That is really a valuable thought; consecrate your engagement to God. Thus, from the very beginning the relationship is based on an enduring spiritual foundation.

Far too many young people actually leave God at the marriage altar. They do not take Him into their homes. I was talking recently with one very troubled woman named Sally whose marriage, she said, was about to dissolve. In the course of our conversation, I spoke about my belief that a praying family will stay together. "Is God ever mentioned in your home?" I asked her.

"Oh yes," she said, "but not in the way you mean."

"Have you ever considered praying aloud with your husband?" I asked, and to this the woman gave a short but conclusive little laugh. "You just don't know my husband!" said Sally.

"Well now," I said, "I have known many men who give that impression. They say they will never pray. But that's an act, I've found, in a great many cases. I want you to try something tonight. At the table before dinner is served tell your husband that you would like to say a blessing. Use that as an opening wedge to bring a spiritual note and then, bit by bit, see if you can't bring additional prayer into your home."

I could see that this lady felt it was a useless experiment, but she agreed to try it, even so. As she reported later the experiment worked. That evening when her husband came home even more morose and grumpy than usual, he buried himself behind his newspaper and refused to talk, except to mumble, "About time!" when the wife finally announced that dinner was ready.

When they were seated at the table she said, "It may surprise you, but I feel like saying a blessing. Do you mind?"

"Well, go on," growled the husband. "It's a free country."

So a little embarrassed, the wife did say the blessing. And at breakfast she said one again. She kept this up for several days until one evening, still in a rough manner, the husband said, "Hold your horses, Sally. You've been saying the blessing at every meal. Who's the head of this house? I'll say the blessing around here." With that he searched his memory and drew out one of the old family blessings that he had heard as a child and, stumbling, he got it off successfully.

This couple had never before heard each other's voice in prayer. As time went on, it became easier to pray together. Eventually they began to say a prayer at bedtime. The last time I spoke with Sally she was able to report that a remarkable new spirit of cooperation and affection had come into their marriage.

Having a prayer centered home is one of the best of all techniques for a happy marriage. I have known couples who have made God central in their home life in a variety of very interesting ways. One woman was having a great deal of trouble with her housekeeping. In my contacts I often hear poor housekeeping mentioned in marital difficulty. This wife did not like housekeeping and as a consequence her home was always untidy and messy. This rankled with her husband who was an orderly and fastidious person.

"I decided that the only way for me to handle my attitude

toward my house," she told me, "was to dedicate my housekeeping to God. The Bible says, 'Let all things be done decently and in order.' (I Corinthians 14:40) This became my housekeeping motto, and the results were really quite pleasing."

Another wife who has tried this technique successfully gets up earlier than her family and "fills her house full of positive affirmations." She stands in the middle of her living room and faces, in sequence, every corner of her house. As she does this she affirms aloud that "this house is a place where God dwells; it is a home full of peace, love and joy." She declares, "The result is really marvelous." Such affirmations become a reality; any home can become a happy place; the toilsome part of housekeeping can be transformed into meaningful purpose. A husband-providing and a wife-keeping house—these are two of the most basic functions of life, and in them, when done in love and harmony, is true happiness.

My own mother had a remarkable ability to turn the chores of housekeeping into creative family experiences. Our house was always full of fun and happy excitement. Mother was a real strategist. No one was aware, for instance, of the fact that the dishes were being washed. Mother's trick was to start a discussion on some lively subject just at the moment that the unpleasant job of dish washing had to be done. Automatic dish washers were away off in the future. We were the dish washers of that generation, and we were not automatic.

When the meal was over, my mother would throw some highly controversial subject into the conversation. In no time, we would all take sides. As soon as the argument had reached a certain crescendo, mother would quietly hand a dish to my father, another one to me, and others to my brothers. She herself would rise and walk out into the kitchen carrying some dishes, all the while constantly stimulating the discussion. Before we knew what was happening we were all out there with her, washing and wiping dishes, and still arguing at full tilt, and having a wonderful time.

In any chapter on successful married life, a discussion of the selection of your mate is important. This is, of course, one of the most single decisions that a person will have to make in his life. Sometimes the decision is wrong, and a lifetime of misery follows. Therefore, I am a firm believer in an engagement of adequate length. A couple has so much to learn about each other. Can they really communicate with each other? Are they interested in many of the same things? Do their family backgrounds mesh gears?

A good friend of mine, Mr. M., a very prominent man, told me that his son Jim came home with the announcement that he was in love. He had fallen head over heels for a "fabulous" girl and was going to marry her right off, just as soon as commencement was over. The boy's family met this young girl and immediately sensed that she was not right for Jim. But to say so would have been wasted energy.

Wisely, the M's decided to let their son discover for himself how he really felt; so at the first opportunity they invited the girl to spend a week with them in their home. Almost immediately it became clear that the girl was not fitting in. She was quite a bit on the sloppy side. She did not get up when the rest of the family did. She would not help with the household chores. She obviously considered herself intellectually superior to the rest of the family, and in general succeeded in keeping herself apart from the rest of the group.

The boy was somewhat disillusioned, but was not ready to admit that he had made a mistake. Then, at Christmas time, Jim's parents strategically insisted that he spend the whole vacation at this young lady's home. They packed him off to her home, not expecting to see him until New Year's Day. But three days later he was back. Bit by bit the story came out. Jim was particularly disturbed by the way his fiancée yelled at her parents. She was difficult around the house and refused to participate in normal household activities. She acted sullen and spoiled.

The parents themselves seemed "neurotic" and were slovenly. Jim said the bathroom soap dish looked as if it had not been cleaned since Hector was a pup. The result of these two visits was that Jim's ardor cooled off entirely. Suppose, however, that Jim had not discovered these facts about his "true love" until after they had been married. Suppose he had insisted upon haste in marrying the girl, only to have his education in her qualities when it was too late to retreat. Love at first sight may have its place, but that doesn't go for marriage at first sight. There are far too many problems to be ironed out before marriage to risk a hasty wedding.

I am going to end this chapter with a "Marriage Mirror" arranged by Dr. Smiley Blanton and Dr. Irwin Smalheiser.

"How well do you know your spouse?" One of the saddest

facts about many marriages is that two people will share the most intimate relationship, yet know next to nothing about each other's outlook on life.

One measure of emotional maturity in marriage is the degree to which you understand your spouse. The following test compares your viewpoints on a number of critical areas.

Part I is to be filled out by husbands. Part II is for wives. After both have completed the test, compare answers to each question and count the number on which you agree.

PART I—For Husbands Only

1. Are you as romantic now as you were on your honeymoon? .... Yes——No——

2. Do you get along amicably with in-laws? .... Yes——No——

3. Are you sympathetic to your wife's household problems? .... Yes——No——

4. Do you put family needs first in budgeting money? .... Yes——No——

5. Do you believe American women are too domineering? .... Yes——No——

6. Do you surprise your wife with occasional gifts .... Yes——No——

7. Do you put your work or career ahead of your family? .... Yes——No——

8. If your wife wanted to work, even though it might not be financially necessary, would you agree? .... Yes——No——

9. Should a husband and wife take separate vacations? .... Yes——No——

10. Do you make the major decisions in your family? .... Yes——No——

11. Are you and your wife sexually compatible? .... Yes——No——

12. Would you resent it if your wife had friends and interests outside the home?.. Yes——No——

13. Do you and your wife agree on how to raise the children?................... Yes——No——

14. Is planning for the future a family project? .... Yes——No——

15. Does your wife strive to keep herself attractive as she was when you were first married? .... Yes——No——

16. Does your wife show an interest in your work? .... Yes——No——

17. Does your wife greet you with a recital of household problems as soon as you come home? .... Yes——No——

18. Does your wife try to run the house as economically as possible? .... Yes——No——

19. Do you feel the children take first place in your wife's affections?................. Yes——No——

20. Does your family take time to renew its spiritual faith? .... Yes——No——

PART II—*For Wives Only*

1. Is your husband as romantic as he was during your honeymoon?.............. Yes——No——

2. Does your husband get along amicably with in-laws? .... Yes——No——

3. Is your husband sympathetic to your problems in running the house?............ Yes——No——

4. Does your husband put family needs first in budgeting money?.................. Yes——No——

5. Does your husband believe American women are too domineering?.......... Yes——No——

6. Does he surprise you with occasional gifts? .... Yes——No——

7. Does he put his work or career ahead of the family? .... Yes——No——

8. If you wanted to go to work, even though it might not be financially necessary, would your husband agree?............ Yes——No——

9. Should a wife and husband take separate vacations? .... Yes——No——

10. Does your husband make the major decisions in the family?.................   Yes——No——

11. Are you and your husband sexually compatible? ....   Yes——No——

12. Would your husband resent it if you had friends and interests outside the family?..   Yes——No——

13. Do you agree on how to raise the children? ....   Yes——No——

14. Is planning for the future a family project? ....   Yes——No——

15. Do you strive to keep yourself as attractive as you were when you were first married? ....   Yes——No——

16. Do you show an interest in your husband's work? ....   Yes——No——

17. Do you greet your husband with a recital of household problems as soon as he comes home? ....   Yes——No——

18. Do you try to run your household as economically as possible?..............   Yes——No——

19. Do the children, rather than your husband, take first place in your affections?..   Yes——No——

20. Does your family take time to renew its spiritual faith? ....   Yes——No——

Agreement on fifteen or more indicates that you understand each other's viewpoint remarkably well.

Agreement on ten to fifteen questions suggests that differences of viewpoint exist, but they are likely to be minor.

Agreement on less than ten questions indicates that many major questions in your marriage have been avoided. A frank, calm discussion of these issues can prevent such misconceptions from developing into more serious problems.

Chapter XIII

LEARN TO LIVE WITH THE SPIRITUAL FORCES AROUND YOU

WHAT WONDERS there are in your mind!

A woman says, "I saw in the paper that so-and-so died of a heart attack."

"What paper?" she is asked.

"I don't know just what paper, but I saw it in the paper." She quotes the item verbatim.

A search of the files of newspapers discloses no such item. Inquiry establishes that the person in question has not had a heart attack. But, three days later, that person dies of heart failure and the newspaper story reads exactly as the woman had quoted it in advance.

And what is this strange power? Precognition.

A little four-year-old girl, during World War I, calls to her mother: "Mommy, Daddy is choking to death! He is down a deep hole!"

Later investigation ascertains that the child's father, at that exact moment, had been down in a cellar under gas attack.

And this is an equally strange power—clairvoyance.

A middle-aged man is driving his car along a New Jersey highway when he feels a terrible pain in his chest. It is so excruciating that he stops his car, thinking he is suffering a heart attack, but eventually it passes.

A few hours later, he learns that his son, driving in Colorado, had been killed at that exact moment, his chest crushed by the wheel of his car.

And this mystic force? Telepathy.

Such phenomena as the foregoing are being investigated by Dr. J. B. Rhine of Duke University, leader in the science of parapsychology, the systematic study of mental activity by means other than the physical senses. What are these things that he describes as precognition, clairvoyance, telepathy? What could they prove? Well, Dr. Rhine believes that these are only some of the powers of the human mind ranging the universe without obstruction of space and time. We mention them here as further evidence of greater capacity within yourself, a capacity that can aid you in living a stronger more effective life.

Now, of course, there are always people who will respond to such phenomena with the flat assertion, "It's impossible." Yet their only reason for saying so is that they have never heard of it before. I met the man who developed the automobile radio. The banker he asked for a loan to finance production told him: "I never heard of such a preposterous idea! There will never be radios in automobiles!" That is how an unimaginative mind often responds to anything that is new.

This author is convinced there is something very great in man that is beyond the physical, beyond the material. We need to see ourselves in vaster relationships in God's great plan. A prominent scientist told me that in higher mathematics if they introduce infinity into the formula it works.

This emphasis on infinity will bring you into closer contact with great forces around you and within you. As you tap these deeper powers you will gain greater victories over the defeated elements in your life.

For example, I have before me a remarkable letter which illustrates graphically what happens to some people when, through positive thinking they make contact with the spiritual forces around them.

I was forty-four years old in June. I have been a professional jockey since 1930. The reason for this letter is an incident that happened to me in October, 1956.

I had been a heavy drinker since 1934. In April, 1955, a copy of your book, *The Power of Positive Thinking,* came into my possession. Incidentally, the man who owned the bar where I drank gave the book to me.

I had practically lost my power of concentration, though I had always been able to keep in shape fairly well physically —had to, to ride. It took me three weeks to memorize the 23rd Psalm—so you can see I was pretty far gone.

I bought a Bible and put your theories to work. It was slow work. I couldn't remember what I read, but I kept on reading and praying. Even memorized a few short psalms.

In the meantime, I had practically cut out hard liquor, but

hit the beer pretty hard. I didn't get drunk as often, but I still got drunk, and I kept on reading my Bible, drunk, or sober, and praying, too.

By fall of 1956 I had made some progress—nothing startling, but noticeable. This brings me up to the point.

I was riding in a race meeting at Spokane, Washington at the time. I lived in a motel a few miles from the track. One night I went to sleep early. I was awakened by a strange feeling starting in the vicinity of my heart, gradually spreading over my entire body. First, all the tension that had accumulated inside me over the years passed, and was replaced by a great feeling of love. My whole body was aglow. I could see my father and mother beside me. They faded away, and I saw many things. I shed tears of joy and tears of sorrow. I prayed for many people who floated through my mind one after another.

I got up and turned on the light so I could look in the mirror. My skin felt like smooth warm satin. I was shedding tears of ecstasy and then of great sorrow.

When we went to work at the track next morning, people would look at me real puzzled. A few said, "What in the world happened to you?" Most of them were good friends of mine so they didn't say anything more. I felt that I could heal any crippled or lame person by touching them. I stayed in this state of illumination about two weeks, then it diminished and would come and go for short periods at a time. It has never gone away altogether.

Now, here's where you come in. The next day I didn't ride any races, so I stayed at the boss's house and mowed the lawn. Everyone had gone to the races. I went by the side of the garage and sat in the sun. A donkey they had there that I could never get close to at all, walked right up to me and stood there and looked at me a long time. I began to cry, and after awhile I got up and cranked the mower and went to work.

All the time I was in this condition there was great emphasis on the most minute details. After I had finished the lawn, I went in the house and took a bath, and lay down on the sofa. I didn't sleep, but seemed to be in a sort of trance of prayer. There were running through my mind many things. Finally your name came to me. It hit me with great force, not once, but many times, one right after the other, with great emphasis upon each one of your names.

Then a little later I was reciting the 23rd Psalm, and when I would come to the last verse, "Surely goodness and mercy shall follow me all the days of my life; and I shall dwell in the house of the Lord forever," a wondrous burst of happiness came over me, with great emphasis on each and every word. I quit smoking in about ten days. By the first of January I had lost all desire to drink. I haven't smoked or taken a drink of any kind since.

I have met this man personally and found him a quiet and intelligent person. He shows a strong desire to help people and seems to go about doing so in a sensible and creative manner.

What a fabulous world we live in! We are surrounded by strange mystic forces which we have only barely begun to understand, let alone use. This jockey was privileged to know a mystical force, the like of which few experience, especially in such a dramatic form, and his life was remade thereby.

But to some degree, everyone of us may identify ourselves with these tremendous forces. In this chapter I am going to share with you some of the remarkable letters I have received dealing with these great matters. I shall not attempt to interpret these letters, but quote them for you to reflect upon. Those who have had these mystical powers touch their lives have many times found an amazing remedy for frustration, hates, weaknesses, sin, even physical ills. Perhaps the experience of others will be of comfort and strength to you.

The following experience was sent me by a professor at a famous New England College:

In my student days, I was bothered by occasional headaches which were always relieved when my grandmother, who made her home with my parents, would place her hand on my forehead. Later, when I began teaching at Amherst College, these peculiar headaches continued to trouble me.

One night, in December of my first year there, the pain obliged me to retire earlier than usual. Toward midnight I suddenly felt my grandmother standing beside my bed. She placed her hand on my head and the pain ceased, *never to return.*

There had been no recent letter from my parents so I had not been told of grandmother's sudden illness. It was not until the following day that word was received saying that she had passed on at the very hour when I felt her hand on my head. I am sure that she thus took the first opportunity to bring me the relief she alone could give.

In a letter written by a reader who lives in Inman, Kansas we are told of an experience that tended to diminish the fear of death.

This past November 18th, I was stricken by an illness and was taken to the hospital in an unconscious state.

The ambulance driver, afterwards, told me it was a miracle I was still alive as he thought that he hadn't gotten me to the hospital in time.

I experienced a wondrous thing. I saw a bright light and as I came nearer and nearer to it, it was like a beautiful sunrise close by, and as I advanced I saw a wide expanse of water and I stood by the edge of the water, finally just looking across at this beautiful light. Then I turned and saw it was such a long way back to the place where I had started.

Is this type of experience unique? By no means. In my files are scores of similar accounts, all pointing to the possibility that death is not the dread terror we think it is. It, too, is surely governed by the amazing forces all around us.

A national magazine ran a remarkable article called, "How Does it Feel to Die?" The article consists of a series of nine statements by eminent doctors on the nature of death. Sir William Osler, the famous physician, once made the statement, "Most human beings not only die like heroes, but in my wide clinical experience, die really without pain or fear. There is as much oblivion about the last hours as about the first and therefore people fill their minds with spectres that have no reality."

Kate Holliday, the author of this article, asked the nine doctors whether they agreed with Sir William's statement and the amazing thing is that not one of the doctors disagreed. "Nature is good to the human race," said Dr. Frank Adair, Associate Professor of Clinical Surgery, Cornell University Medical College. "The haunting fear which the average person carries all through life is dissipated by the approach of death."

And Dr. H. D. Van Fleet, President of the Los Angeles Academy of Medicine, says, "I have sat with dying men of every race and creed—Hindus, Shintoists, Catholics, Protestants, Jews and Mohammedans. They die in peace and I have found that the sweetness of death is intensified in all men by a childlike faith in their religion. Except for their own interpretation of religion, what men cling to is the same throughout the world."

Dr. Johannes Neilsen, Associate Clinical Professor of Medicine at the University of Southern California says, "People who dread death do so because they imagine they're going to be snuffed out of life suddenly. That isn't the way it is at all. As you become more and more ill, whether it is from anemia or cancer or even accident, you become more and more absorbed with the problem of the moment, the condition of your own body. Even doctors who are dying experience this. Their circle of interest grows smaller until they are concerned only with the immediate challenge, until life at last is merely a question of whether or not they will breathe again. And when the circle becomes too small, they go to heaven . . . The circle, in other words, has drawn in to such a degree that even fear is shut out. When you meet eternity all trivialities, even fear, fade into nothing."

So, it would seem from Kate Holliday's research that the fear of death is not as realistic as we have supposed. It is acute to us in the fullness of life, but in sickness and disability the world recedes and God provides a blessed anesthetic for the mind and spirit. The final end is not a painful experience, nor a frightening one, though the illnesses preceding death may be painful indeed. The fears which we attach to death are strongest while we are still very much alive and healthy. But when people approach the experience itself and are weak and ill, it seems that life constricts, ordinary concerns lose their value and death itself becomes so natural that it no longer frightens.

Who knows how near those on the other side may be to us. Readers almost shyly tell how departed loved ones seem to brush their lives for what reason we cannot know. But it does suggest that great and good forces are around us. Some years ago I was driving with my wife from Asbury Park, New Jersey to New York City. At Asbury Park I had attended an auction of household furnishings from an estate called Shadow Lawn, made famous as the summer White House of President Woodrow Wilson. I purchased a pair of beautiful hurricane lamps. While I got them at a bargain price, still I paid a rather good sum for them and perhaps felt a bit guilty. But since they were intended as a birthday gift for my wife, Ruth, I thought the expenditure justified. They were packed and put into the luggage compartment of the car and we started for home.

Midway on the trip we stopped at a Howard Johnson roadside restaurant for lunch. The place was crowded but we got two stools at the counter. I finished first and to give someone else a seat, I told Ruth I would wait for her at the car.

As I stepped into the brilliant sunshine outside, I suddenly had an overwhelming sense of my mother's presence.

She had crossed to the other side several years before. I felt rather than saw her smile, and sensed her warm loving personality as distinctly as any feeling I have ever had. Then came the sound of her voice with all the old time familiarity and strength. She said something about Ruth being a wonderful girl and that she deserved those beautiful hurricane lamps and not to worry about things, but be happy and keep on doing good. Then it all faded but I was stirred and moved to the depths of my being. I stood speechless and totally unconscious of surroundings except for a sharp clear beauty in everything.

I wept and believe me I am not the weeping kind. I hurried to the car and when Ruth found me, she was shocked to find me weeping and unable to talk. We drove for several miles before I recovered myself and told her the story. Why should my mother have contacted me at such a time and place and about a seemingly trivial matter? Who knows the logic of the amazing forces around us. That we were together in that vibrant moment, personally I have no doubt, and from this meeting I have drawn a strange peace and strength.

Such things are not uncommon and there is certainly no need to be reticent about relating these experiences. I had a letter from Mrs. Mark Clark, the wife of the famous World War II general. In part it read:

> On many occasions I have heard my grandmother and mother relate the story of the death of the former's twenty-five year old son, Elmer.
> Elmer had typhoid fever and in 1900 that was often fatal. A twin sister, Eva, to whom Elmer was devoted, had died two years previously with the same disease.
> For many days my uncle had been in a coma, too weak to move. Suddenly he sat up straight in bed with arms extended to the heavens, his face radiant with happiness and cried out in a firm clear voice, "Eva"—then he died.

Cecil B. DeMille told a wonderful little story of an experience which gave him insight into the nature of life and death and life again. "I was up on a lake in the Maine woods. The canoe was drifting. I was reading, resting, searching for an idea. I looked down in the water, for my little craft had drifted where the lake was only about four-inches deep. There in a world of mud and wet, were water beetles.

"One crawled up on the gunwale, stuck the talons on his

legs into the woodwork and died. I let it alone and turned to my reading. The sun was hot. In about three hours I noticed my water beetle again. He was parched. His back was cracking open. I watched, and out of the back of that dead beetle I saw crawling a new form—a moist head—then wings. A most beautiful dragonfly. It scintillated all the colors of the rainbow. As I sat watching, it flew. It flew farther in a second than the water beetle had crawled in days. It hovered above the surface, just a few inches from the water beetles beneath. They did not know it was there.

"I took my fingertips and moved the shriveled water beetle husk from the canoe's gunwale. It fell back into the lake and sank down to the mud-covered bottom.

"The other water beetles crawled awkwardly to see what it was.

"It was a dead body. They backed away from it.

"If God does that for a water beetle, don't you believe He will do it for me?" asked Cecil B. DeMille.

This is a sound description, to my way of thinking, of the nature of death. Death is simply a change, not an ending, and that we shall emerge into a better form of life it seems logical to assume.

All of the experiences related to me, dealing with extra sensory phenomena, seem to stress continuity.

On May 2, 1914, our beloved mother was dying. She was in a weakened physical condition due to diabetes. She had not gotten up since May 1st and gradually sank into a coma.

Father was sitting at the head of the bed, holding his opened-face watch in one hand, his fingers on mother's pulse with the other. I was gone from the room for a few minutes, leaving my sister standing at the foot of mother's bed. As I came from the hallway to the open doorway, facing the foot of the bed, I stopped suddenly, in astonishment at what I saw —then I slowly walked to the bed and stood silently beside my sister at its foot—to the end. I never mentioned to her what I had seen lest she imagine she saw the same thing. I wanted her to tell me.

Two weeks after mother was buried, my sister and I were quietly sitting on the porch, occasionally speaking. After some time she spoke, saying: "I saw the strangest, most unusual thing as we stood at the foot of mother's bed shortly before the end came." I did not interrupt her. When she had finished I said: "Yes, I saw the same. I have waited for you to tell me." The following is what we saw:

Directly over and about nine or so inches above mother

was a thin sheet of grayish-blue mist, the color one sometimes sees at twilight in the mountains. This mist, side edges blending into the air like a water color painting, was very slowly moving from foot to head; as it moved upward the bottom edge was even—straight as this paper's edge.

Mother's gown was open carelessly at the neck to several inches on her chest. The flesh seen *through* the mist was the color of life, but as the mist passed upward, over her flesh, the color was of death, both colors visible in passing.

Just as the mist passed over her head, father, eyes never raised from his watch, fingers yet on her pulse, said sadly: "Mother has gone." The mist vanished immediately into the atmosphere of the room. No outside door nor window was open. We two saw her life pass from her visibly.

These two women believe that they "saw her life pass from her visibly," as if the life itself were a separate entity that continued outside of the body. The incident seems to indicate that death is a passing of the personality or soul from one state into another.

The scores of experiences which have been told to me indicate further that the change in life called death is not without beauty. Always the spiritual forces around us seem to be concerned for us.

A reader from Stratford, Connecticut, wrote me about an incident related by a medical doctor. A woman had been hit by a car and lay by the roadside. Those who gathered thought she was dead. When the ambulance came bringing the doctor, he knelt and lifted the woman's head. She opened her eyes and asked if he was the doctor. When he replied that he was she said, "Well, I want to tell you to tell all my friends; if this is dying, it is the most beautiful experience I ever went through," and with that she dropped her head back and she died.

God has built into us the will to live and the love of life. It is our nature to resist the death of the body to the very last. But can we not believe that God has also arranged our lives so that when they are finished in this world, they shall pass into a better place. Those who live with God in this life need have no fear of the next one. This is the testimony of the hundreds of sincere people who have described their experiences, in one form or another, as to the spiritual forces around us.

Such experiences are related to me with great frequency and they invariably are reported as having aspects of beauty.

For instance here is a letter from a lady who lives in Hamilton, Ohio.

> When I was twelve, a simple tonsil operation touched off terrible hemorrhages. In those days transfusions were seldom given and I was already home from the clinic. My mind was clear; and since children seem singularly unafraid of such occasions, I only wished the ordeal were over.
>
> I saw that my mother's face was gray as she brought more basins; the doors of my bedroom were filling up with people, even Grandma had managed to get up the stairs. . . . Suddenly they were all gone, and I was alone. I was standing in a dark corridor, unafraid, just hesitating. In the darkness of it, at times, people would brush against me, rushing forward, together, to the end of the corridor, where shone a wondrous light, more bright than any I had ever known. They were all happy people.
>
> I went forward a little, until I could see "outside." No crowds, only a beautiful field of great white daisies, shining under a radiant sky, and in the field a little girl, smaller than I, was sitting and picking the flowers.
>
> All my short life, since a visit to an uncle's farm, I, a city girl, had always thought a field of daisies shimmering on a breeze-swept hill under a bright sky was the most beautiful thing I had ever seen. I knew for certain the daisies were for me; and the brightness of all that lay beyond that corridor, beyond that hill, was mine.
>
> Then, like a curtain dropped against the light, the words came: "Mama needs me." I shall not trouble you with why I believed this, but it was so. . . . I woke, to find my head cradled on my mother's breast; she was softly calling me, over and over again. In the ensuing days, I alone was sure that I would get well.

Such experiences may offer some hint of the nature of life on the other side. And note that they are vivid and bright and joyous experiences without exception. Do they provide a glimpse of reality that is usually known only after death?

Extra-sensory perception must be another of God's kindly gifts supplying occasional glimpses into the true nature of reality. There is something extra wonderful that is just beyond our usual mortal reach but which can effect our lives even so. It is given to us only in flashes and in fragments of insight to remind us that while we are physical beings in a mortal world, we are also part of a greater world.

Do we understand these mystic laws? Not as yet. We do not even understand to any great extent the physical laws which surround us, much less these profounder spiritual laws. C. B. Colby writing in the White Plains *Reporter Dispatch* posed the following question:

Have you ever wondered what ultimately becomes of the waves that radio and TV stations send out into space twenty-four hours a day? Do they fade and vanish, or do they keep going forever? We do know that sometimes pictures appear mysteriously, long after a program has finished. One of the most famous of all such weird happenings was in England in September, 1953.

Suddenly in many parts of England television screens blossomed out with the identification card and call letters of TV station KLEE in Houston, Texas. Even today transatlantic programming is but a dream, so several viewers took pictures of the image to prove the happening.

What really startled the TV world was the fact that when British broadcasting engineers advised KLEE in Houston of the unusual event, they were told that the station had been off the air since 1950. No KLEE identification card had been shown for the past three years.

Where had that picture been for three years? Why did it appear only in England and how did it get back from wherever it had been? Does make you wonder, doesn't it?

We are surrounded by phenomena—even physical phenomena—which we cannot easily explain. And strange happenings give hints of a fantastic world of spirit in which we are doubtless nearer to the true realities of our universe and which also defy explanation. What, for example, is the relationship of those on the other side to our lives? Do they sometimes draw near in strange and wonderful ways to help us?

Over the years many instances have been reported which suggest the protecting and supporting aid of the strange forces about us. From a practical point of view it bears out our conviction that the broader life in which we dwell will undergird us with extra power if we go confidently about our duty.

Dr. Smiley Blanton gave me a letter from an enthusiastic reader of his fascinating new book *Now or Never*. This reader tells of a controversy in a community meeting years ago in which the local Episcopal minister opposed an action which was violently advocated by a rough sort of man named Sam——. When the vote was taken the minister's position was sustained. Enraged, Sam shouted, "I'll kill you for this!"

Since this man's character was known to be violent, some men said to the minister, "We will walk home with you for you have to pass that lonely wood lot and we aren't too sure Sam won't try to carry out his threat."

But the minister said no, he would go without them as he was never alone . . . there was Someone who would watch over him.

A number of years later the minister was called to Sam's deathbed. He said, "Reverend, there is something I must confess before I die. You remember the night I swore I'd kill you? Well, I intended to and I waited for you in the wood lot with a bar in my hand."

The minister asked, "Why didn't you, Sam?"

Sam looked at the pastor in surprise, "How could I with those two big men on each side of you?"

There is no magic in the universe. But God is there and His powers are vast indeed. We have long since learned and accepted that fact in the world of materiality. What men once called "Miracles" are now everyday facts. No wonders of any kind astonish us, for so many wonders occur almost daily in the realm of science.

Why, then, should we doubt the workings of a whole world of phenomena in the psychic sphere? That isn't miraculous either, for without doubt it will be found to be operating according to law. This is a law abiding universe. We call a phenomenon a miracle until we understand its relationship to law. Instances such as I cite are not presented as bizarre curiosities but are given to indicate that, as spiritual beings in a spiritual universe, we are related to immense forces which we do not comprehend. Their meaning is that, if we live normal humble lives, walking by faith, living in unbroken contact with God, we shall be strangely supported all our days.

Then, by the same forces, we shall enter into that even larger life, which impinges on this one so closely, which we call the eternal. We cannot separate mortal life from eternal life. Eternity means all of time. We are in eternity now. When mortality ends, immortality beings; but there is no break in the flow of time.

The mortal is only an aspect of the spiritual. The body is but a temporary tool of the real person, who is spirit.

Dr. J. B. Rhine cites many cases of physical phenomena

bearing on this matter, for example, this from a school teacher:

It occurred in the first school where I taught. I was then just eighteen and doing my practice teaching. There was a young lad (he was fourteen) who insisted on knowing where I was going to teach. I didn't know at the time. He made it very emphatic on several occasions that no matter where I taught, he was going to my school and no other.

I was seated at my desk shortly after our afternoon studies began when a voice said "Hello, Miss Long." Glancing up, I saw him standing there, smiling at me, hat in hand, holding onto the door. "I told you that no matter where you taught I was going to your school and here I am." Pleased as well as startled I smiled back, exclaiming, "Truman, how did you get here?" He replied, "Oh, I just came. Where can I sit?"

I was aware of the dead silence in the room and every pupil seemed frozen in their places, mingled emotions stamped on their faces, all eyes watching me. Ready to reply I noticed that instead of a solid substance, as he had first appeared, the figure was fading and I could see the details of the room through him. Shaken, I, who hadn't thought of him before, couldn't get this out of my mind.

A few days later a letter from my mother telling of Truman's sudden death made me have the creeps. He had been only slightly ill for a few days and his mother was planning on sending him to school the next day. He had been downstairs eating his noon lunch. At 1:30, the time I saw his apparition, as he started to go back upstairs he collapsed and died, hanging on the stair post.

Such phenomena are remarkable in that they are repeated with frequency and similarity of detail. That they indicate a world beyond our senses seems not unreasonable. And since every phenomenon in God's created universe is intelligent and purposive we cannot but feel that we are related to these amazing powers, that their values may contribute to man's well-being.

Dr. Rhine, in his collection of experiences of pre-recognition, tells the startling story of a Los Angeles streetcar motorman who dreamed one night that he was driving over a new route. As he passed a streetcar coming from the opposite direction, a green truck shot across the tracks. In his dream, his streetcar struck the truck; two men were killed instantly and a woman was badly injured. "You could have prevented it!" the woman screamed at him. He saw that her eyes were bright blue.

The next morning the motorman reported for work, still musing over his dream. "I'm giving you Jim's route this morning," the dispatcher said to him. "He's just phoned in sick." As the motorman drove over the new route he suddenly became aware that it was the very route of his dream. He broke out in a cold sweat. Then he saw a streetcar coming toward him. Instinctively, he slammed on his brakes. At that moment a green truck shot from a side street and darted across the tracks. The streetcar squealed to a halt, missing the truck by inches. In it were two men and a woman. As they passed close to him, the woman's bright blue eyes caught his. She said nothing, but slowly closed her thumb and forefinger in the familiar gesture of "okay."

These experiences would seem to indicate that our usual concepts of time and place are not based on total reality. There are, apparently, other ways of receiving knowledge than through ordinary sensory reactions. One of the top technical experts in the United States, Charles F. Kettering, said that a great mistake of education today is that it does not place sufficient emphasis upon intuitive knowledge. He cited the case of a professor of organic chemistry at Darmstadt about one hundred years ago. This professor had a dream or vision in which he saw the complete atomic structure of a molecule of hexametabenzene. He wrote it down, but he died with people still ridiculing it.

In a research laboratory only recently, a scientist took a picture of a molecule of hexametabenzene. And there, precisely as the professor had seen it by pre-cognitive insight one hundred years ago, to the exact detail, was the outline of its atomic structure!

We seem to be part of some immense spiritual mechanism which, occasionally, in spite of ourselves, we grapple with. A practicing neuropsychiatrist in New York Ciy, Dr. Russell G. MacRobert, wrote an article called, "Science Studies Intuition," for *Tomorrow* magazine. In it Dr. MacRobert said:

The following experience occurred to a woman in April, 1949, while she was being given gas anesthesia in the office of a prominent New York dentist. The patient had a dream under the anesthetic and when she awakened she was very upset. In her dream she saw her friend, Mrs. Manuel Quezon, widow of the first President of the Philippines, ambushed and murdered on a lonely mountain road near Manila, halfway around the world. Allowing for the difference in time between New York and Manila, the dream occurred ten hours before the same crime was actually committed—a very ample margin of knowing beforehand as well as seeing something true at a distance without the eyes.

Weird [concluded the dentist's report to me] especially coming from a very intelligent, two-feet-on-the-ground type of person.

That's the kind of report that makes one pause. And note, these experiences do not necessarily come to the spiritualist; often as not they are experienced by the most conservative personalities. And sometimes they are extremely well documented. One of the editors of our own *Guideposts* magazine happened to be in Boston a few hours after the occurrence of an amazing example of mental telepathy. This editor himself interviewed the people involved, cross-examining them carefully for any possibility of intentional or accidental "exaggeration," and came away convinced that he had just seen a genuine illustration of the fact that the human mind is capable of mysterious extensions of itself. This is the story:

On the afternoon of June 14, 1955, Thomas Whittaker, a welder from Boston, got a sudden and strong hunch. He had the felling that something was wrong. He didn't know what it was, but he sensed it so strongly that he quit work and got into his car and just started driving. At various stoplights along the way, he tried to turn his car toward his own home, but the intuition kept him from doing so. Time after time instead of turning toward home, he turned toward Washington Street where his company was also doing some work.

"This is ridiculous," he kept telling himself. "That Washington Street job has been suspended." But he kept edging toward the area just the same.

It's a good thing that he did. When he finally got there, he looked down into a fourteen-foot deep trench that had been dug down the center of the street, and there in the bottom, he saw a cave-in. The sides of the trench had collapsed. And projecting out of the tons of dirt, sand and debris, was a human hand!

Whittaker jumped down into the trench and tried to claw away the dirt with his own hands. He dug down deep enough to uncover a wrist watch, and immediately he recognized it as belonging to his best friend and boss, John H. Sullivan, owner of the Stoneham Welding Service. The hand moved.

Frantic now, Whittaker scrambled to the top of the trench and called for the fire and police to help dig Sullivan out of the hole.

Several hours later, safe, if not entirely sound after his ordeal of being buried alive, John Sullivan told the *Guidepost* editor how he had decided to go, alone, to the Washington Street job to finish up some work, and how the sides of the trench had suddenly given way. He was buried. The only thing that saved him from immediate suffocation was the fact that he had on his welder's mask, and inside of it there had been captured enough air to keep him alive until help came.

Had he called for help? Indeed he had. At first he called out loud, and then, when it became clear that that would do no good, he began sending out mental distress signals like an S.O.S. "God send someone," he prayed. "God send someone. God send someone." Over and over again he said these words. And it was while he was thus praying that Tommy Whittaker began to get his strong urge to visit the Washington Street scene. It seems logical to assume that John Sullivan called Tommy Whittaker to his aid by means that are not usually available.

What has all this got to do with everyday life?

Perhaps some day it will be possible for us to bring these spiritual processes under control for the use of mankind, just as we have controlled natural processes the very thought of which our forefathers regarded as miraculous, even ridiculous. Whoever thought that man would fly or send pictures through the air? The Creator placed these powers in the world for man to find and use for his betterment.

Apparently these strange forces around us have been known and used for centuries. For example, in the writings of the early Spanish explorers and adventurers who fought the South American Inca Indians, there are strange reports that indicate the Incas knew the secret of controlling mental telepathy. The Spanish armies would move out on a secret expedition only to discover that the Incas knew exactly when they were leaving, with how many troops, and with what intent. It drove the Spanish mad. There was no evidence of drums, or smoke signaling or of any other form of physical transmission of information. The Spanish concluded that the Incas had the secret of passing information to each other through a form of telepathy.

But even if the day of our practical use of such phenomena should be far off, we cannot avoid the belief that man will become ultimately master of forces in the psychic realm as he is in the material. This is an amazing world God has set us in. It is a world that is ruled by physical laws which are being used in ways almost incredible, as for example outer space exploration. But also around us and within us are spiritual laws which are hardly being used at all in comparison with potential possibility.

We are part of an alive, vibrant universe where the true reality is spirit. When we learn to live in harmony with this spirit, and catch its rhythm, then we will be in tune with power as never before. The end result will be to bring us closer to God and to the exciting knowledge that our existence with Him is not tied to the physical world but to a far greater spiritual world. We shall find that we are part of His immortal spirit and thus are greater and more important than we think. It will make us know that the Lord does not intend us to be weak or little or defeated but to walk the earth in the power of God's great spirit.

You and I have the power to live truly great lives. The strange and powerful forces all about us and within us were surely designed by God to enable His children to master life rather than to be mastered by it. And these forces are infinitely greater than all our weaknesses and sins, our fears, hates and inferiorities.

The power to live with joy and victory is available to you and to me. This power can lead you to a solution of your problems, help you to meet your difficulties successfully and fill your mind and heart with peace and contentment.

The life which the Good God created for us is not little and mean and limited. It is big and beautiful and unlimited. Its possibilities are boundless.

Chapter XIV

You Can Become Strongest in Your Weakest Place

YOU CAN become strongest in your weakest place. That is a fact of vast importance to you, to me, to everyone. Repeat that amazing statement aloud, allowing it to sink deeply into consciousness. It is absolutely true—you can become strongest in your weakest place.

That people can become altogether different—strong where they were weak, right where they were wrong, is demonstrated by the experience of a twenty-year-old boy. From his letter it seems he had been a "delinquent," but he is certainly that no longer. Read his letter:

> I have just read your book *The Power of Positive Thinking*. It has made a new man out of me. I am only twenty years old, but I never realized how badly I have wasted those years. All I have ever done with my life is try to be bad, such as fighting, drinking and swearing, because all my friends did it. But I see now how mistaken I have been and I have really been trying your ideas. They have done wonders for me. I have quit smoking and drinking and looking for fights. I have stopped hanging around with people that do those things. I have turned to sports which I greatly enjoy, but best of all I have started going to church again because I have learned to believe in God.
>
> I have found a girl friend that really loves me and we believe in the same things. She is a good girl, not like the girls I have known before. I have learned love and respect with her help, which is something I never had much of, for anyone but myself, before. And I am making more and more friends because I am using your ideas. Truly I have never been happier in my whole life than I have been since reading your book.

Many people have demonstrated in various ways how you can become strongest in your weakest place. There was Glenn Cunningham, whose legs were so badly burned as a

209

child that he was told he would not walk again. But he became one of the fastest Olympic milers in history.

Glenn Cunningham told me that faith and positive thinking are 85 per cent of an athlete's success; in other words, believing that you can do it. "You have to perform on three
levels," he explained, "physical, mental and spiritual. And
the spiritual helps you to draw on power from the Master
to help pull you through. And," he added, "I don't believe
there is such a thing as an impossibility."

Paul Anderson was a sickly, puny weakling. In back of his
house in Tacoma, Georgia, he constructed a homemade
weight-lifting outfit. It consisted of blacksmith weights tied
on the end of a stick. Paul Anderson became the strongest
man in the world, breaking strength records that had stood
for decades.

Positive thinking looks upon weak places in people as
challenging opportunities. You can turn them into your
strongest points. The process of so doing is somewhat like
that of welding. If a piece of metal breaks and is welded together, the weld is stronger than the metal which surrounds
it. At the point of intense heat the molecular structure of the
metal flows together.

A cabinet maker once told me that when two pieces of
wood are reversed and glued together under heat, the wood
will crack elsewhere before it will break at the glued point.
This same process can, and often does, take place in personality. Through the intense application of right thinking and
strong faith, a weakness can actually become one's strongest
point.

Well then, how do we go about turning a weak point into
a strong point? The following six-point formula has been
used most successfully.

1. Isolate your weakness; then study and know it thoroughly.
Plan a real campaign against it.
2. Precisely specify the strength results you wish to attain.
3. Picture or visualize yourself as becoming strongest at your
weakest point.
4. Immediately start *becoming* the strong person you wish
to be.
5. Act as though you are strongest where you have been
weakest.
6. Ask God to help you and believe that He does.

This formula was developed by H. C. Mattern, one of the

most thoroughgoing positive thinkers I have known. H. C. Mattern himself is an example of how a man can change a serious weakness into real strength. He was thoroughly negative, in fact so negative that on a balmy night some years ago he walked into a lonely meadow on Long Island and tried to commit suicide. Life was worthless. There was no hope left. He had with him a vial of poison. He lifted it to his lips, drank it and slumped to the ground.

The next thing he knew he was opening his eyes and staring with astonishment into a moonlit sky. At first he wondered whether he were dead. He never did know why he did not die. He always believed, simply, that God wanted him to do a job in life. When he realized that he was still alive, suddenly he wanted very much to live. He thanked God for having spared him and dedicated himself to a life of helping other people.

Mattern became a unique positive thinker. He made it his whole mission in life to encourage others.

What weakness do *you* want to conquer? Is it fear? Anger? Hurt feelings? Inferiority? Disappointment? Is liquor your weakness? Or woman? Whatever it may be, one thing is sure, it does not need to keep on defeating you. Remember this powerful fact; you can become strongest in your weakest place.

Let us look at some examples of people who have turned weakness into strength.

This letter is from a young man who lives in New Mexico.

Dear Dr. Peale:

I don't know how to start this letter. I live on a ranch here in New Mex. For the last ten years I have spent most of my time in bars and night spots. And I was getting in bad shape. I have tried three times to kill myself. I had no friends of my own. And no girl would have anything to do with me. And I don't blame them. I have no one to blame but myself.

But things have changed for me now. I was in Lubbock, Texas, to see my brother. Him and his wife left me there one night to take care of their kids so they could go to the show.

While the kids were asleep, I went into the bedroom to see how they were. On the floor was two of your books about positive thinking. I picked them up and looked at them. I went back in the living room and sat down.

Began reading them. I had found what I was looking for. A new life. I have been without God for a long time. I have now been going to church every Sunday and Bible Class every Wednesday night. The people here in town sure have changed toward me now. I have lots of friends, new ones. But I lost a lot of my old bar buddies. They think I've lost my mind. I just wish and pray that they could follow me and find what I have—a new life. Without God's help I could not have done it. And I have you to thank, too.

I still don't have a girl friend, but I understand that now. Because here in the Southwest a ranch hand or cowboy isn't too well liked. I don't have too much school, but I am not going to let it get me down. If I live by God's way, which I will, there will be a home for me up there if I cannot have it here on earth—because I have faith and believe and have confidence in myself and God. Be content with what you have, for he has said, "I will never fail you nor forsake you." I carry these books with me all the time. Never a day goes by that I do not learn a verse from one of them.

I am thirty-two years old. I am sending a picture of me taken here on the ranch last summer. I am so happy I had to write this letter to let you know what your books have done for me. I will close this letter. And pray for me.

P.S. Please overlook my writing. I don't know how to spell very good. I have to write with pencil. I make mistakes. I have to cross out a lot.

The life of this young man was transformed by a sudden exposure of his mind to the power of God through positive, creative ideas. If a person has a weakness which he wants to get under control and seemingly cannot, but is willing to take into his mind the best positive ideas, he will find that the power of such ideas to affect his life is amazing indeed. This explains many of the dramatic changes that happen to people through religious faith. A new and powerful thought has burst into the mind, shattering old weaknesses, breaking them to bits. It is in the mental processes that all motivation changes take place. The phrase "a change of heart" really means a profound change of mind. The heart is only a muscle to pump blood. It is the mind that accepts the new concept that changes. And faith is an idea so powerful that it can set the entire life going in a new direction with new and amazingly increased strength.

This is why you should read the Bible, the most powerful accumulation of life changing thoughts ever assembled. This is why you should go regularly to church and hear the great words, the words of God which, if received deeply into your mind, have the power to change your life. Dynamic, powerful, positive thoughts take a bold step forward in the conquering of an individual weakness.

Some time ago I was lecturing in Los Angeles when I ran across a most interesting example of a young lady who was ruining her life by the use of the wrong kind of words—words as symbols of a destructive idea. If you constantly use negative or deprecatory words about yourself, you are implanting equivalent destructive concepts in your mind.

On this particular day, after my lecture, I was at the front of the auditorium greeting quite a number of people. In this line was an attractive young lady who took my hand with a timid little shake and greeted me with this shocking sentence. "I so much wanted to speak to you," she said. "But of course I'm a nobody. You wouldn't know me. I don't amount to anything, but I have read your books and I just wanted to shake your hand."

I say this statement was shocking, for it minimized and depreciated God's highest form of creation, a human being.

I was a little tired of hearing so many people say they were "nobodies." It happens time and again across the country that people speak this way of themselves. So I stopped this young lady and said, "Miss Nobody, will you do me a favor? Will you please wait until I am through here . . . I'd like to talk with you." A little later I turned and found that sure enough she was there waiting.

"Now, Miss Nobody," I said. "I'd like a few words with you."

The girl laughed. "What did you call me?" she asked

"Miss Nobody," I said. "Because that is what you called yourself. Do you have some other name?"

She said yes and gave me her proper name.

"Just why did you tell me you are a Nobody?" I continued. "You say you've read about positive thinking, but you evidently haven't gotten very much out of it, else you'd never think of yourself as Miss Nobody. These books are designed to make people realize who and what they really are. Now, obviously, you have been telling not only others, but what is more serious, you tell yourself that you do not amount to much of anything. But I can see that you are wrong for, obviously, you have many qualities which are admirable. Certainly you are attractive. You have a good, clear eye. You know how to dress well. You have a charming smile. I think you are a very fine person and I don't think you should be carrying around a 'nobody' complex."

This young lady and I talked for some time about her ambitions and hopes and about the fact that it is very important not to weight these hopes down with negative thoughts. Her weak spot was a deep-seated "nobody complex" and she was compounding the difficulty with negative words. The cure for her situation was a reversal of the concept of herself.

I gave her the formula for overcoming her weakness and told her how to apply. I also suggested that she use the following affirmation: "I am the temple of God. In God I live and move and have my being. I am a child of God. I will think and act like a child of God."

She agreed to say this affirmation a dozen times every day and at the same time to visualize herself as being as the words describe. Months later, when I was again in California on a speaking engagement, an attractive young lady appeared before me and said, "You used to know me, but you don't now." That was an unusual thing to say and I turned to look carefully. To my astonishment who should it be but "Miss Nobody." "I have found that I can do things," she continued. "I have gotten out of that awful habit of thinking of myself as a Nobody and I just wanted to thank you for helping me change my identity."

As we talked it became very clear that she had, indeed, changed noticeably. Here was a girl who overcame a weakness through the use of positive ideas. She had become strongest in her weakest place; she had had a depreciatory and inferior attitude toward herself.

This self-depreciatory weakness is none that a great many face under the name of inferiority . Such feelings of inferiority can be extremely painful and self-defeating. Believe me, I know from hard, personal experience. When I was a boy I was what they used to call "bashful." That word isn't used much any more, but under whatever name, the feeling of being abashed by life is certainly painful. And the trouble is very widespread judging from the number of letters I receive on this subject. Here is one, for example:

Dear Dr. Peale,

I have been wanting to write to you for a long time. I surely do need help, but do not know if anyone can help me or not.

This is my problem. My husband is custodian of our church and I assist him, but I do not feel accepted among the women. Many times when I go to church I sit alone. The women will come in and sit in front of me or behind, but not in the pew with me unless all the others are filled up.

We do not dress as well as they do and I think the main reason is because I am not as bright as they are. I am quiet and sometimes say things that I should not and I do not mean it the way it sounded.

The women do not have me work with them in sewing or anything they do in groups. I have volunteered my services, but they say they are saving me for a time when I am needed. Still I hear them asking others to help.

My relatives seem to be ashamed of me or something. They do not introduce me to their friends or do not care to have me go to church with them. We have lived here in this community for a year and only one neighbor has been in.

I surely would appreciate it if I could learn how to be accepted among the women and have friends.

This is a typical letter showing tragic glimpses into the suffering of men and women who have become victims of the feelings of inadequacy. Very often (and I think this was true of the custodian's wife) these painful weaknesses are self-imposed. Notice in the above letter that this woman puts herself into a position where she asks to be hurt. She deliberately arrives in the church early, sits in the pew where people will either have to say to her, symbolically, "I like you" or "I do not like you." Now, the mathematics of the situation are very much against her. If one hundred people came to the church, only two can sit next to her and ninety-eight have to sit somewhere else. But she interprets the action of each of the ninety-eight as being against her.

Why is it that so many people actually seek out this feeling of inferiority? Psychologists tell me that one of the most common weaknesses of personality is that people often *do not want to succeed!* Somewhere along the line they have learned that it is a dangerous thing to succeed as it imposes upon them the burden of responsibility to live up to a success status. So they deliberately, though unconsciously, seek ways to keep themselves inferior by emphasizing their weaknesses.

Now it is a fact of life that each person is made up of stronger and weaker areas of personality. The question is, which are you going to dwell on? Which are you going to emphasize? If you specialize on the weaker areas in your personality you will become weak; if you stress the stronger areas you will become strong. It is as simple and certain as that.

But we must be careful not to confuse real weaknesses with self-assumed ones. Learning to accept ourselves is the first step in overcoming the weakness of inadequacy. Most of us, at least those of us who are troubled with the inferiority complex, pay far too much attention to ourselves, to our self-assumed weaknesses and drawbacks. We become self-conscious about things which are not important. We feel that everyone is noticing them when in reality they are not.

Not long ago I had an unusual opportunity to test this theory. I had been receiving a great deal of mail from people all saying the same, pathetically inferior thing: "No one likes me because of this or that."

One girl was ashamed because she was too fat; another because she was too thin. One boy felt that his ears were too big; another that his ears hugged his head too closely. Still another boy was self-conscious because he was too tall and another had painful inferiority feelings because he was short. I even recall one letter from a young girl who complained that she was too pretty. Nobody liked her for herself, but only for her body.

Now it happened that one of these typical complaints came to me from a young boy in our city. "Dr. Peale," he said, "nobody likes me because my nose is too big."

I had heard so much of this sort of thing that I decided then and there to make an experiment. "Name six of your acquaintances who do not like you because your nose is too big," I said to this boy. He gave me six names and a little later I took the time to place a call to each of these young people. As soon as I got them on the phone I asked them to name the outstanding characteristic of this young man's personality. Each one had to think a while, but this was the result of my inquiry. One told it was his friendliness; another that he was unusually good in arithmetic. A girl said he was a marvelous dancer. And so it went. Not *one* of these people signaled out this boy's nose as his outstanding characteristic. Apparently no one but he himself had any consciousness of that nose.

So it is true that many of us pick out some little characteristic which we consider to be a weakness and spend a great deal of effort convincing ourselves that *because of this weakness we cannot succeed*. The solution of the problem lies in realizing that God intends you to be a happy, successful, strong person. You must decide whether you will emphasize your weak points or your strong points, for you have both. The choice is up to you. Just as soon as you start emphasizing your strengths, your inferiority will diminish and a new sense of capacity will replace your old weakness and inadequacy.

Let us take a look at another common weakness and at solutions that were found; and this weakness is that of discouragement. So many times discouragement spells the difference between success and failure. If only you had carried on a little bit longer! Or harder! But discouragement made you give up just short of something really great. How tragic to quit when one more extra push would have brought success.

The fact of ups and downs is something we have to deal with in life. But positive thinking handles that problem. My friend Frank W. Kridel, General Manager of the great Manhattan and Astor hotels in New York, is a good example of the power of positive thinking in meeting potential discouragement. Referring to the helpfulness of prayer and guidance in practical problems, he said, "It is terrific how the whole pattern has worked out. And we've had some tough problems too, but it's a fact that when you trust God and keep plugging, while you have your ups and downs, with positive thinking you can turn your downs into ups." What a tremendous truth: "You can turn your downs into ups." That is to say, we must know how to turn our negatives into positives.

It is in problems of difficulty and discouragement that positive thinking has had some of its most amazing results. Another friend of mine, Ruth Hardy, also a hotel proprietor, runs the Ingleside Inn in Palm Springs, California. This is a little gem of a place set amidst lush gardens of bougainvillea, orchid bushes, palm and orange trees. Nestling in the lee of towering San Jacinto, it basks in the golden sun and balmy desert air. At night, when a silvery moon rises over the mountains, the place is almost ethereal in charm and peacefulness. It is one of my favorite spots.

But there has been struggle here as well as beauty. Indeed, how can there be any real beauty without struggle?

This charming Inn came into being through faith and positive thinking. Mrs. Hardy had plenty of troubles before making a success of her enterprise. She knew that she needed spiritual strength to do it and searched everywhere for guidance. She found help through Ernest Holmes and others.

To a friend, who passed the letter along to me, she writes:

It is strange how Norman's teachings came to me. Away back in 1942, when I was left alone, I decided I had to have some plan of living or something to go by. I have read everything that I could find in metaphysics that seemed to have some of the answers. Then along in the 40's someone sent me some of the literature from the Marble Collegiate Church. To me it made sense, and I thought that if this theory that I believed in really works then I should depend on it. And from that time on I have attempted as near as possible to run Ingleside along the plan for living that Norman advocates. Norman has told me many times that his theory is in the proving stage. He believes it and he knows it works, and he is always looking for evidence and proof that it *is* the way of life.

You know, by all the rules of aerodynamics, the bumblebee cannot fly! But the bumblebee doesn't know it and just keeps on flying! He is too fat, too big, and his wings are too short, but he just keeps going. In all the hotel books it says that any American Plan hotel under fifty rooms cannot exist, as there is not enough income to make it survive, as it is too small an operation with a dining room. Yet for twenty-six years I have run a small American Plan hotel, and it has worked. And the more I go along the lines of Norman's teachings, the better it works. I find I don't have to hurry and strain and be tense— I find that it is a very relaxing, happy life, all because I ask God for guidance and get it. I read my Bible and my books and apply the theory. The greatest thing that ever happened to me was to have Norman's literature fall into my hands.

Positive thinking has been responsible for many a successful battle against failure by turning another prevalent kind of weakness into strength. One man, today a successful and respected executive, had to battle a dull sense of inferiority. When I first met him he seemed an extremely retiring young man. In fact, he was retiring to the point of shrinking. It was a real weakness which hampered him greatly. By it he minimized himself and gave the impression that he lacked force and ability.

He was with a large business organization in the personnel department. One day he was notified that his services were no longer required—this after eight years with the company. He was crushed and dazed. He had accumulated very little money, the future was dark, he was keenly discouraged. But then a strange thing happened; now that he had to depend upon himself, now that he was faced with a real crisis, he turned his weakness into strength. He remembered some of the things we had been saying about positive thinking, and he resolved to put these theories to work.

I heard of his difficulty and said, "I want to help you. I have some contacts and maybe we can do something."

But to my surprise he replied, "I do not want you to do a thing, not a thing. I am going to put your principles of positive thinking into effect. You just forget me except to pray for me; that is all. If these principles are workable, they will work whether you help me or not, and if they will not work, then your help will not do me much good." I liked that as it showed strength coming up.

A few months later he told me of the results of his experiment. He said, "For the first time in my life I was forced to do some real creative thinking. Here I was, no job, none in sight and a family to support. But I visualized that somewhere was a future for me. Indeed, I intended to find it. I had to use my brain and my faith to do it."

So what did he do? Simply this; he secured the names of the presidents of one hundred firms. He read *Who's Who* and other types of directories in order to form an insight into the thinking of each executive whom he wanted to contact. He studied what type of businessmen they were. He investigated their personal attitudes, their likes and dislikes. He developed a comprehensive analysis of the mental slant of each man.

To each of them he then wrote a personal letter saying that he was trained for personnel work and outlining his experience. He told the prospective employer, modestly but specifically, what he had to offer. He outlined how he felt he could help that employer. He slanted his sales presentation of his own services to the employer's self-interest. He was not bold, but neither was he shrinking. He presented his qualifications objectively. And he received a number of replies expressing interest.

He held on to his mental picture of the work he wanted, continuing to think positively, and his contacts produced a choice between two good positions. He accepted a job at twelve hundred dollars more a year than he had received in the business he had left. After he started his new job I said to him, "It is really a miracle, the thing that happened to you."

"Miracle, not at all. It's merely a demonstration of the power of positive thinking which you teach. I've discovered by the acid test of personal experience that positive thinking is practically and scientifically sound. I know now why the Bible tells us to have faith, for when you believe, really believe, your mind becomes clear and then you can think your way through your difficulties. And besides," he added, "an experience like this isn't all bad. Maybe I needed something to shake me out of the mouse-like, half-scared rabbit that I was. I feel more self-confidence now." He had, in fact, become strongest where previously he had been weakest.

The most effective way for developing strength from weakness is through the life changing process of a positive faith. Evidences of this fact are multiplied daily; so much so, that selection among illustrations is most difficult. Dramatic demonstrations of people who out of weakness were made strong seem to be without limit.

Oftentimes I have mentioned this process of change to people struggling with a weakness and they say to me, "But I go to church, I contribute to charities and read my Bible. It seems to me that I am living with an active faith and it doesn't help at all." But, you see, the really important thing is a spiritual experience of God's power. It requires much more than religious formality to do the powerful job necessary in building real strength out of weakness.

Take the case of Bill Carter. I will call him that though Carter is not his name. Bill was having a great deal of trouble with alcohol. He tried every known method of curing himself of this weakness, with no results at all. One day his physician told him rather bluntly, "Bill, I am sorry but there is nothing more that I can do for you."

"You mean my case is hopeless?"

"Yes, unless you get top expert help."

"But, Doctor, who knows more about alcoholism than you?"

"Well," said the doctor, "I know of one specialist who might be able to help you. He is very high priced, however, and you'll have to be willing to pay. He takes everything you've got, but He can cure you for sure."

Bill sat straight up in his chair. "Who is this specialist? I will pay whatever is necessary if I can just get a hold on myself and solve this drinking problem."

"Bill," said the physician, "this specialist I'm talking about keeps office in the New Testament. You know who He is. And I doubt very much that you are willing to pay the price He asks. I know that you go to church, say your prayers; you even read your Bible, but you are not paying the price required for change. And what does this Doctor charge? Yourself, your whole self. You're holding out, that's why we can't get a cure in your case. You won't let go of that last 5 per cent of yourself. I've got the alcohol boiled out of you, but that area of 5 per cent of your brain, that I cannot reach. Only the Great Physician can get in there and cure the weakness that licks you and will continue to lick you.

"You see, you have to go all out, give all of yourself. Do that and you will really get strength."

He was a doctor! He was a doctor of the mind and soul as well as body. It is true that a great many of us actually are giving just a part of ourselves to our faith. It takes the whole man, the whole heart and soul, to make religious faith effective in this deeper sense. Bill Carter finally took his doctor's advice. He said a simple prayer which, however, was a prayer he had never before been able to say. Here is what he said —and meant:

"Lord, I am no longer going to hold on to this 5 per cent of resistance. I am going to give You the whole of myself. You take charge. I no longer belong to me. Do with me what You will. Amen."

As a result, spiritual power began to come. In time Bill's ability to cope with the problem of alcohol strengthened. Today he is a sober and effective person because he learned how to give all of himself to God's will. "When I let God take over," he said, "I could actually feel that old weakness being burned out of me." It is a basic fact about faith that it will work with power when you give *all* of yourself to what you believe. Withhold nothing. Have no reservations. Believe *positively* with all your heart, all your mind, all your spirit and no weakness can be too great for you to master.

In this chapter we have been looking at the methods used by actual people to transform weakness into strength through positive thinking. We have paid particular attention to anger, inferiority, discouragement, moral defeat.

The same principles can be applied to any weakness, whatever it is. Bring your own particular problem into the patterns suggested by this chapter. First, get your problem into a clear focus so that you know specifically what weakness it is you are trying to combat. Then focus on the results you wish to attain; specifically, what is it that you wish to accomplish? Start right away to become the person you wish to be. Practice expecting to be strongest in your weakest place. And you will be. Always persevere in your efforts to attain this goal. Don't give up. Continue—continue—continue.

If you feel your energies flagging, reread this chapter; notice in particular how others who have faced similar weaknesses have carried on to victory. And, finally, keep forever before you the firm belief that God does not intend you to be victimized by weaknesses. Believe this, for it is true. Believe that the natural way for you to face life is with courage and strength. Believe that God built potential strength into you which you have not been using. But now you are going to start using it.

Isolate your weak spot, specify the results you wish to attain, picture yourself becoming strong, start being the strong person you wish to be. Act as though you are now changing into strength, believe you can attain the results you seek, humbly trusting in God to help you. This is the pattern, the tremendous pattern of deep personality change. Apply it to your own particular problem and you, too, can become strongest in your weakest place.

In fact your whole life can become stronger and happier in every particular. As you study and apply the teachings of this book, great things will happen to you because something great will have happened within you. Your stronger faith, deeper understanding and greater dedications will open up a wonderful new life for you. You will become a vital personality well able to handle all your own problems. And you will have enough extra strength and insight to be a creative influence in the lives of many others.

No more defeat, no more failure, no more dull hopelessness. Life won't suddenly become easy or superficial—not at all. Life is real. Life is earnest and it is full of problems. But thank God it now becomes full of the overcoming of problems. Through the formulas of thinking and acting outlined in this book you need no longer be mastered by your difficulties. You can now master them. The difference is due to that Master who has entered into your life to make you a very different person. So to you, as to the others, will come the amazing results of positive thinking.

Epilogue

I COULD GO ON and on telling of the amazing results of positive thinking. So many others than those mentioned in this book have experienced great personal victories. And I would like to tell you about all of them. But there is a limit to the length of a book. And we must close.

But before doing so there is just one final thing I want to say: Never become discouraged with yourself or with your life. Never give in to defeat, never lose heart.

There is a way out, there is a way around, there is a way through any problem, any difficulty. And that way is by positive thinking and positive action. It is accomplished by spiritual motivation.

What others have done—with the help of God—you also can do. And how to do it has been stated with sincerity, and, I hope, with clarity in this book. On page after page are formulas and techniques used by others to turn defeat into victory.

Now that you have read the book go back and practice it. This, unlike most books, is not merely a reading book. It's a practicing manual. It will work, but only when you work it. For best results disciplined and prayerful perseverance is required.

I dedicated this book in sincere prayer. I dedicated it to God with a prayer that it might help you. And the book *can* help you as others have been helped. Faithfully practice its teachings as suggested and you too can have the amazing results of positive thinking.

With friendly good wishes and a sincere God bless you, I am

Cordially yours,
NORMAN VINCENT PEALE

NEW FROM FAWCETT CREST